Black Republicans:

The Politics of the Black and Tans

by

HANES WALTON, JR.

The Scarecrow Press, Inc.
Metuchen, N. J.   1975

Library of Congress Cataloging in Publication Data

Walton, Hanes, 1941-
    Black Republicans.

    Bibliography: p.
    Includes index.
    1. Republican Party--History.   2. Negroes--Pol-
itics and suffrage.   I. Title.
JK2356.W34   329.6'00975   75-6718
ISBN 0-8108-0811-0

To
Clarence Holte
The Black Bibliophile Par Excellence

The word bibliophile means "one who loves books, especially for their binding and style." Mr. Holte is a bibliophile, but not in that sense. He is a seeker of the truth, a searcher in the Darkness for Light, and a groper in the backways, the byways and lowways for the Black Past.

Most Blacks who have received applause and acclamation for insights into the Black Past have been scholars like Woodson, Dubois, and Hansberry. The insights they have given us grow in part out of their intellectual commitment. But in some rare instances, a layman, like yourself--a man who earns his way outside of academia--contributes to the growing intellectual wisdom, that Blacks are not without a past worth speaking of before the coming of the white man.

The Clarence L. Holte Collection on Blacks stands as a testimony, a witness, a monument to the Black Past as second to no past civilization. Alone, and without the comfort of cloistered academia, you have searched and found the truth, not its bindings or style. And the Clarence L. Holte Collection, like the Black Past, is second to none.

So, Clarence L. Holte, I salute you and place you with Woodson, Dubois, and Hansberry. In a way your commitment and insights are much greater than theirs--for they were partly motivated by their academic backgrounds--you rose from the masses, the "Soul" of Black People.

iii

FOREWORD

The path to Black Liberation has been described as multi-faceted, many splendored and variegated. There is no single pattern or design for securing the ultimate liberation of Black people. Indeed, the political direction of the Black Community itself has taken many forms and shapes, and the myriad contours and directions can not be enumerated in this Foreword. But one can say without danger of contradiction that the African inhabitants of this country have explored nearly all possible avenues in the pursuit of their freedom. These different approaches have, in our opinion, advanced the Black political struggle in America.

The predominant strains of political thought--assimilation, pluralism, nationalism--all have roots in the Black community, north or south, urban or rural. The urban north and rural south are populated with organizations dedicated to the liberation of Black people. The call for liberation, of course, is not a recent phenomenon; the desire to be free has been a constant refrain in the annals of African-American history. The truf has been treacherous and the trek bloody and hazardous, but African-Americans have persisted and kept their eyes on the prize--their ultimate liberation. The journey has been rewarding and disappointing, exalting and disgusting, futile and joyous, painful and redemptive--indeed, it has been a journey of superhuman proportions. No one document or presentation illuminates and conveys the valiant struggle of Black people in this country. The nature of this struggle does not lend itself to a monlithic interpretation or characterization. Its complexities and frustrations present a collective challenge--to scholars and non-scholars alike.

Dr. Walton's treatment of the Black and Tan Republicans is one such contribution to that collective effort--the struggle for human dignity and freedom. His seminal and systematic treatment of the Black and Tan Republicans is a timely and long-awaited study of a unique American political phenomenon. He has captured and illuminated the plight and experiences of a group of Black Americans struggling and transforming the party of Abraham Lincoln--the Republican Party. Dr. Walton has also recaptured a significant segment of the political history of Black people in this country. His study reminds me in a number of ways of Joseph Walker's excellent play, The River Niger, which is a commentary on the glorious and righteous struggle of Africans in this country. One of the characters in the play points out that the history of Black people in America is a poetic one--and in a real sense Professor Walton has related the political struggle of a group of African-Americans in a poetic-political manner. Dr. Walton has systematically dealt with the poetry and politics relationship in another volume, The Poetry of Black Politics. We are not attempting to analyze the present work in that context, but it is instructive to look at Professor Walton's most recent offering from that perspective.

Black Republicans: The Politics of the Black and Tans is a detailed analysis of the various Black and Tan Republican parties throughout the old confederacy, including the State of Florida. He recounts the Black involvement within the Republican Party from shortly before the Civil War until the last Black and Tans participated in the 1956 Republican National Convention. This account is thought-provoking, lucid and well-reasoned--a prime example of top-rate scholarship. He has done a masterful job of describing the constant tension and competition between the Black and Tan Republicans and their counterparts, the Lily-white Republicans. This treatment of a significant era of African-American political history and involvement is another stepping-stone in the process of total liberation for Black Americans. Dr. Walton's latest contribution provides intellectual light for all of this country's citizens--both black and white.

Leslie Burl McLemore
Department of Political Science
Jackson State University

vi

TABLE OF CONTENTS

Foreword, by Leslie Burl McLemore   v
Introduction, by Prince A. Jackson, Jr.   xi
Preface   xiii

1. The Emergence of Black Republicanism   1
      Race and Intra-Party Conflict   1
      Black Republicans Before the Civil War   3
      The Republicans and Colonization: 1851-1860   9
      The Republicans and Black Suffrage   10
      Blacks and Abraham Lincoln   12
      Black Political Action and Attitudes and the
        Party: 1858-1877   14

2. The Roots of Black and Tan and Lily-White   30
      Republicanism   30
      The Republican Party in the South: The
        Foundations   31
      Intra-Party Factionalism   34
      Democratic Violence, Fraud and Intimidation   35
      Presidential Policies Toward the Southern
        Republican Party After Reconstruction   38

3. Black and Tan Republicans on the State and
      Local Levels   45
      Georgia   47
      Texas   62
      Louisiana   67
      Alabama   69
      North Carolina   86
      Virginia   92
      Florida   98
      South Carolina   105
      Tennessee   116
      Arkansas   123
      Mississippi   128
      The Southern States: Summary   137
      Other States   140

4. Black and Tan Republicanism: Nationally and
   in Decline   151
   Republican National Conventions   151
   Decline and Fall   163
   Goldwater, Nixon, and Black Republicans   164

Appendix: Tables   169

Bibliography   180

Index   193

TABLES AND DIAGRAMS

Tables

I. Southern Black Delegates to Republican National
Conventions, 1868-1944   170

II. Votes for Black and Tan Republicans in South
Carolina--1936, 1944 and 1952   177

III. Votes for Black and Tan Republicans in
Mississippi--1928, 1936, 1940, 1944, 1948,
1952 and 1956   178

IV. Number of Black Delegates to Republican
National Conventions, 1868-1972   179

Diagrams

I. The Nomenclature of the Southern Republican
Party's Coalition Before and After 1877   33

II. The New and Emerging Southern Republican
Party's Coalition   42

INTRODUCTION

In recent years, especially during the past eight years, there has been no shortage of literature for and about Blacks in the United States. Much of this writing has been in sociological and philosophical areas. Needless to say, this relatively new and avid market emerged largely as a result of the civil rights movement of the sixties and the scarcity of writings of Blacks in white institutions. Even in Black institutions, there were, and still are, relatively few Black collections of any consequence. And where abundant materials on Blacks can be found, there are still very few works of merit about Blacks in the political arena.

When the author asked me to write the Introduction to this work, I was extremely pleased and happy. I have had the unique opportunity to work with him as a fellow faculty member and as his President. I have followed religiously his efforts to "push back the frontiers of knowledge" through prodigious commitment to research and herculean dedication to forging a place in the sun of American history for Blacks. He has been eminently successful; reading all of the author's works so far, it is obvious that three principles have been his beacon: 1) Nescire autem quid antequam natus sis acciderit, id est semper esse puerum (To be ignorant of what happened before you were born is always to remain a boy); 2) Veritas vos liberabit (The truth shall make you free); and 3) Veritatis simplex oratio est (The language of truth is simple). In applying the Aristotelian law of the Excluded Middle to his works, one can see immediately that they are scholarly and excellent.

This work, Black Republicans: The Politics of the Black and Tans, comes at a time when the whole American political process is under question and examination because of the Watergate excesses. It is particularly interesting that the Republican Party is deeply involved at a time when Black Republicans consider themselves separate and distinct from the National Party. Never before has it been more imperative

xi

to know why and how this separation came about.   Hanes
Walton, Jr. provides us this necessary knowledge in the pages
which follow.   Starting with the birth of Black Republicans
(circa 1854), he leads his readers through the evolution which,
some 120 years later, has changed the Republican Party from
its early posture of the party of all colors and creeds to the
almost lily-white posture of republicanism today.   The author
has shown that the evolution was not the result of intra-party
factionalism alone, but that it had generous assistance from
the Democratic Party.   The reader will also benefit from
learning of the great impact on this evolution of several presidents of the country, including Hayes, Garfield, Harrison,
and McKinley.   In the latter part of the work, Walton ex-
amines the influence of Goldwater and Nixon in shaping republicanism into its present form.   In concluding the work he
prognosticates, since it is obvious that the Republican Party
must find a policy which can regain Blacks and, at the same
time, be attractive to the South.

      The author has demonstrated a quality which is diffi-
cult to find in works of this type.   That quality is objectivity.
He has not allowed bitterness, experienced by all Black writers, to creep into his pen.   This work should be read by all
who are interested in the history of the Republican Party and
Blacks in America.   It is my hope that Hanes Walton, Jr.
will extend his research and writings to a similar work on
Blacks in the Democratic Party.   Such a work, perhaps,
would demonstrate the principle of the need for collaborative
efforts and division of labor expounded by the great Dominican,
St. Thomas Aquinas, in his work, De Regimine Principum.

Prince A. Jackson, Jr., Ph.D.
President
Savannah State College
Savannah, Georgia

June 24, 1974

PREFACE

Black Democrats and Republicans have not been ana-
lyzed and studied in a systematic and comprehensive fashion.
This volume represents the first scholarly look at Black Republicans in general, and the Black and Tans in the Republican Party in particular. It covers the time period from
1854 to 1972, and represents a pioneer effort to bring to
light the fortunes and efforts of those Black Americans who
were participants in the Republican Party.

Professor Paul Lewinson, writing in 1932, stated that
the "origins of the modern Lily-white movements are shrouded
in the mists of obscure local factionalism."[1] Black political
scientist Ralph Bunche, writing in 1940, indicated that Lily-
whiteism in the South dates back further than 1928. In fact,
as far back as the Taft Administration, white Republicans in
the South began to assert their impatience with being identified as "Nigger lovers." Therefore a concerted movement
began among them "to take control of the Republican organizations in the South into their own white hands."[2] On the other
hand, Professor Alexander Heard has indicated that "the term
'lily-white' was first used in 1888 in Texas. A Negro Republican leader, Norris Wright Cuney, so dubbed a faction
seeking to take control of the party from him."[3]

Prior to Heard's statement, Black political scientist
William F. Nowlin saw the emergence of the "lily-white movement" on the national level in 1908.[4]

What all four men are trying to describe is a political
movement of white Republicans in the South. As can be gathered from their remarks, the exact date of the emergence of
this political phenomenon is not known or cannot be pinpointed
with any great degree of accuracy--or at least they were unable to do so. If the origin of the movement is fuzzy, it was
nevertheless very important and a significant factor in both
Southern and national politics. Despite its importance and impact on the American political arena, there are, however, no

full-length studies of "Lily-white Republicanism." It is discussed only in a very few works and articles dealing with Southern politics, and in hardly any which deal with national and convention politics. There is even less coverage devoted to the Lily-whites' counterparts, the Black and Tan Republicans.

"The Republican party in the South," writes Professor Key, "came to be branded as a Negro party and therefore unattractive to most whites." But, "when whites moved into it, the issue of white versus Negro control of the party arose, and every state was plagued by the question of Black-and-Tan versus Lily-white."[5] The Black and Tan Republicans, nevertheless, are little discussed. They have received less coverage than the lily-whites, although in some states they existed longer or at least as long as the lily-whites, and in some states their achievements were much more important than those of the lily-whites. Moreover, the Black and Tans played major roles at the Republican National Conventions of 1892, 1908, 1912, and 1928. It was due to their influence that several Republican Presidents secured their nominations. Today the Black and Tans are gone, their organizations defunct and their rank and file membership depleted, while in some states the lily-whites still exist. But Black and Tanism was a consequence of lily-whiteism and vice versa.

This book is the first comprehensive and systematic study of the Black and Tan Republicans, their origin, existence, accomplishments, and the forces which led to their decline. It deals not only with the movement on the state level, in all eleven of the southern states, but also with the politics of the Black and Tans on the national level, at each convention from 1892 through 1956. The study starts with the rise of Republicanism in general and the emergence of Black Republicanism in particular--in both South and North but concentrating primarily on the former.

In a way, this work is also a study of the Lily-whites because no comprehensive study of the Black and Tans could be made without dealing with their raison d'être--the Lily-whites. The two groups are inextricably involved. They confront each other at every step of the political journey; one cannot be viewed without the other.

Since this is a study of factional politics, it necessarily covers the lives and political activities of Black, as well as some white, Republican leaders. To discuss the Black and Tan organizations without dealing with their leadership would be to present an incomplete picture, for some Black political leaders, like Perry Howard in Mississippi and Ben Davis in Georgia, were prime forces in and out of their state organizations. The group's activities cannot be understood apart from their leadership.

In writing about a political faction like the Black and Tans, which covers a period of more than a half century, continuity is often difficult to follow. These groups rarely kept records or minutes. Not being permanent organizations in the strictest sense of the word, they appeared, disappeared, and reappeared from time to time for four- or two-year intervals. In many instances there are only limited newspaper accounts of them, where any records exist at all. The groups were particularly difficult to follow from the 1870's to 1900. After that period the national activities of the groups mushroomed and the newspaper accounts, Republican proceedings, and journalists' remarks are plentiful. The story "state by state cannot be satisfactorily compressed because the very details of greed and doctrine and personality and bickering comprise the heart of the trouble."[6] Despite the scattered source materials on some states, an attempt has been made here to put into focus and describe the entire story for each state. The major stages of the movements in each of the eleven Southern states have been covered.[7]

To cover a recurring four- and sometimes two-year political movement in eleven states is no mean task. Having made the attempt, I am indebted to a host of scholars, laymen, and political observers. It is not possible to mention all of those who helped at various stages of this two-year study, but I do want to acknowledge some of the more important contributions.

First and foremost, I owe a debt of gratitude to Miss Luella Hawkins who helped me gather and assemble the data for the eleven states from many diverse sources. Although her facilities were limited, she went above and beyond her duty in securing all the essential data. To her assistant, Mrs. Allen, I am also appreciative, for she helped in Miss Hawkins' absence. Cooperation of the first order was given by Mr. Andrew McLemore, Head Librarian at Savannah State College.

Xavier University's librarian also extended me courteous assistance in using that institution's facilities. It is at Xavier in New Orleans, Louisiana that the only full statewide study of Black and Tan Republicans exists.

I must also thank Mr. Walter Fisher, Program Chairman of the Association for the Study of Negro Life and History, for his encouragement and insistence that I present a portion of the first chapter at the 55th Annual Meeting of the Association in October, 1970. That portion, entitled "Black Republicans Before the Civil War, 1856-1860," was well scrutinized at the meeting and valuable comments and suggestions were given to strengthen it in its final form. Professor Tobe Johnson of Morehouse College did much at the meeting of the Association to improve the final product.

Professor Harold Gosnell assisted from time to time with words of wisdom, loans of materials, guidance to further resource materials, and general encouragement. Professors Samuel Cook, Leslie McLemore, Thomas Byers, Brenda Mobley, John McCray, and Abbie Jordan aided me in a number of ways. For typing and retyping the work, I must extend generous thanks to Miss Lillie Mae Key, Mrs. Mattie Haynes and Miss Betty Lawton, who continued to work for two years at what must have seemed a never-ending task.

To the members of my family, Mr. & Mrs. Thomas Walton, my parents; Mr. Thomas N. Walton; G. Richardson; Marjorie Walton, Spencer, Stevie, and April Walton; Margaret Guest; Katie, Joe, Phil, and Bonnie Hampton, their encouragement and help shall always be remembered.

The research here reported was assisted by a grant awarded by the committee on Minority Research Awards of the Social Science Research Council. However, the two grants made under the Minority Research Awards Program are in no way responsible for any of the conclusions, presentations of facts, or errors in judgment. These, in the final analysis, are mine and I assume full responsibility.

H. Walton, Jr.

August, 1973

Notes

1. Paul Lewinson, Race, Class and Party: A History of Negro Suffrage and White Politics in the South (New York: Russell & Russell, 1963), p. 170.

2. Ralph Bunche, "Political Status of the Negro" (unpublished

manuscript prepared for the Gunnar Myrdal Study), p. 1176.

3. Alexander Heard, A Two-Party South (Chapel Hill: University of North Carolina Press, 1952), p. 222.

4. W. F. Nowlin, The Negro in American National Politics: A Study of the Negro in America National Politics since 1868 (Boston: The Stratford Company, 1931).

5. V. O. Key, Southern Politics in State and Nation (New York: Vintage Books, 1949), p. 286.

6. Heard, op. cit., p. 221.

7. Even two recent studies fail to give any significant data on the two factions. They are: Richard B. Sherman, The Republican Party and Black America: From McKinley to Hoover 1896-1933 (Charlottesville: Univ. Press of Virginia, 1973), and Thomas R. Cripp, "The Lily-white Republicans: The Negro, the Party and the South in the Progressive Era" (Unpublished PhD. dissertation, 1967). The Sherman volume explores only National Republican policy towards Blacks, while Cripp looks at the Lily-whites up to 1912.

CHAPTER 1

THE EMERGENCE OF BLACK REPUBLICANISM:
1854-1877

Race and Intra-Party Conflict

Political parties are primarily electoral devices which
must appeal to the general electorate for the right to adminis-
ter the government of a state. Before a political party can
gain control of the government, it must, through numerous
appeals, form a coalition of voters from as many sectors of
the population as possible.

According to Professor Pendleton Herring, "the task of
the [political] party is to achieve a working combination of
sections of interest and also of the liberal and conservative
within its own ranks."[1] However, after the pary forms a
coalition of diverse groups and individuals, the party leaders
must "attempt to iron out friction among the elements, to re-
assure the interests traditionally associated with it, and by
other means, to form its battalions for the assault against
the opposition."[2] Party cleavages and disunity, which occur
when the pragmatic coalition collapses, mean disaster and
political losses on election day.

The factors which cause internal cleavage and disunity
have been of constant concern to party leaders and political
scientists alike. Discussions and analyses of these cleavages
--which involve ideological, class, sectional, incentives, and
patronage factors--abound in the literature of politics, and
most of them center on how these internal cleavages affect
the electoral potential of the party and what can be done about
it. For instance, political scientist V. O. Key developed the
concept of factionalism--i.e., "any combination, clique, or
grouping of voters and political leaders who unite at a particular time in support of a candidate"--to describe intra-party
cleavages and competition, primarily in the South. While

1

Key's theoretical concept was developed for the Southern party scene, it has relevance, though, for each region of the country. Where intra-party cleavages result in three or more factions, this is known as multifactionalism. Where intra-party cleavages result in two factions with a high degree of cohesion and continuity, a state of bifactionalism exists. [3]

Political analysts and political scientists have so far been concerned mainly with characterizing existing intra-party cleavages and offering some theoretical generalizations about how party loyalty and cohesion can be secured. Few data are available on how race and racial beliefs have caused or provoked internal cleavage, and even less is to be found specifically on intra-party conflicts that have arisen out of racial concerns. Much can be found on how race has solidi-fied southern politics on certain issues and on how the racial issue had divided political parties or men of the same party, but little is available on the nature of the impact of race on party structure and competition. Put otherwise, although the Negro issue has occupied a central place in the development of the national party organizations and in the formation of political alliances, its effect upon intra-party cleavages has been dealt with in only a peripheral and superficial manner.

The omission in the literature of race as a significant factor in causing intra-party cleavages does not mean that cleavages have not happened for this reason. In the Southern Republican party during the 1880's a major intra-party split occurred wholly on the basis of racial beliefs and resulted in the formation of two minority organizations or factions in the Republican party: the Black and Tan Republicans and the Lily-white Republicans. [4] These two factions, in each of the eleven southern states, competed with each other for more than a half century for the right to be designated as the regular party (i.e., as the party leadership) and for the right to control and dispense national patronage within the boundaries of each state involved. [5]

In this intra-party struggle between the Black and Tans and Lily-whites, both groups employed political tactics that varied from state to state and from one election and convention to another, in an attempt to gain the party leadership and con-trol of national patronage for the state. Before we explore the politics of the Black and Tans in those states, however, let us turn our attention to the emergence and rise of Black Republicans.

Black Republicans before the Civil War

In 1854, when those who dreamed of a Republican organization began to put their plans into motion, Free Blacks
had the legal right to vote in all of the New England states
except Connecticut; more than 1200 qualified as voters in New
York City and environs, and those with a greater admixture
of white blood had the right to vote in Ohio. In several
places within some other states, such as Wisconsin and Michigan, Blacks were permitted to vote illegally due to a laxity
of law enforcement. And from 1838 to 1860, Free Blacks
voted illegally in Rapides Parish, Louisiana, even though the
state legislature had curtailed the right in 1812.

Recent analyses of the political behavior of these Free
Blacks have revealed that they were in the main abolitionists
and strong supporters of the anti-slavery political parties and
politicians. When the Republican party organized in Ripon,
Wisconsin in 1854, although no Blacks were present, the issue
of Black Americans (slave or free) loomed heavy in the air.
Among the different groups, "the Free Soilers, Independent
Democrats, Conscience Whigs, Know-Nothings, Barn Burners,
Abolitionists [and] Teetotallers" were strong and diversified
in their opinions regarding Blacks, and especially on the issue
of slavery. In regard to the slavery issue, the Know-Nothings aggregation in the Republican Party was pro-slavery in
its outlook, [6] while the Abolitionists and Independent Democrats and Whigs wanted a destruction of the slave institution.
In short, when the Republicans organized in 1854, the array
of opinions regarding Blacks (slave or free) ranged from complete indifference to advocacy of complete freedom and equality. [7]

With this variety of racial attitudes, the Republican
party at first didn't evoke much comment or concern from
the Free Blacks in the North. Although one Black abolitionist, Frederick Douglass, carried an announcement of the
formation of the party in his newspaper, Frederick Douglass'
Paper, [8] "there was no indication that any special effort was
made to attract Negro voters or to interest the American
people in extending suffrage to Negroes."[9] It seems highly
probable, says Professor Charles Wesley, "that Negroes were
not interested in a party which at first resolved to interfere
only with slavery extension in the territories."

As events progressed and debate over the slavery issue
grew more intense, comment from the Black community about

the Republican party began to appear. Douglass indicated
some of the thoughts of the Black community about a year after
the party had been formed in a speech in July, 1855, which
stated that "we [the Black community] rejoice in ... the great
Republican movement which is sweeping like a whirlwind over
the Free states. "10   But, he said, "we cannot join the party
because we think it lacks vitality"; because "it does not go far
enough in the right direction"; because it is willing to "let
slavery alone where it is. " In Douglass' view, and probably
that of the rest of the Black community, slavery should have
been attacked where it existed. However, Douglass didn't write
off the Republican party because of its position on slavery in
1855; he went on in his speech to state that the Black community was "hopeful that the Republican party as it grows in
number will also grow in the knowledge of the truth, " and
would become a truly anti-slavery political organization.

The Republicans themselves, eager to grow and enlarge
their chances for political success in 1856, were constantly
searching for new allies and converts. To many of the new
Republicans, who were anti-slavery advocates and had been
members of the anti-slavery Liberty and Free Soldiers party11
that had received Black support and participation, an appeal
to the Free Blacks who could vote, was a natural way to enlarge the ranks of the party. Since many Free Blacks were
abolitionists themselves, they would be an immediate source
of additional support and votes. 12

In late 1855, therefore, such an appeal was made to
the Black community by several of the abolitionists in the Republican party. Douglass' reply to the request, in his newspaper on December 7, 1855, is indicative of the request and
its reasoning.

In their appeal to the Black community for support, the
white Republican abolitionists had criticized Douglass for not
urging Black voters to strongly support the Republican party.
These abolitionist Republicans felt that Douglass, "by keeping
a certain number of men [Blacks] within the sphere of his influence from voting [for the Republican party] where their votes
will count against slavery, will indirectly aid the causes which
he depreciates. "13   Douglass asserted in his editorial, "The
Republican Party--Our Position, " "that the Black community
couldn't accept the abolitionists' invitation to join the Republican party because, due to its position on slavery, it does
not go far enough in the right direction" for the Black community.

Douglass urged the abolitionists who wrote the request, and other members of the Republican party, "to take a higher position, make no concession to the slave power, strike at slavery everywhere in the country and not wait for a pro-slavery Supreme Court to proclaim the acceptable year ... throughout all the land. "

Early in 1856 the political alternatives available to Black voters were indeed few and unpromising. The existing anti-slavery liberty party was becoming smaller and even more inconsequential in American politics. The Radical Abo-litionist Party, which was formed in June, 1855, failed, de-spite its title and lofty objectives, to attract the mass of Black voters and justified the rumors and predictions of its poor chance of success. The Whig party had practically dis-appeared, and the American Party (Know-Nothings) was also in the throes of dissolution over the slavery issue.

The Republican Party, which had achieved several notable electoral victories in some northern states before 1856, began early that year to make preparations to run a candidate for the Presidency. On February 22, 1856, Republican lead-ers met in Pittsburgh, planned a national convention for June, and drew up an "Address to the People of the United States. " But the Address revealed to the Black community that the Re-publican party still hadn't changed its position on slavery and consequently was offering little more than the other political parties.

Douglass, in reviewing the document, indicated that since nothing was said of "The Fugitive Slave Bill, nothing said of slavery in the District of Columbia, nothing said of the slave trade between states, nothing said of giving the dig-nity of the nation to Liberty, nothing said of securing the rights of citizens from the northern states, or the constitu-tional right to enter and transact business in the slave states, "[14] he could only urge Blacks to support the Radical political abolitionists and Liberty Party candidates, despite their limited possibilities. Douglass and several other Black abolitionist leaders, including J. W. Loguen, Amos Beman, and J. McCune Smith, attended the political convention of the Radical Abolitionists which was held on May 18, 1856 in Syra-cuse, New York. At the convention Douglass' name was put in nomination for the Vice Presidency.

If the Black abolitionists and other Black voters re-sponded negatively to the Republicans "Address to the

People...," the Republicans, at their convention in June, 1856, remained cognizant of the slavery issue and responded to those who criticized them.

Edwin D. Morgan, the National Chairman, in calling the delegates to order, "You are here today to give direction to a movement which is to decide whether the people of the United States are to be hereafter and forever chained to the present national policy of the extension of human slavery ... [and] in its consideration let us avoid all extreme--plant ourselves firmly on the platform of the Constitution and the Union, taking no position which does not commend itself to the judgment of our consciences, our country, and mankind."[15]

Judge Robert Emment of New York, who as temporary chairman of the convention, gave the keynote address, asserted that the other parties "may laugh at us." He continued, "they may call us Black Republicans and Negro worshippers. Why, if they were not traitors and buffoons, they would find something better than that to apply to us [cheers and shouts of 'That's it' rose from the audience]."

Given such directions and challenges, the platform committee, chaired by David Wilmot (author of the Wilmot Proviso), avoided extreme and violent proposals on the question of slavery. A platform was drawn up and adopted by the Convention which declared in part that "the rights and the union of states be preserved, that Congress must exercise its sovereign power over territories to prohibit slavery [and] that Kansas should be admitted as a Free state...."[16]

Following the platform adoption, John C. Fremont was nominated for President and "his moderate but not radical opposition to [the] extension of slavery" enabled him to become the party's Presidential candidate on the second ballot. Professor Franklin Burdette, characterizing the convention, states that it was basically guided by "moderation in action but evangelism in purpose."

After the convention the Republicans launched a campaign which emphasized "Free Speech, Free Press, Free Men, Free Labor, Free Territory, and Fremont." In Illinois, Abraham Lincoln, who campaigned in behalf of Fremont, declared that the major differences between the two parties centered upon one single question: "Shall slavery be allowed to extend into the national territories now legally free? Buchanan [the Democratic candidate] says it shall and Fremont says it shall not."

With so much heat over the slavery issue being generated in the campaign, one of the major spokesmen of the Black community, Frederick Douglass, added fuel to the fire when he reversed himself and endorsed Fremont on August 15, nearly a month and a half after the campaign had started. In his newspaper, <u>Frederick Douglass' Paper</u>, Douglass urged Blacks "to support, with whatever influence we possess, little or much, John C. Fremont and William L. Dayton, the candidates of the Republican party for the Presidency and Vice Presidency of the United States, in the present political canvass."[17] Whether Douglass' endorsement was motivated by sincere conviction or political opportunism is not known, but it is known that in a letter to Gerrit Smith on May 13, 1856, he indicated that his newspaper was in financial trouble. Since it was opposed "to the Republicans of fifty-six ... therefore Republicans look coldly on it, "[18] he said, and couldn't be expected to help him pay off the fifteen hundred-dollar debt. Douglass did, however, accompany his endorsement of Fremont with a long and careful explanation of the reasons for his political reversal.

In subsequent editorials Douglass enlarged upon his reasons and continually called upon the Black voter to support the Republican party. His well-defined reasons for his political reversal didn't satisfy all of his readers, and by September, numerous criticisms of his support of the Republican party began to appear. In fact, they became so numerous that he devoted an entire editorial to them, which he entitled "A Brief Response to Our Assailants." This editorial was unable to quell his critics and in September, 1856, in an editorial entitled "The Republican Party," Douglass tried once again to quiet the bitter attacks upon him for his endorsement of Fremont.

This editorial also didn't muffle his critics, but the controversy which Douglass had started with his endorsement of Fremont and call to Blacks to support the Republicans, as well as the furor that the Fremont candidacy was causing in the white community and the South, were by now attracting the attention of the Black community. Douglass' call to Black voters to support the Republicans must have been effective because a convention of Blacks in Boston, held August 26, 1856, adopted a resolution stating that "we, the colored citizens of Boston, will support with our voices and our votes, John C. Fremont ... as President of the United States and William L. Dayton ... as Vice President. "[19] However, the Blacks qualified their endorsement in another resolution stating that "we do not pledge ourselves to go further with the Republicans than the Republicans will go with us. "

In Ohio, a group of Blacks, meeting shortly after Douglass' pleas began, "voiced their support of the Republicans because the opposing party was 'the black-hearted Apostle of American Slavery. ' "[20]

On October 3, 1856, at the State Convention of Colored Men in New York, convention leader Henry Highland Garnet urged "New York State's six thousand Black voters to come out for the Republicans. " As the campaign progressed and the Democrats continued to apply the epithet "Black Republican" to the new party and denounce it, Black support of the new organization became even more solid. As one observer put it, "These speeches were heard by thousands of Negroes, and they very naturally took up the idea that they had a great friend in that Mr. Mont to whom they heard the epithet 'Free' so constantly applied. And that he was to free them all as soon as he was elected. " In fact, "many Negroes sympathized with the Fremont ticket and those who could vote were reported to have voted for it. "

Despite Black support, the Republicans lost in 1856. Buchanan, the Democratic candidate, received 1, 838, 169 popular votes and 174 electoral votes to Fremont's 1, 341, 264 popular votes and 114 electoral votes. The Republican party's defeat, however, by no means disposed of the slavery issue or the problems of Black Americans.

Although Black support had been tentative and limited (due to the limited number of Black voters), it was clear to the Republicans that they had to find a new platform and position in regard to Black Americans. Two basic issues increasingly dominated party thinking from 1856 to 1860: colonization and the granting of suffrage rights. [21] Pro-slavery Republicans generally supported colonization, while anti-slavery Republicans argued for the granting of suffrage to the Black man. The former hoped that all Blacks might be sent out of the country and thus solve the issue of Blacks permanently. The latter saw granting suffrage to Blacks as a way to increase the Republican party's chances of victory. Involved in the whole matter of suffrage rights, also, was the notion that once the Republicans were elected to office, they could abolish slavery through legal means. But this idea-- equalitarianism --was mixed with notions of power, as we shall see later on.

The Republicans and Colonization: 1851-1860

As Professor Eric Foner sees it, within the Republican Party prior to 1861 there was wide acceptance of plans
for colonizing Blacks outside the United States. Although this
"solution" to the race problem had been advocated and pursued for many years and had apparently failed to gain sufficient support, not all of the pro-slavery or anti-slavery Republicans were discouraged. The plan had been referred to
briefly by the Republicans during the Fremont campaign, but
gained little acceptance. After the 1856 election, however,
colonization "became a major political issue" for most Republicans who "contemplated on areas closer to home."[22]

The chief architects of the "Republican colonization
plan were Francis P. Blair and his sons Frank and Montgomery." Basically, the "Blairs were anti-slavery slave-
holders who shared the assumptions of their class regarding
race and who attacked slavery primarily because of its effects
upon southern white labor." The Blairs wanted a Republican
party organization to emerge in the South and saw the poor
whites of the region as the main support and advocates of such
an organization. They felt that the chief obstacle to the establishment of such an organization was the fear of the poor
whites that emancipation of the Blacks would lead to equality
and the intermixing of the races. Thus, "the idea of liber-
ating the slaves and allowing them to remain in the country,"
Blair asserted, "is one that never will be tolerated." When
the non-slaveholders of the South were convinced that Black
freedom and Black removal would go hand in glove, then the
Republican party would emerge as a power in the region.
Thus, Black removal or colonization in Blair's scheme was
not only a technique for destroying slavery, but also a method
by which a Republican party organization could be established
in this region of the country.

If anti-slavery Republicans saw these virtues in colonization, pro-slavery Republicans saw colonization as a way
to keep America a nation of white men. With virtues and
benefits appealing to both pro- and anti-slavery Republicans,
colonization as a "solution" was vigorously pursued. Blair
and other Republicans held that past colonization efforts had
failed because the removal plans were too remote. He proposed to settle Blacks in Central America; here the Federal
Government could buy land and grant Blacks free homesteads,
free transportation, and financial aid in establishing farms
and businesses. With such government support the colony

would flourish and would thereby attract more Free Blacks to
settle there.   As the slaves were emancipated, Blair argued,
they could be transported to the Black colony, to help improve and enlarge it, and establish new ones.   In time, all
Blacks would have been removed from the United States.

Having devised their scheme, the Blairs and Doolittle
"engaged in an extensive propaganda campaign within the party
on behalf of their proposal. "[23] Blair gave public addresses
on his colonization plan in New York, New England and the
Northwest, while Doolittle, in campaign speeches in Wisconsin
and Iowa, tried to convince westerners to endorse and adopt
the Blairs' colonization scheme.

The pleading and exaltations of the Blairs and Senator
Doolittle were not in vain.   According to Professor Foner,
"by early 1860, Governors of Iowa, Wisconsin, Illinois, and
Ohio had come out for colonization, as had an impressive list
of Republican congressional leaders including Preston King,
Henry Wilson, Lyman Trumbull, Hannibal Hamlin, James
Halan, Ben Wade, C. C. Washburn, Charles Sedwich and
James Ashley. "[24]   Republican newspaper support for Blair's
colonization scheme came from the Times, Evening Post, and
Albany's Evening Journal in New York, the Cleveland Leader,
the Wisconsin State Journal, the Chicago Tribune and Press,
and the Boston Daily Bee and Atlas.   In the Black community,
several Black nationalists, such as Martin Delany, H. Ford
Douglas, and William H. Darcy, favored Blair's proposals for
nationalist reasons.   But other Blacks, notably Frederick
Douglass, strongly opposed the scheme.

The Republican party platform of 1860 did not mention
colonization.   Fearing a probable intra-party fight and the
problems involved in writing a colonization plank, because it
was "too large a scheme and involved too many details, " the
pro-colonization Republicans didn't insist at the convention.
The lack of a platform didn't dampen their enthusiasm because
both Republican nominees were sympathetic to their proposals.
And Abraham Lincoln, during his first year in office, supported the idea. [25]

The Republicans and Black Suffrage: 1850's--1860's

Not all Republicans were pro-colonization.   Many individuals, such as John R. Hale, Francis Gillette, Charles
Sumner, William H. Seward, Thurlow Weed and Thaddeus

Stevens, came to the Republican ranks with a long history of support for Black rights, especially suffrage rights. While these individuals were a minority within the party, they still made efforts to advance the rights of Blacks to suffrage.

Moreover, Black voters had long supported the antislavery parties and their candidate on the state, local, and national levels. [26] Many of these former candidates and supporters of anti-slavery parties, who had won office because of Black votes, continued to urge Black suffrage rights now that they were Republicans.

In 1857, the Republicans in the New York legislature, after numerous petitions had been received, enacted a constitutional amendment providing for equal suffrage. [27] In Iowa the question of Black suffrage was debated at the constitutional convention of 1857. A minority of the Republicans present persuaded the convention, over Democratic opposition, to adopt a plan for a referendum on Black suffrage. [28]

In Ohio the Republican newspaper, the Ohio State Journal, and several Republican legislators tried unsuccessfully to get a measure on Black suffrage through the state assembly. A similar situation prevailed in Illinois and Indiana. In September, 1857, Blacks in Wisconsin again petitioned the state legislature, as they had done continuously since 1849, for their suffrage rights.

In Oregon, in 1857, there was no meaningful sentiment in favor of granting electoral privileges to Blacks. And in Minnesota, while a considerate element in the Republican party favored the elimination of discrimination on the basis of color from the text of the state constitution, they were too small in number to be effective.

The upshot then, is that Republicans in Iowa, New York, Wisconsin, Ohio, Illinois, and Minnesota favored equal suffrage before the Civil War. In many cases Republicans were instrumental in getting referendums passed by at least one house of the legislature or debated in the state constitutional or party conventions. But in all cases, these pro-Black Republicans failed to generate enough public enthusiasm to get the referendums passed. In fact, usually through fear of losing political office and popularity, some of these earlier Republican supporters of Black suffrage withdrew their endorsement of the measure at crucial times. Despite their timidity, though, the Republicans did carry the issue of equal suffrage

rights for Blacks to the people and did give it their tacit
approval.

The Democrats, on the other hand, emerged in state
after state as the main opponents of Black suffrage. They
unequivocally opposed giving Black men the same voting privileges that whites had. It was mainly due to this staunch
Democratic opposition that the measures which would have
extended the franchise to Blacks were defeated. It should be
kept in mind, however, that in all the states mentioned earlier, conservative Republicans allied themselves in many instances with Democrats to defeat Black suffrage.

Colonization and Black suffrage are just two examples
of the diversity of thought and action that existed within Republican ranks. The ambivalent and divergent viewpoints
within the Republican party, on Free Blacks and the slaves,
eventually dovetailed and converged in one individual, Abraham
Lincoln, who also expressed much ambiguity on the Black
issue.

Blacks and Abraham Lincoln

Linclon's rapid rise in the Republican party ranks and
his acceptance by the Republicans as their standard-bearer,
in spite of his loss of the senatorial contest in Illinois to
Stephen Douglas, the Democratic candidate in 1858, is indicative of his moderation and of his paradoxical actions and
views on the Black problem in America.

Stressing this same point, Professor Franklin Burdette
asserts that "in Abraham Lincoln ... the Republican party
found a leader of amazing effectiveness. Part of his extra-
ordinary capacity was his quiet, carefully-planned, well-
reasoned preparation for his announced political positions. "
Professor Eric Foner has written that, "by the eve of the
Civil War there had emerged a distinctive Republican attitude
towards the Negro [and] as on other questions, it was well
represented by Abraham Lincoln. " But despite his diverse
views as to the Black problem in America, Lincoln, like
many members of the Republican party, had some clear-cut
ideas on colonization and Black suffrage. [29]

In regard to colonization, Lincoln had quite definite
views, long before he became president. He asserted: "There
is a moral fitness in the idea of returning to Africa her

children, whose ancestors have been torn from her by the
ruthless hand of fraud and violence. "[30] In fact, Lincoln became such a firm believer in the value and promise of colonization that "he quietly managed in 1856 to reduce the influence of abolitionist elements of the Republican party" in
Illinois. [31]

Upon his assumption of the Presidency, the question of
colonization arose again, especially in relation to the problem
of what to do with the large number of slaves who began to
attain freedom as the war of secession progressed.   Lincoln,
in his first annual message to Congress, urged Congress to
consider colonization as a solution for "Free colored people"
and to aid them in their desire to leave the country.   At his
request, Congress appropriated $100,000 on April 16, 1862,
to aid in the resettling of persons of African descent.   On
August 14, 1862, Lincoln gave an audience to a number of
Blacks who had established an Emigration Society and encouraged them in their efforts.

Beyond his second annual message to Congress, urging
them to support colonization, Lincoln included remarks about
colonization in his Emancipation Proclamation of January, 1863.
In the Proclamation Lincoln said that he would propose to
Congress at its next session a practical measure to "colonize
persons of African descent with their consent, upon this con-
tinent or elsewhere with the previously obtained consent of
the government existing. " In sum, Lincoln, "without being
an enthusiast, was a firm believer in colonization.   And although his political ideas included colonization and emancipation, they always rested upon a voluntary basis. " If colonization was rather clearly stressed in Lincoln's thought and
political action, his position on the issue of suffrage was not
nearly as clear.

In his debate with Douglas in 1858 Lincoln repeatedly
asserted his opposition to enfranchisement of Black Americans.
"But in 1864, after emancipation and after thousands of Negroes had fought and died for the Union cause, he spoke favorably of limited Negro suffrage--perhaps on the basis of
intelligence and military service. " Lincoln met in 1864 with
Black representatives from New Orleans and North Carolina
who urged the President to aid them in securing the franchise.
He was so impressed with the former group that he penned
"a private letter to Michael Hahn, the newly elected Governor
of Louisiana" expressing his thoughts on the matter.

Lincoln's suggestion had no impact because the new Louisiana constitution granted suffrage only to white males. One year after transmitting these private thoughts on the matter, Lincoln, in his last public address in 1865, speaking of the failure of the new Louisiana constitution to give Blacks suffrage rights, said, "I would myself prefer that it [suffrage] were not conferred except on the very intelligent and on those who served our cause as soldiers."[32]

Professor Quarles succinctly summarized Lincoln's position on suffrage when he said that "Lincoln undoubtedly sympathized with the disfranchised. But as a rule he believed that the people of a state should themselves take the lead in matters affecting their welfare. On the suffrage ... Lincoln believed in federal non-interference. He wanted the states ... to confer the ballot on Negroes ... but if ... a state was unwilling to enfranchise the colored men, Lincoln was not willing to penalize her."

Lincoln's views before 1860 on colonization and Black suffrage made him acceptable to a majority of the Republican party. His views fitted confortably into the wide range of opinions that existed within the Republican party in regard to Free Blacks and slaves.

Black Political Action and Attitudes
and the Republican Party: 1858-1877

As the Black responses to the Republicans in the 1856 election reveal, Blacks give only tentative support to the new party because it didn't seek the complete destruction of the slave institution. It is easy to understand why most Blacks returned to support the regular anti-slavery parties (the Liberty Party and the Radical Abolitionist Party) on the local level in 1857.

When fifty-five Black delegates from a score of towns and cities in New York met in Troy, New York on September 14, 1858, at a state-wide Negro Suffrage Convention, they thoroughly discussed the Dred Scott decision and the possibility of supporting the Republican party on the state level. The Convention members advised "the eleven thousand colored voters of [New York] to concentrate their strength upon the Republican ticket for Governor, now before the people." The convention appointed William T. Watkins as a traveling solicitor to drum up votes for the Republican party in the state.

In Ohio, at the state convention of Ohio Colored Men meeting in Cincinnati from November 23-26, more than fifty Black state leaders condemned the Dred Scott decision, resolved that they would "rejoice at the declension of the Democratic party in the North and that its defeat presages the down fall of slavery, and urged support for the Republican party. "[33] Watkins, the traveling solicitor of the New York Convention, attended the convention in Ohio and helped to convince the convention that the Democratic Party had to be defeated.

By 1859, the Republican Party was enjoying a great deal of support from the Black community, and the support continued to grow. In fact, on August 2, 1859, many Black men and women from New York, New Jersey, Pennsylvania, Illinois, Canada, and all five of the New England states met in Boston in the New England Colored Citizens Convention, denounced the "unrighteous Dred Scott decision" and endorsed the Republican Party. [34] As the convention adjourned, the delegates were urged to return to their own states and localities and urge their followers to cast their support and influence for the Republican party. [35]

Despite vacillation on the part of some Black leaders, many Blacks "in several northern cities formed Republican clubs" and affirmatively supported the Republican organization. In fact, "the Colored Republican Club in Brooklyn raised a 'Lincoln Liberty Tree' in July, 1860. The colored 'West Boston Wide Awakes' marched in a massive Republican parade in Boston. "[36] And Blacks elsewhere, like Samuel Smothers, a Black educator in Indiana, wrote letters urging support of the Republicans.

Even after this strong endorsement of the Republican party by numerous Black leaders and conventions, as well as the increasing support within the Black community, Republicans at their second National Convention on May 18, 1860 in Wigman, Chicago, failed again to draw up a strong platform on Black rights.

One of the leaders of the Black community, Frederick Douglass, responded to Lincoln's nomination and the Republican platform in the June issue of his newspaper. In his editorial, Douglass stated that Lincoln was a promising prospect and that, while the Republican party wasn't fully committed to the dictum of "all rights to all men, " the prospect of the Democrats taking such a position or the anti-slavery parties

offering a meaningful challenge, led the Black community to
"desire the success of the Republican candidates. "

However, the Republicans made no efforts to win the
Black vote, although they "were attacked by the Democrats"
during the campaign as being "Nigger worshippers. " Since
the Republicans remained aloof from the Black community despite its continuous support, Douglass and several other Black
leaders attended the Convention of the National Political Abolitionists in Syracuse on August 29, 1860; at the Convention
Douglass declared that the Republicans and their platform
were "more unsatisfactory to the people than the Republican
convention of 1856. "

After being chosen as one of the presidential electors
for the party, Douglass later advised his newspaper readers
that "10, 000 votes for Gerrit Smith would do more for the
abolition of slavery than two million for Lincoln or any man
who stands pledged before the world against all interference
with slavery in the slave states and who is not opposed to
making free states a hunting ground for men under the Fugitive Slave Law. "[37] Thus, Douglass and several other Black
leaders urged the Black community to support the anti-slavery
parties, rather than the Republican party, because even after
Black endorsement, the Republicans had failed to make any
kind of meaningful overtures or policy changes for Black
Americans.

But pleas by Douglass' and other Black leaders came
too late. According to Professor Benjamin Quarles, "By
election time in 1860 the Negro vote was almost solidly Republican. "[38] In fact, dissatisfied as he was with the inade-
quacies of the Republicans, Douglass, as he had in the Fremont campaign, changed his mind about the Republicans and
ended up "campaigning for Lincoln in Michigan, Wisconsin,
and Iowa. "[39] When the election results came in, Lincoln and
the Republicans had won. The Republican victory raised a
ray of hope and optimism in certain segments of the Black
community.

As this account has revealed, Blacks took notice of the
newly formed Republican party from the outset in 1854, and
by 1856 they cast their votes and campaigned for the party.
By 1858 the Republicans began receiving strong endorsement
from the Black community. Although there was some Black
criticism and denunciation of the Republican party, Blacks
formed Republican clubs and strongly supported the party in

1860. Black Republicanism before the Civil War was largely
the result of a lack of effective alternatives in the existing
political system. Blacks joined and supported the Republican
ranks simply because, compared to the Democrats and anti-
slavery parties, it seemed the best of the lot. It seems to
have been more of a negative choice than a positive one,
stimulated not so much by Republican party appeal and action
as by Democratic accusations and the weakness of the anti-
slavery parties. The emergence of Black Republicanism was
firmly rooted, in the final analysis, in the desire of Blacks
to destroy the slavery institution, and a large factor was the
lack of verbal commitment or action toward this goal among
other political parties.

After the firing on Fort Sumter, the nature of Black
Republicanism's connections to the party became more positive, a shift concomitant with the changes in policy positions
which the events of the war led the Republican party to make.
As social historian Lerone Bennett says, "men in the mass
are taught not by books [nor speeches, campaigns, or plat-
forms] but by events."[40] In particular, "in the time of revolution, the real position stands out ·clearly, as if lit up by
lighting."

Moments of crisis and revolution, Bennett feels, reveal
the character and selflessness of groups and individuals. The
Civil War and Reconstruction created events and crisis situ-
ations to which the Republicans responded with decisive acts
--acts which caused the Black masses to bestow their ·allegi-
ance to the Party.

The first event, of course, was the beginning of the
war in April, 1861 and Lincoln's refusal to dissolve the Union.
As the war progressed, contrabands became a problem and
Lincoln moved from limited emancipation to compensated
emancipation and finally to full emancipation on January 1,
1863. The Act of Emancipation Proclamation, although limited
in scope, won thousands of Black supporters for the Republican Party and Lincoln. While some adverse criticisms of
the Republicans continued within the Black community, the
anti-Emancipation stand of the Democrats lessened its intensity and potential growth.

A militant minority of Black leaders in both the North
and the South, however, had not been won over to the Republican banner by the symbolic acts of Lincoln and other individual Republicans; they remained critical of Lincoln's con-

servatism and other Republicans' racist-oriented attitudes.
These militant Blacks "pointed to Lincoln's reluctance to take
decisive action against slavery in 1861-1862, his suppression
of emancipation edicts issued by his generals, his efforts to
colonize the Negroes, the injustices to Colored troops and reconstruction policy which would restore the former rebels to
power and leave the freedman little more than a peon on the
soil of his old master."[41] This group of Blacks plus a few
white radicals met in Cleveland on May 31, 1864--several
days before the National Republican Convention--and nominated
John C. Fremont and John Cochrane as their standbearers on
a platform of equal rights for Blacks in the South, an uncom-
promising prosecution of the war, constitutional prohibition of
slavery, reconstruction to be administered exclusively by
Congress, and the confiscation of rebel lands to be divided
among soldiers and actual settlers. One major Black leader,
Frederick Douglass, gave his blessing to the Cleveland Convention and strongly endorsed its proceedings.[42]

After the Democrats nominated McClellan on a peace
platform, however, Douglass immediately endorsed Lincoln
and urged the rest of the militant minority Black leaders to
do the same.

Total endorsement of the Republicans by Black Americans did not come until ten days after Fremont's withdrawal,
at a National Convention of Colored Men which gathered in
Syracuse, New York for the first time in more than a decade.
One-hundred and forty-four delegates from eighteen states,
including seven slave states, were present. Douglass was
elected president of the Convention, and in the main address
urged the delegates to support the Republican party at the
polls in November. Before the Convention adjourned, the
delegates reorganized themselves into the National Equal
Rights League and set the attainment of the ballot as their
major goal.

After the Convention, criticisms of Lincoln and the
Republican party dissipated in the Black community. The
militant faction which had decided to support Fremont now
came out for Lincoln. One Black publisher, Robert Hamilton
of The Anglo-African, told northern Blacks, a day after the
Convention, that "you and me may have thought that Mr. Lincoln has not done what we think he could have done for the
overthrow of oppression in our land, but that is not the question now. The great and overshadowing inquiry is, do you
want to see the many noble acts which have been passed dur-

ing Mr. Lincoln's administration repealed and slavery fastened
again upon Maryland, Louisiana, Tennessee, Virginia, and
portions of states now Free? This is the only question now,
and if you are a friend of liberty you will give your influence
and cast your vote for Abraham Lincoln, who, under God, is
the only hope of the oppressed. "[43] There was rejoicing
throughout the Black community, North and South, when it
was announced on November 21st that Lincoln had been tri-
umphant in the election.

Five months after Lincoln's inauguration the war ended,
on April 9, 1865. This event became another symbol of Republican goodwill for the Black community; meetings were
held throughout the country and joy sounded throughout the
Black community. Slavery, at long last, was dead. But in
the midst of jubilation the Republican party acquired a
martyr--a man who had attained great stature in the Black
community. Moreover, Lincoln was assassinated by a white
who was sympathetic to the Southern cause.

The mood of Black Americans was one of despair and
sorrow. Jack Flowers, a Black freedman on the South Carolina Sea Islands, expressed this mood: "It 'pears we can't be
free, nohow. The rebs won't let us alone. If they can't kill
us, they'll kill all our frien's sure."[44] Another Black freedman argued that Lincoln would be immortalized in the Black
community and his memory preserved for future generations.[45]

According to Professor Quarles, the grief-stricken
Black community translated their sympathy and indebtedness
into support for the Republican Party.[46] He asserts, "having
identified Lincoln with the ballot, the Negroes found the next
step much easier--that of linking him firmly to the Republican
party. The chieftains of the G. O. P. soon found that the name
Lincoln cast a spell over the Negro voters," a charm that
would lose its potency only after nearly three quarters of a
century. Blacks in effect tried to "keep Lincoln's memory
alive by voting the straight Republican ticket." Although
events arose which tested the Black community's allegiance
to the Republican party, other events and symbolic policies
restrengthened it. In the North, the Republican Party sponsored equal suffrage referenda, while in the South, Republican
congressional reconstruction led to the emergence of Black
politicians and public officers, which had an even greater
effect, gaining many new supporters for the Republican party
in the Black community.

The national election provided another chance for the
newly enfranchised southern Black, as well as northern Blacks
to support the Republican party. The electoral campaigns of
1868 clearly showed which party had at least some interest
in the plight of the Black community.

When the Republican National Convention convened at
Chicago in May 20-21, 1868 there were four Black delegates.
They were from North Carolina, Louisiana, Texas and South
Carolina. This was the first time in American political history that Blacks had been able to attend a political convention
of a major political party. Although their number was small,
even this token of recognition represented a signal advance
for Blacks, north and south. At the convention, moderate
Republicans, cognizant of the 1867 election defeat of Black
suffrage amendments, used this as an excuse to rally their
forces to nominate on the first ballot the military hero, General Ulysses S. Grant, in preference to the champion of Black
suffrage, Chief Justice Salmon P. Chase. Although Grant was
acceptable to most radical Republicans because they felt that
his flexible political position would permit them to win him
over to their point of view, they clashed with the moderates
on the issue of universal Black suffrage. "In the November
elections Grant won with a plurality of only 300, 000. The
Southern Negro vote, " argues Professor William Gillette,
"exceeding 450, 000, was indispensable to a Republican popular, but not electoral, majority. "[47]

After the election, Black leaders throughout the country
discussed the possibility of calling a national convention early
in 1869, to "discuss the major problems confronting their
people. " For in the several northern states Blacks still
didn't have the ballot, and in the South, the Democrats' attempts to coerce Black voters during the 1868 elections made
it clear that the Black voter needed protection, possibly in
the form of another amendment. On January 12, 1869, Blacks
from more than twenty-two states met in Washington, D. C. in
a truly national convention, with two purposes: to prod members of Congress who were indicating that they might throw
their support behind the proposed Constitutional amendment to
grant Blacks their suffrage rights, and to discuss their mutual
problems.

After numerous resolutions describing their difficulties
and handicaps, the Black delegates issued an address to the
people of the United States stressing the need for a guaranteed
franchise, and created two committees, one to visit the Pre-

sident and request his support for the amendment, another to
visit Congressmen and urge them to support the proposed
fifteenth amendment.   Each committee reported back that it
had met with a "favorable reception. "

The convention must have had an impact because, on
February 25, 1869, the fifteenth amendment had received the
necessary two-thirds vote in both houses of Congress and was
submitted to the state legislatures for their ratification.   The
jubilant Black leaders intensified the agitation for ratification
of the amendment, at the same time singing the praises of
the Republican party within the Black community.

During the campaign to get the fifteenth amendment
ratified, the Republican party extended further rewards to the
Black community.   Black Republicans who had been expelled
from the Georgia legislature by white supremacist Democrats,
were restored to their places with back pay.   Grant, in an
unprecedented act, appointed several Blacks to political office,
the chief appointment being Ebenezer D. Bassett as minister
to Haiti.   When November came, Black Republicans were
elected to the House and Senate for the first time in American
history.

The crowning symbolic act of the Republicans came
however on March 30, 1870 when a Republican president,
U. S. Grant, proclaimed the adoption of the fifteenth amendment, a Republican-sponsored piece of legislation.   According
to Professor Foner, "the Negro people and their friends were
jubilant.   Celebrations were the order of the day. "   Ten days
after the ratification of the fifteenth amendment, the American Anti-Slavery Society met for the last time and the Black
masses and leaders took this occasion to express their untold
gratitude to the Republicans.   Douglass, speaking at the meeting, remarked, "I am a Republican--a Black Republican dyed
in the wool, and I never intend to belong to any other party
than the party of freedom and progress. "

The legislative acts ranging from the Emancipation
Proclamation and the Freedmen Bureau to the Thirteenth,
Fourteenth, and Fifteenth Amendments were the chief measures by which the Republican party secured the allegiance of
the Black community.   These pieces of legislation had a meaningful impact upon the Black community: each measure meant
something specific--freedom, voting privileges, and the emergence of Black public officials.   These Republican-sponsored
measures were concrete examples, tangible results of Repub-

licans' interest and concern for the Black community. Black freedmen and officeholders were no illusion, and even the illiterate Freedmen could make the connection between these positive features and the benefits of Republicanism and the party.

In addition to its legislative enactments, the Republican party had appeal as the party of the martyred Lincoln and of numerous outspoken radicals like Sumner and Stevens, whose names became associated in the Black community with the cause of freedom and liberty.

Further, beyond symbolic legislative acts and charismatic and impelling personalities, the Republican party had organizations like the Union League and the Freedom Bureau which reached even the most illiterate and remotely isolated Blacks. These organizations carried the news of Republican greatness to places where Black leaders and newspapers had no sway, where "word of mouth" needed reinforcement, proof that it was really true. These organizations provided the personal contact that is always significant in persuasion and was necessary then to overcome dependency and the master-servant relationship.

Added to these factors were the recognition, political appointments and general courtesy that Republican party leaders extended to influential members of the Black community. Republican presidential and Congressional leaders met with Black delegations, listened to their problems and responded favorably in near-crisis times. The acceptance of Blacks at Presidential inaugurations, at national political conventions, and their appointment to several political offices, no matter how minor, were revolutionary changes and had a tremendous impact upon the emerging freedom-conscious Black community.

To these factors one could add other minor pieces of legislation sponsored by the Republican party, such as one giving Blacks the right to vote in the District of Columbia, the repeal of laws barring Blacks from carrying mail, and attempts to remove legal discriminatory barriers. These also had some effect upon the most literate of the Black community.

The Republicans were also active at local levels. In state after state they sponsored legislation to grant Blacks their suffrage rights, and some Republicans even campaigned on "equal suffrage" platforms. Moreover, numerous Repub-

lican newspapers strongly advocated and supported Black suffrage rights and freedom.   From 1865 to 1870, Republicans
on the state and local levels supported, in varying degrees of
intensity, many issues beneficial to the Black community. [48]

What one sees from 1854 to 1870 is an evolving progressive posture on the part of the Republican party toward
the Black community.   While political expediency, ambiguities,
timidity, and slowness were surely present in Republican actions and programs and proposals, the cumulative effects of
their policies and activities were far more significant and had
a great deal more influence than their retrogressions.   Moreover while these retrogressions, ambiguities, and negative
policies might have been known to the most sophisticated Black
leaders, the masses only saw the positive consequences.
While the essence of Black Republicanism stems from progressive Republican measures up to 1870, it was during the
era of Black Reconstruction, in which more and more Black
public officials served as symbols or examples of Republican
concern, interest, and dedication to the idea of freedom, that
Black Republicanism took even deeper roots.   Black politicians
themselves became the final link connecting the Black community to the Republican party.   They not only served the
Black community but helped to stimulate, motivate and maintain Black allegiance to the Republican party.

The Republicans themselves did not stop assisting the
Black community during Black Reconstruction.   The enforcement Acts, dubbed the "Force Bill," were passed and sponsored by Republicans in 1870 and 1877.   The Civil Rights Acts
of March 1, 1875, sponsored by the Republicans, guaranteed
individuals, regardless of their color, "the full and equal enjoyment of the accommodations, facilities, and privileges of
inns, public conveyances on land or water, theatres, and other
places of public amusement."[49]

In addition to their positive actions and activities, Republican efforts to capture the allegiance of the Blacks community had help from another quarter.   Their opposition--the
Democratic party--was a major source of aid.   The Democrats, almost from the beginning in 1856 to 1876 and beyond,
opposed almost all of the great humanitarian and equalitarian
concerns of the Republican party's leadership.   The Democrats
appeared almost always as the antagonist, the culprit, the evil
and sinister opponents of progress and concern for the Black
community.

On the local and state levels, the Democratic leadership led the fight to prevent Black suffrage and Black freedom.
According to Professor Forrest Woods, "Although many Republicans were indeed frequently inconsistent and equivocal on
the issue, their resistance to universal suffrage would best
compare to that of the Democrats. In the first place, Republican resistance never became a sustained crusade, with
racism an essential ingredient of the party's national campaigns or platforms. "[50]

Clemenceau, a French observer of the American situation, said as late as 1867, that "any Democrat who did not
manage to hint that the Negro is a degenerate gorilla would
be considered lacking in enthusiasm. "[51]

On the national level Democratic Presidential and Congressional candidates became identified with pro-slavery positions such as "squatter sovereignty, " and opposition to the
Civil War, the Emancipation Proclamation, and the thirteenth,
fourteenth, and fifteenth amendments. During the Civil War
their cries of "peace at any price" made them appear suspicious and untrustworthy to the Black press and top Black
leadership.

The voluminous output of miscegenation propaganda by
Democratic pamphleteers and writers during the 1864 campaign and thereafter left no doubt about their position on social
equality. [52] It is easy to understand, in this light, the emergence of a regional position--i.e., the Southerners' assumption
that the Democrats were a "white" man's party and the de-
fenders of white supremacy.

At least in the South, the Democrats translated these
beliefs into violent action from the 1870's on. The violence
which the Democrats unleashed against the Black community
during the era of Black Reconstruction, to recapture and regain their seats of power, also accounts in part for the Black
community's continued attachment to the Republican party despite its shortcomings.

In summary, a clear-cut delineation between the two
parties arose almost immediately in 1856, and continued almost unchanged until the turn of the century, if not thereafter.
Black politicians and the Black community could not but be
well aware of the differences.

The negative image the Democratic party had acquired

prior to the 1870's was enhanced by the violent and fraudulent policies and programs of segregation and discrimination
that it backed in nearly every southern state after Reconstruction.   Even after recapturing government offices or forcing
Blacks from the political arena, Southern Democrats went on
to establish Jim Crowism and the caste system of segregation.
The party's every action took it further and further away from
the Black community.

In conclusion, then, the roots of Black Republicanism
were laid in the Republican party's promotion of humanitarian
policies before 1870.   Whether the policies were the result
of expediency or ideological commitment, they nevertheless
aided the suppressed and nearly captive Black community. As
a Black clergyman, Reverend Peck of Pittsburgh, noted, the
Republican party had done the Negro good, but they were doing
themselves good at the same time. [53]   Republican sponsorship
of numerous policies and programs attracted the allegiance of
the Black community, and the intransigence and repression of
the Democrats enhanced that allegiance even as the Republicans lost some of their more progressivism and idealism.
Blacks simply had nowhere else to turn despite Republican
shortcomings; there was no third parties during this period
which offered a meaningful alternative.

Notes

1.   P. Herring, The Politics of Democracy (New York:
      Norton, 1940), p. 133.

2.   V. O. Key, Politics, Parties and Pressure Groups (New
      York: Thomas Y. Crowell, 1958), p. 501.

3.   Allan P. Sindler, Political Parties in the United States
      (New York: St. Martin Press, 1966), pp. 31-42.
      V. O. Key, Southern Politics (New York: Vintage
      Books, 1949), pp. 298-314, and Allan P. Sindler,
      "Bifactional Rivalry as an Alternative to Two-Party
      Competition in Louisiana, " American Political Science
      Review (September, 1965), pp. 641-662.

4.   For a brief analysis of the Black and Tans in Texas and
      Louisiana see H. Walton, Jr., Black Political Parties
      (New York: Free Press, 1972).

5.   The eleven states involved in this analysis are Georgia,

Florida, Alabama, Tennessee, Texas, Louisiana, Mississippi, Arkansas, North Carolina, South Carolina, and Virginia.

6. See Hanes Walton, Jr., The Negro in Third Party Politics (Philadelphia: Dorrance, 1969), pp. 22-29.

7. For an excellent discussion of the variety of racial attitudes that existed within the Republican organization prior to the Civil War, see Eric Foner, Free Soil, Free Labor, Free Men (New York: Oxford University Press, 1970).

8. Frederick Douglass' Paper, August 1, 1854, September 8, 1854, October 13, 1854.

9. Charles H. Wesley, Neglected History: Essays in Negro-American History (Wilberforce, Ohio: Central State College Press, 1965), p. 76.

10. Philip S. Foner, ed. The Life and Writings of Frederick Douglass, Vol. II (New York: International Publishers, 1950), p. 365.

11. Wesley. Neglected History, pp. 75-76.

12. For information on how Blacks participated in, supported, and voted for the early anti-slavery parties, see Walton, "The Negro, " pp. 9-21.

13. Quoted in Foner, Frederick Douglass, p. 379.

14. Quoted in Foner, Frederick Douglass, p. 82.

15. Proceedings of the Republican National Convention, 1856-1896 (Minneapolis, 1893), p. 15.

16. Franklin L. Burdette, The Republican Party: A Short History (New York: D. Van Nostrand Company, 1968), p. 20. See also Kirk H. Porter & D. B. Johnson, eds. National Party Platforms 1849-1964 (Urbana: University of Illinois Press, 1966), pp. 27-28.

17. Foner, Frederick Douglass, p. 396. As early as August 8, Douglass stated in his newspaper that he was looking forward to the Liberty Party and Radical Abolitionists party's joint convention on September 17.

"The issue, " he stated, "presented by the Republicans
for the restriction of evil is too narrow, " Frederick
Douglass' Paper (August 8, 1856), Ibid., 551, fn. 42.

18.   Ibid., p. 395.

19.   Quoted in H. Aptheker, ed., A Documentary History of
      the Negro People In the United States (New York:
      Citadel Press, 1969), p. 388.

20.   Quarles, Black Abolitionists, p. 189.

21.   For an excellent discussion of how the Republican party
      vacillated between colonization and suffrage rights
      before 1860, see Eric Foner, Free Soil, Free Labor,
      Free Men, chapter on "The Republicans and Race, "
      pp. 261-300.

22.   Ibid., pp. 276 & 268.

23.   Ibid., p. 276.

24.   Ibid.

25.   See Charles H. Wesley, "Lincoln's Plan for Colonizing
      the Emancipated Negroes, " Journal of Negro History
      (January 1919), pp. 11-12.

26.   Walton, The Negro in Third Party Politics, Chapter II.

27.   Emil Olbrich, The Development of Sentiment on Negro
      Suffrage to 1860 (Madison: University of Wisconsin
      Press, 1912), pp. 126-127.

28.   R. Dykstra and H. Hahn, "Northern Voters and Negro
      Suffrage: The Case of Iowa, 1868, " Public Opinion
      Quarterly (Summer, 1968), p. 207

29.   For a greater insight into the paradoxes that Lincoln
      represented for the Black community, see Benjamin
      Quarles, Lincoln and the Negro (New York: Oxford
      University Press, 1962), and W. O. Douglas, Mr.
      Lincoln and the Negro (New York: Atheneum, 1963).

30.   Quoted in Charles H. Wesley, "Lincoln's Plan for Colo-
      nizing the Emancipated Negroes, " Journal of Negro
      History (January, 1919), p. 8.

31. Burdette, The Republican Party, p. 23.

32. Brainerd Dyer, "One Hundred Years of Negro Suffrage,"
     Pacific Historical Review (February, 1968), p. 3.

33. Aptheker, Documentary History, pp. 412-413.

34. Ibid., p. 434.

35. Quarles, Black Abolitionists, pp. 189-190.

36. James M. McPherson, The Negro's Civil War (New
     York: Vintage Books, 1965), p. 10.

37. Wesley, Neglected History, p. 76.

38. Quarles, Black Abolitionists, p. 190.

39. Foner, Frederick Douglass, pp. 528-529.

40. Lerone Bennett, Jr., What Manner of Man (Chicago:
     Johnson Publishing Company, 1964), p. 156.

41. McPherson, The Negro's Civil War, p. 303.

42. Foner, The Life and Writing of Frederick Douglass,
     Vol. I, pp. 43-44.

43. Anglo-African (September 24, 1864), p. 1.

44. Quoted in McPherson, Civil War, p. 307.

45. Ibid., p. 300.

46. Quarles, Lincoln and the Negro, pp. 245-246.

47. Gillette, Right to Vote, p. 40.

48. Glenn M. Linden, "A Note on Negro Suffrage and Re-
     publican Politics," The Journal of Southern History
     (August, 1970), pp. 411-420.

49. R. Logan, The Negro in the United States (New Jersey:
     D. Van Nostrand, 1957), p. 34.

50. F. Woods, Black Scare (California: University of Cali-
     fornia Press, 1968), p. 92.

51.   Ibid.

52.   For a complete analysis of the prejudicial and anti-Black
      basis of the Democratic party, see Woods, pp. 53-
      80.

53.   Gillette, op. cit., pp. 119, 165, 175.

Chapter 2

THE ROOTS OF BLACK AND TAN AND
LILY-WHITE REPUBLICANISM

With the passage of the Fifteenth Amendment in 1870,
anti-slavery societies disbanded, many of the old Radical
Abolitionists had passed on, and efforts on behalf of the Black
man slackened as interest began to fade. The crusade was
all but over. "Regarding the ballot as a panacea," says Professor Gillette, "whites could in good conscience leave
[Blacks] alone now because [Blacks] could protect themselves
with the ballot and without the help of government."[1] But the
job was hardly over, for, as Radical Republicans and Abolitionists dismantled their battle equipment and demobilized their
forces, the whites of the South were reorganizing, developing
strategies and structuring a crusade to rid themselves of
"nigger domination." As one group of troops marched home,
feeling that the war had been won and victory secured, another
group was marching to battle. "The plan reduced Negroes to
political impotence. How? By the boldest and most ruthless
political operation in American History. By stealth and
murder, by economic intimidation and political assassination,
by whippings and maimings, cuttings and shootings, by the
knife, by the rope, by the whip. By the political use of
terror.... By fear."[2]

While these activities were carried on underground,
aboveground the Democratic attempted to control the votes of
their former slaves. The plan and organization succeeded.
"White rule was restored in Tennessee in 1869; in Virginia,
North Carolina, and Georgia in 1870; in Alabama, Arkansas,
and Texas in 1874; and in Mississippi in 1875. Thus, only
South Carolina, Louisiana, and Florida remained to be 'redeemed' in 1876."[3] Black Reconstruction was on its way to
ending and Black allegiance to the Republican party, while not
wavering, was beginning to enter an era of profound reassess-
ment as the Democrats continued their battle against the Black

30

voter. Since the National Republican party had turned its
attention to other issues in society, the task of furthering
Black rights fell to the state Republican parties, which were
ill-equipped to accept the mantle.

The Republican Party in the South:
The Foundations

The foundations of the early Republican party in the
South rested upon a political coalition of Scalawags (white
southerners who became Republicans during Reconstruction),
Carpetbaggers (Northern politicians or adventurers who went
South after the war and sooner or later became active in politics as Republicans) and Black Freedmen.   This political
coalition was for all practical purposes cemented together by
the Reconstruction Act of 1867.   With this Act, the Congressional Radicals took over the reconstruction of the South from
the President, Andrew Johnson, and reorganized the South into
military districts, thereby giving impetus and political power
to the Republican sympathizers and supporters.

Prior to the Military Reconstruction Act, the three
components of this political coalition existed as distinct and
separate political coteries.   The Blacks, with no political
power, were organized in the Equal Rights Leagues and other
such associations.   Another element in the political coalition,
the Carpetbaggers, remained separate and distinct prior to
the Act because of their diverse interests and reasons for
adopting the South as a new home.   Some Carpetbaggers pursued their business endeavors and dreams, others sought out
opportunity and personal advancement, and yet others pursued
humanitarian impulses and motivations.

The final element in the coalition--native whites
(Scalawags)--were also loosely organized and separated from
other possible Republican groups in Southern society.   This
disorganization was due in part to the fact that the Scalawags
were made up primarily of four separate and distinct groups
in Southern society.   One group was the Unionists, Southerners who had supported the Union cause before the war and who
suffered during the period that the secessionists were in
power; and who now wanted to retaliate and to participate in
government.

Another Scalawag faction were "the poor whites and
yeoman farmers" who resided in the upland and hill country

and harbored a natural animosity for the Delta farmer and
planter class.   "The cleavage between the planters of the
Delta and the rednecks of the hill, " says V. O. Key, "has
persisted for half a century and even yet appears from time
to time. "[4]

   "A third source of Scalawag strength came from
Southerners engaged in business enterprises and from those
living in regions which were rich in natural resources and
had an industrial potential. " And the last group of Scalawag
supporters were the upper class Southerners who had supported the Whig Party before the Civil War.   This group, being more affluent and socially secure individuals in Southern
society, saw the Republican party as heir apparent to the
Whig tradition.

   It was questionable from the beginning how long such
a fragile political coalition could hold together, and from the
outset, a major positive disruptive factor was present. Among
two of the groups that comprised the Scalawags there were
negative feelings about Blacks.   "A very large proportion of
[the] Unionists Scalawag element had little enthusiasm for one
aspect of the radical program: the granting of equal civil and
political rights to the Negroes. "[5]   Among the poor whites and
yeomen farmers, race prejudice was very intense: "As men
of low status and low income ... [they] were keenly aware
that the Negroes were potential social and economic competi-
tors. " Race prejudice was not the central focus of the Carpetbaggers and the Whig-Scalawags element: "They too believed in white supremacy but they seldom made the crusade
to keep the Negroes a subordinate caste the central purpose
of their lives. "[6]

   At the beginning the anti-Black feelings and prejudices
were submerged in order to further the Republican organization and its promise.   But when competition and pressure
arose and were applied, the fragile coalition very quickly came
apart at the seams.   The submerged and repressed race feelings immediately surfaced.   But we shall discuss this factor
later [see Diagram 1].

   As the Republican party continued in the South, more
and more stress was placed upon it and four major factors
eventually caused the fragile coalition to fall apart.   These
factors were: 1) intra-party factionalism: 2) violence, fraud,
and intimidation by the Democrats; 3) race prejudice from
without and within; and 4) Republican Presidential policies toward the southern party.

DIAGRAM I

The Nomenclature of the Southern Republican Party's Coalition
Before and After 1877

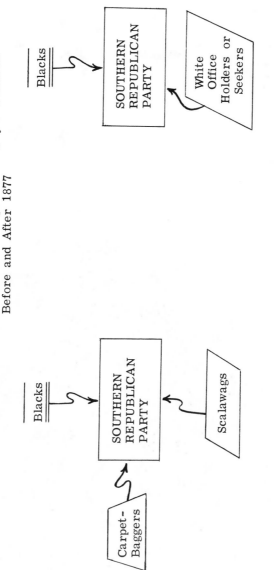

Intra-Party Factionalism

"Every coalition," argues Professor William Riker,
"has internal conflicts over the discussion of spoils."[7] Almost from its inception, the Republican party's coalition in
the South began to be undermined by internal rivalry over the
distribution of party favors and patronage. "When pressure
from an opposing coalition is great, so great in fact that the
opposition may win and thereby deprive the coalition of any
spoils to distribute, these internal conflicts are minimized.
But when pressure from the outside diminishes, there is less
urging to settle the internal conflict amicably."[8] This was
definitely the case with the Republican coalition in the South
because there was little competition from the Democrats, who
were scattered, divided, and disorganized. Moreover, the
Military Reconstruction Act of 1867 enabled the new military
government to disfranchise most of the Democratic supporters.[9]

Hence, with little outside competition, the Carpetbaggers and Scalawags battled each other for spoils and positions
and other fruits of the Republican party victories. In South
Carolina, a feud broke out between the two groups when an
honest and conscientious Carpetbagger replaced a corrupt
Scalawag governor. In Georgia the Scalawag governor, Joseph
E. Brown, who used his office to become president of a
steamship company, a railroad, a coal company, and an iron
company, antagonized both the members of his own group and
the Carpetbaggers as well; both groups tried to dislodge him
and his supporters from the helm of the party in the state.
In Mississippi James Alcorn, a Scalawag who became the first
Republican governor of the state, collaborated with the Whigs
and tried to give them control of the party. This action drew
the wrath of other Scalawags and Carpetbaggers and they combined to put a Carpetbagger governor in office in 1873. In
Alabama, upland or hill whites fought the Whigs and Blacks
for property in the rich delta planter region of the state. In
Louisiana the pro-Grants and anti-Grants fought each other.

In other states, rival Republican business groups fought
each other for legislative favors, while rival Republican reform groups sought to destroy each other over desired policies
and programs. Factionalism also arose because of rivalry between two prominent political leaders who sought to gain control of the party apparatus. Last but not least, factional dis-
content emerged as Blacks began to assume more and more
political offices. This increase in Black politicians would

cause white party leaders to conspire to limit or fix the number of offices Blacks could hold or the type that they could
aspire to.   When Blacks didn't accept the quotas set by whites,
further trouble accrued within the party apparatus.

Intra-party fights and divisions resulting from these
factors greatly strained the Southern Republican political coalition and dissipated much of the party strength.   But when
the National Republican party split during the 1872 election
between the Stalwarts and Liberal Republican and decreased
the patronage which the party could disperse, the intra-party
rivalry intensified over the meager spoils and diminishing
fruits of victory. 10   However, intra-party competition was not
the only factor that wrecked the party's fragile coalition.
Another factor which wrecked the coalition was the resurgence
of the Democratic party.

Democratic Violence,   Fraud and Intimidation

Southern Democrats began to regain their strength in
1870 when the Republicans lost 41 seats in the House and six
in the Senate, and thereby, partial control of Congress.   In
1872 Congress, under pressure from the Liberal Republicans,
passed a general Amnesty Act that finally removed the political restrictions upon most of the South's pre-war leadership
and restored the right of officeholding to the vast majority
who had been disqualified under the provisions of the fourteenth amendment.   Once these individuals began to assume
power, they sought to overthrow the Republican coalition, and
in fact, they applied pressure to each segment of the coalition as well as upon the entire party.

Democratic Klansman "broke up Republican meetings,
threatened radical leaders, whipped Negro militiamen, and
drove Negroes away from the polls. "11   Democratic terrorism
became the order of the day and was perpetrated on Black
and white Republican alike.   The pattern of violence that conservatives [Democrats] developed became generally known as
the "Mississippi Plan, " or sometimes as the "shotgun policy."
Taking the Mississippi state election of 1875 as an example,
one can readily see how systematic force and terror were
used to capture political office.   On election day, Blacks either
hid in the swamps or stayed in their cabins or showed up at
the polls with Democratic ballots.   Those who were brave
enough to bring Republican ballots to polling places were fired
upon, driven away, misled, or fraudulently manipulated so
that their ballots didn't count.

Violence was not the only tool. Economic coercion
was also employed against Black and white Republicans. For
instance, in Henry County, Alabama, landlords required Black
laborers to sign political contracts before they could acquire
a job. The contract stated "that said laborers shall not
attach themselves, belong to, or in anyway perform any of
the obligations required of what is known as the 'Loyal League
Society' or attend elections or political meetings without the
consent of the employer. " In short, to vote meant the loss
of a job, medical aid, credit, food, supplies, and materials.

Beyond violence and economic coercion loomed fraud
and manipulation. According to social historian Lerone Bennett, "Ballot box manipulation reached an artistic height.
Polling places were located in bayous and on islands, in barns
and fodder houses. "[12]

This still wasn't all: the Mississippi Plan had some
additional techniques for use against white Republicans.
"White Republicans were ostracized. Their children were
hounded in school. Their wives were cut to the quick at
church. "[13] The end effect of these tactics was that the fragile political coalition within the Republican party began to dis-
integrate and White Republican southerners started to switch
back to the Democratic party.

"Many of the parting scenes, " states John Lynch, a
Black politician in Mississippi during Reconstruction, "that
took place between the colored men and the whites who decided to return to the fold of the Democrats were both affecting and pathetic in the extreme. " Describing one such parting, Lynch says that the Black president of a local Republican
club, Sam Henry, was urging a white ex-Confederate Colonel
James Lusk to stay within the Party ranks for the benefit of
all:

" 'Oh! No, Colonel, ' Henry cried, 'I beg of you do not
leave us'.... If you leave us, hundreds of others in our immediate neighborhood will be sure to follow your lead. We
will thus be left without solid and substantial friends. I admit that with you party affiliation is optional, with me it is
different. I must remain a Republican whether I want to or
not.... I plead with you don't go. '[14]

" 'The statement you made, Henry, that party affiliation with me is optional, ' the Colonel answered, 'is presumed
to be true; but, in point of fact it is not. No white man can

live in the South in the future and act with any other than the
Democratic party unless he is willing and prepared to live a
life of social isolation and remain in political oblivion. ...
Besides, I have two grown sons. There is, no doubt, a
bright, brilliant, and successful future before them if they
are Democrats; otherwise, not. If I remain in the Republican
party--which can hereafter exist at the South only in name--
I will thereby retard, if not more, and possible destroy their
future prospects. Then, you must remember that a man's
first duty is to his family. My daughters are the pride of
my home. I cannot afford to have them suffer the humiliating
emergencies of the social ostracism to which they may be
subjected if I remain in the Republican party. '[15]

     " 'The die is cast, ' Lusk insisted. 'I must yield to
the inevitable and surrender my convictions upon the altar of
my family's good--the outgrowth of circumstances and conditions which I am powerless to prevent and cannot control.
Henceforth, I must act with the Democratic party or make
myself a martyr; and I do not feel that there is enough at
stake to justify me in making such a fearful sacrifice as
that. ' "[16] Thus, Lusk bade Henry and the Republicans farewell and switched to the Democrats. And whites all over the
South, like Lusk, "crossed over Jordan. "

     In state after state the Democrats "redeemed" the state
for and in the name of white supremacy. Tennessee, Virginia, Georgia, and North Carolina were redeemed by 1871,
and the remaining seven southern states fell to the systematic
pattern of violence, fraud, intimidation, and social ostracism
before 1876.

     Black Republicans and their allies put up a good fight
but their resources were meager. White Democrats controlled the money, the land and the credit facilities. [17] The
fragile Republican political coalition collapsed under systematic and sustained Democratic terrorism and soon the Southern Republican party became composed of only "faithful, loyal
and sincere colored men, who remained Republicans from
necessity as well as from choice, and a few white men, who
were Republicans from principle and conviction, and who were
willing to incur the odium, run the risks, take the chances,
and pay the penalty that every white Republican who had the
courage of his convictions must then pay. "

     As the Republican coalition of Carpetbaggers, Scala-
wags, and Blacks deteriorated under the resurgence of the

Democrats a realignment took place. The new Republican
coalition, which basically emerged in each state as Democratic
redemption took place, became one primarily of Black and
white federal office holders and seekers. As Diagram One
reveals, this new or second political coalition was well under
way by 1877, after the disputed election had finally enabled
the Democrats to redeem the last remaining states of South
Carolina, Florida, and Louisiana. The whites who remained
in the party after the onset of the Democratic restoration
tactic were those who had gained sufficient rewards or
had been promised that they would be shortly forthcoming.
Without rewards such as federal patronage, in terms of
office, federal contracts, subsidies, loans, or appointments,
whites had little reason to continue to act with Blacks in the
face of nearly overwhelming opposition from the rest of the
white community.

        Even this second Southern Republican coalition didn't
last. It came under renewed attack by the Democrats and by
various Republican Presidents from 1877 until three decades
into the twentieth century.

Presidential Policies toward the Southern
Republican Party after Reconstruction

        The Republican political coalition in the South changed
during Reconstruction because of resurgent Democratic Bour-
bonism. The coalition underwent even greater change after
Reconstruction due to the southern Republican policies of
Hayes, Garfield, Arthur, and Harrison. While each President
had a different southern policy, the final effect of each was
the subordination of Blacks and an appeal to southern whites.

        Hayes' policy of wooing southern whites, Garfield's
policy of education and limited support to independents,
Arthur's policy of total support for the Independents, and
Harrison's policy of seeking to organize a southern Republican
Party on the basis of protection tended to elevate the remaining whites in the Republican party to positions of dominance
and power. In so doing, it completely polarized the organization in the South. This trend toward polarization began with
Hayes and neared culmination under Harrison, who actually
recognized several "lily-white" Republican organizations in
the South, notably in South Carolina, Alabama, and Louisiana.
In several other southern states where the Independent movement was fairly effective and had achieved some small mea-

sure of success, Harrison gave them the assent to head up his new Republicans.   In all, Harrison's policy was a logical conclusion to those of Hayes, Garfield and Arthur.   Together, their policies had built a new southern Republican party that was not heavily dependent upon Blacks.   To build such a party, top organizational and leadership positions had to be given to whites to attract them to the organization; and these new white Republicans, since they had to compete effectively with the Democrats, generally known to be the white man's party, felt it necessary to purge their party of its Black supporters and leaders.   This move, however, was only one aspect of the larger trend which had been emerging in the South: the demand for white supremacy in all areas and the insistence that politics was white men's business.

The ideology of white supremacy had permeated southern society and any organization which did not uphold this principle could not be effectively supported by local whites. The emergence of a "lily-white" Republican party in the South resulted, therefore, not just from Republican Presidential policies; it was also the product of inherent demands and the customs of southern life-styles.   It was, in a word, inevitable.

"Black and Tan" Republicanism was born of two similar forces.   First, the white supremacy principles and policies, as well as the violent actions and terrorism of the Democratic party, precluded any significant shift by Blacks into the Democratic ranks.   Blacks, even if they had accepted white supremacy, could not switch en masse because the Democrats were determined to remove Blacks from the political arena, by whatever means available.

Secondly, the Republican Party, because of its actions from the Civil War to the end of Reconstruction (as discussed in Chapter 1), had tied both Southern and Northern Blacks to it.   Their civil rights program, the Emancipation Proclamation, the Reconstruction Act, etc. had drawn the Black man deeper into the party ranks and even the Republicans' new shift in the South didn't, comparatively speaking, evoke much criticism from the Black community.   After Reconstruction, Black criticism of the Republican Party was kept at a minimum through the judicious use of patronage and appointing of Black leaders.

Thus, for a variety of reasons, the Southern Republican Party had begun to polarize itself on the basis of race--

white and Black.   When McKinley came to power in 1896 the
Republican Party had two clearly identifiable factions (a lily-
white and a Black and Tan) in the South.   And the Black and
Tan faction had a rapidly dwindling number of voters.

In 1890 Mississippi called a constitutional convention
to rewrite the constitution that had been drawn up under the
Reconstruction Acts and that had given Blacks the right to
vote.   The new constitution of 1890 stripped Blacks of their
right to vote, with numerous legal devices ranging from
grandfather clauses to reading and interpretation tests.   Mississippi's new constitution, in effect, legally barred Blacks
from the polls.   The only Black delegate to the convention,
Isaiah T. Montgomery, a wealthy and conservative businessman, greatly approved of the new constitution's elimination of
Black voters on the basis of lack of education and property.

The most significant impact of the Mississippi plan
was that it became the "American way" in the South. [18] State
after state followed Mississippi's lead in disfranchising Blacks
on one ground or another.   During the ten years or more of
this process Black voting in the South declined appreciably.
In fact, the Black and Tan faction, each year after the 1890's,
became less and less a viable vote-getting organization and
more and more small coteries and cliques of officeholders
and patronage seekers.   The Black and Tans became self-
seeking little groups, looking to Washington, D. C. for support
rather than to their own communities, because the era of disfranchisement effectively destroyed their local bases of community support.

Even as the Black and Tans began to decline, the lily-
whites never really grew at any significant pace.   The Democratic hold over the populace of the South was nearly un-
breakable except during the Populist Era of the 1890's, and
even this group returned to the Democratic fold before 1900.

McKinley continued the Harrison policy of supporting
the lily-whites and appointing a few Blacks to federal office,
but instituted a new policy at National Republican Conventions.
This dualism in McKinley's southern policy was helped by two
factors.   Booker T. Washington's Atlanta Exposition speeches
in 1895, in which he urged Blacks to drop their interest in
politics and seek to accommodate to the white man's politics,
helped to perpetuate segregation and limited demands from the
Black community for equal treatment.   In addition, a Supreme
Court decision in 1896 declared "separate but equal" to be

constitutional, and thus legally sanctioned dualism in American life. This decision, coming prior to McKinley's nomination, provided obvious justification for his support of the separate Republican factions. These two factions came to play a major role in the making of national convention strategy, and McKinley's strategy would remain as a policy at least until 1932.

McKinley's new policy toward the Southern Republican party emerged during the 1892 national convention, when he was in the running for the Republican Presidential nomination. At that convention he didn't receive enough convention votes to win, but it became evident to him and his political manager, Mark Hanna, a millionaire industrialist, that the two Republican factions which had begun their seating challenges at the national conventions could be useful in securing his nomination. Just prior to the 1896 convention, Hanna made a tour of the South, seeking to commit one of the factions in each of the southern states to his candidate at the national convention. To get a faction committed, money and promises of patronage were offered. The tactic succeeded: McKinley was nominated on the first ballot in 1896.

At the convention were nine Black delegates from six southern states. They were crucial in gaining McKinley the nomination. Recognizing the "crucial support of Negro delegates in the national nominating convention"[19] McKinley adopted a policy of playing off one faction against the other in order to secure his next presidential nomination. (This will be discussed in greater detail in Chapter 4.) McKinley's southern Republican policy in this respect--i.e., maintaining two distinct factions, especially the Black and Tans when they had no real vote value--was continued by each Republican President who followed until Hoover's nomination in 1932. After 1932, Hoover capitulated entirely to the lily-white faction and did all he could to destroy the federal basis of support of the Black and Tans. While Black and Tanism finally died shortly after Hoover's new policy change, one or two factions like that of ole "tireless" Joe Tolbert from South Carolina continued until 1956.

In summary, the first southern Republican coalition collapsed during Reconstruction and a new one began to take its place after Reconstruction. As Diagram II illustrates, not only did a new readjustment take place within the Republican party; it began to polarize into two major and clearly defined factions during the era of President Harrison and after the Southern policies of Hayes, Garfield, and Arthur.

DIAGRAM II

The New and Emerging Southern Republican Party's Coalition

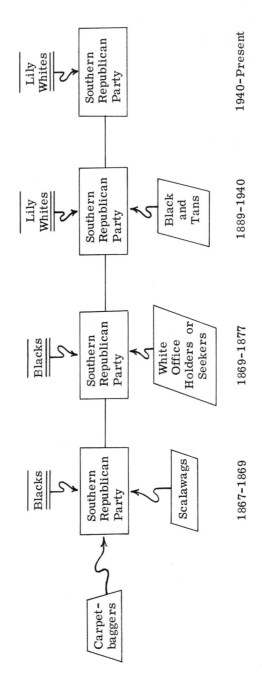

Carpet-baggers → Southern Republican Party ← Scalawags	Blacks → Southern Republican Party ← White Office Holders or Seekers	Blacks → Southern Republican Party ← Black and Tans	Lily Whites → Southern Republican Party
1867–1869	1869–1877	1889–1940	1940–Present

President McKinley and subsequent Republican Presidents continued the policy of a bifactional or dual Republican organization in the South because of the possible usefulness of one or the other--the lily-whites or the Black and Tans--at the national nominating conventions. Either one faction or the other could be persuaded, by money or patronage, to support a particular Presidential candidate for the nomination. This support became significant when there were numerous contenders for the party's nomination. Any prospective candidate who could arrive with assurances that a certain number of delegates would back him had half the game, if not all of it, won. The scramble for convention delegates became the primary reason that the Black and Tan faction remained a force, even when they had no possibilities of capturing state voters to the Republican organization. Southern Republicans became Presidential Republicans, useful primarily at the national conventions. For their cooperation, the rewards were indeed significant: numerous federal posts ranging from postmasterships to consul posts and ambassadorships with prestige and large salaries. For these rewards the two factions struggled with each other, for supremacy in the state, recognition by the national party and President, and control of the patronage for the entire state.

Notes

1. William Gillette, The Right to Vote (Baltimore: Johns Hopkins Press, 1969), p. 162.

2. Lerone Bennett, Jr., Before the Mayflower (Baltimore: Penguin Books, 1968), p. 197.

3. Rayford Logan, The Negro in the United States (New Jersey: D. Van Nostrand, 1957), p. 32.

4. V. O. Key, Southern Politics: in State and Nation (New York: Vintage Books, 1949), p. 230.

5. Kenneth M. Stampp, The Era of Reconstruction 1865-1877 (New York: Vintage Books, 1965), pp. 162-164.

6. Ibid., p. 196.

7. William Riker, The Theory of Political Coalitions (New Haven: Yale University Press, 1968), p. 66.

8. Ibid.

9. William A. Russ, Jr., "Registration and Disfranchise-
    ment under Radical Reconstruction," Mississippi
    Valley Historical Review, XXI (1934), pp. 163-180.
    See also his "Radical Disfranchisement in Georgia,
    1867-1871," Georgia Historical Quarterly (Septem-
    ber, 1935), pp. 178-207.

10. Patrick W. Riddleberger, "The Break in the Radical
    Ranks: Liberal vs. Stalwarts in the Election of
    1872," Journal of Negro History (April, 1959), pp.
    136-157.

11. Stampp, Era of Reconstruction, p. 200.

12. Bennett, Before the Mayflower, p. 216.

13. Ibid.

14. John R. Lynch, The Facts of Reconstruction (New York:
    Bobbs-Merrill, 1970), p. 121.

15. Ibid., p. 127.

16. Ibid., p. 123.

17. Bennett, Before the Mayflower, p. 217.

18. C. Vann Woodward, The Origin of the New South, 1877-
    79 (Baton Rouge: Louisiana State University Press,
    1951), p. 321.

19. Clarence A. Bacote, "Negro Officeholders in Georgia
    under President McKinley," Journal of Negro History
    (1959), p. 219.

Chapter 3

BLACK AND TAN REPUBLICANS
ON THE STATE AND LOCAL LEVELS

The term "lily-white" Republican was coined by a Black Republican leader, Norris Wright Cuney, in Texas after a riot occurred at the State Republican Convention on September 20, 1888. [1] The riot grew out of a clash between Black and white Republicans when the latter group attempted to wrest control of the Party organization from a Black, Cuney. In addition to the fight for party control, there was also fighting "between the colored and white factions ... over placing a ticket in the field. "

The use and perpetuation of the phrase "Black and Tan" Republican can be linked to numerous Southern newspapers. In Louisiana the term "Black and Tans" was applied to the Regular state organizations after the lily-white had withdrawn. "This name was applied to this group by newspapers and by general popular use and was never officially recognized by the regular organization itself. "[2] Louisiana served as a model for other states: in state after state whites withdrew from the regular party organization which was dominated by Blacks and formed their own lily-white groups or clubs. Once the lily-white group had become a reality, the regular organization was then generally referred to by all the newspapers and public media as the "Black and Tan" group.

The term "lily-white" referred not only to political organization but also to its set of beliefs. This organization condemned and denounced the Negro in general and his participation in Southern politics in particular. Lily-white Republicans upheld the idea of white supremacy and the social system of segregation in the South.

Black and Tanism, on the other hand, endorsed Black suffrage, Black participation in politics and Black equality.

45

As a newspaper euphemism, it also referred to the wide range
of skin colors and hues that existed with the Black groupings.
Black and Tan Republicans not only didn't condone segregation; they protested it.   The Black and Tans tried continuously
to improve their lot and, from time to time, the poor conditions of the Black community, too.   However, the former
role--i. e., improving their lot with better patronage, positions and larger salaries--became their chief concern as disenfranchisement removed more and more Black voters from
the political arena.   In some localities, indeed, the Black and
Tan organizations became merely self-seeking groups with no
concern for the welfare of the Black community.   Because
the Black and Tan leaders had no constituencies, like the
lily-whites, they became primarily presidential rather than
local groupings; the local Republican electorate was not strong
enough to enable them to win state offices.   Although each
group coalesced or fused with the Populists, Democrats, or
Prohibitionists in varying degree from state to state to win
some election or other, neither group alone could attain enough
votes for any significant state or local electoral victories.

In addition to the lack of a constituency, the self-cen-
tered outlook of the Black and Tans was also fostered by the
nature of politics itself.   Politicians are generally more concerned with getting elected and re-elected than with the promotion of social, economical, and racial justice, and the
Black and Tans were politicians first and Blacks second.   The
environmental and political circumstances of the South severely
limited their social and racial consciousness.

In a paradoxical way, however, racial and social consciousness did find expression at the state and national conventions.   In fighting each other for control of patronage and
the right to be seated at the national conventions, both sides
issued charges of racial discrimination and claims that they
had the backing of the community.   In these intra-party battles, racial discrimination and the needs of the Black community were used by both groups to belittle or eliminate the
positions of their opponents in the struggle for power.   And
out of these power struggles some small benefits would at
times accrue to the Black community.

For instance, the "lily-whites, in order to avoid the
charges of racial discrimination from the national committee,
solicited a small Negro membership but quite consistently with
the avowed objectives of the lily-whites, the colored members
had no voice in the government of the organization. "[3]

The Black and Tan faction also had a mixed composition, many whites remaining within it for reasons of ideology
or ambition. In South Carolina, a white man, Tireless Joe
Tolbert, led the Black and Tan faction for more than forty
years. He and his Black followers were either delegates or
contestants for seats at every Republican national convention
from 1900 to 1956.[4] In other states Black and white leadership alternated and there were some where Black leadership
prevailed exclusively.

While some Black and Tan organizations had white
leaders, the lily-white organizations maintained a limited
Black membership only to avoid charges of racial discrimination at the national convention, since such charges could
hamper their efforts to get seated, in preference to the contesting Black and Tan delegation. Thus, they included Blacks
out of necessity. It may be noted, though, that some Blacks
joined the lily-white Republican organization, not out of fear
but out of their basically conservative outlook:[5] they accepted
the tenets of white supremacy.

Despite their limited base and lack of constituency,
despite their mixed racial composition, and despite their
chances of achieving electoral victories within their respective
states, the Black Tans and the lily-whites continually fought
each other for recognition by the national committee as the
official party in the States as well as for control over state
patronage. Each group employed a number of political techniques, ranging from electioneering and propaganda to legalism and fisticuffs, to eliminate, suppress, or discredit its
opponents. It is with these political techniques, and with the
emergence of the Black and Tans on the state and local level,
that the rest of this discussion is concerned.

GEORGIA

For nearly two years after the Civil War, "there was
little discussion of party politics in Georgia."[6] The impact
of the war had been devastating and men and women were too
"busy in the herculean task of bringing order out of the chaos
which surrounded them to spend very much time in discussing
politics." President Johnson had appointed a provisional governor and numerous political leaders had not yet been par-
doned; thus, Party lines did not develop immediately.

During the last months of 1866 and all of 1867, how-

ever, political activity in the state was intense, in anticipation
of the emerging state Republican organization. Basically
speaking, the unionist elements of the state, anti-secessionists
and Whigs, the Carpetbaggers and the Blacks began three separate paths toward political ascendancy which culminated in
the first Republican Party organization and state convention at
Atlanta on July 4, 1867. [7]

At first the southern element--i.e., the Unionists,
Whigs, and anti-secessionists--began its own organization with
the formation of a Union League. Blacks, on January 10,
1866, formed the Georgia Equal Rights Association, while
Carpetbaggers fused with one or the other of the two organizations depending upon their ideology and moral convictions.
At first, each of these Republican-oriented groups in Georgia
began going its own separate way.

The passage of the Military Reconstruction Act in February, 1867 brought these groups together into one political
unit--the Republican Party. They united under a common
banner because of the prospects in the upcoming election and
constitutional conventions which were feasible as a result of
the Reconstruction Acts. The promise of political rewards
brought together this unwieldy and precarious coalition.

The Republicans during their first state convention in
1867 adopted platform planks which made it clear that the
party would "appeal to the Negroes and to the whites in North
Georgia [hill whites] and in the Wire grass country [marshes]
of South Georgia." With this "delicate allegiance of Negroes,
yeomen, white farmers, and the few railroad and industrial
promoters," the Republican party was able to stay in power
from 1867 until 1871 in Georgia.

During 1871 intra-party disputes badly divided and disorganized the party. There was antagonism between the Carpetbaggers and the native whites, antagonism between native
whites and Blacks, between officeholders and office seekers.
"The political activity of the Negro," claims Professor Olive
Shadgett, "was a primary cause of splits and fractional fighting and of defection from the ranks." Many whites "who had
aligned themselves with the Republican Party and acquiesced
in the Reconstruction Acts, including the requirements of
Negro suffrage, had never subscribed to the doctrine that this
gave the Negroes full political equality and the right to hold
office." It was on this basis that white Republicans and Democrats came together in the Georgia House of Representatives

on September 3, 1868 to expel twenty-five of the twenty-nine Black members. Later, they expelled two of the remaining four. However all these Black members were reinstated, with back pay, by the federal government in 1869.

Externally, the party was beset by charges of malfeasance and corruption in office, and the delicate coalition which was so vital to the party's success collapsed. The Democrats redeemed the state in 1872 and Democratic governor, James M. Smith, was inaugurated on January 12 that year. Ever since, for over one-hundred years, Georgia has always had a Democratic governor.

Although the Democrats installed a governor in 1872, the total "redemption" of the state didn't come in a single political campaign; it was a slow, torturous affair. Once the Democrats regained hegemony over the Republicans in the state, however, they didn't relinquish it. They made every effort, from 1872 on, to further suppress and weaken the Republicans.

In addition to Democratic repressions, internal problems and a tainted public image, "the Republican national committee disposed of" the party in Georgia in 1872, "rejected [its] pleas for aid and left the shattered remnants of the state party to their own devices." The last Republican candidate for governor in Georgia was nominated in 1876 and there was never any real chance of winning the presidential electoral vote after 1868. [8]

Under the pressures of Democratic resurgence and repression, whites began a general exodus from the Republican party in 1872. To continue to work in the Republican ranks "meant to work with Blacks, to meet with them, to be classed with them" in the public eye, and this was unpalatable both to most native whites and to most of those who had come to Georgia from other parts of the country. From 1872 to 1932 the Republicans more and more were a party of Blacks, with few white officeholders or office-seekers.

With this white exodus the Black and Tan faction became a reality. From 1872 until 1880, the party was like a pyramid, with a few white leaders on top in control and the masses of Blacks as the base, furnishing the political muscle and content with the small fragments of patronage thrown their way. The arrangement was apparently so satisfying during this period that there was no clash between the two races within the party.

This odd state of affairs caused the leading Democratic paper in the state, the Atlanta Constitution, frequently to express surprise that Blacks would submit to the control of the few whites who dominated the party. The paper took pains to point out in 1876 that there were many Black men "of fine manners and more than ordinary education ... mental powers of no mean merit, "[9] who deserved to lead the party organization.

Under such Democratic chiding and prodding, and with the emergence of new Black leaders, Blacks at the Republican state convention in 1880 took advantage of controversies among the few white leaders and seized control of the party machinery. This seizure caused a breach in the party ranks and provoked proposals by several whites for a separate white Republican party in Georgia.

The origin of the Black and Tan faction in Georgia can be dated from April 21, 1880 when the state party convention convened in Atlanta. J. E. Bryant, the white Carpetbagger who was General Superintendent of the Freedman's Bureau and chief organizer of the Black Georgia Equal Rights League in 1876 and its president thereafter, expected to be re-elected as state chairman and sought to enhance this possibility by profusely stating his loyalty to his Black friends. "Ordinarily Bryant was known as a shrewd and successful operator with the Negro element but on this occasion he made a blunder which was to cost him his leadership in the party. "[10]

Bryant, trying to stave off a discussion of the method of selecting a chairman and to conciliate the Black delegates, offered a resolution on how patronage should be disbursed in the state. Hoping that his resolution would capture the convention's attention (because, with all chance of state patronage gone and little hope of elective offices remaining, federal patronage was all that remained), Bryant suggested that the division of federal offices in Georgia should be on a fifty-fifty basis between the races. However, "others immediately suggested that three-fourths for Blacks would be more in line with the racial composition of the organization. "

A Black, Edwin Belcher from Augusta, offered a substitute proposal to test the sincerity of Bryant and other whites. Designated as the last speaker in the state convention, Belcher moved that three-fourths of the delegates to the forthcoming national convention in Chicago should be Black delegates. This motion drew great cheers from the Black

delegates and was quickly passed since Blacks were in a majority at the meeting.

The white delegates, failing to get Belcher's motion
tabled, tried to keep the committee on delegates from sub-
mitting a report in conformity with Belcher's resolution. They
took this action primarily because to have a resolution about
patronage adopted by a convention that didn't control it had
little meaning, but to have another resolution slip by that instructed the convention on its choice of delegates was indeed
significant.

But even the white delegates' move to short circuit the
committee on delegates' report went haywire. When the list
that appeared was not in conformity with the Belcher motion,
Blacks asserted themselves and had the list revised to include
fourteen Black and eight white members. Of the four delegate-at-large positions, Blacks got three. This latter move
was particularly significant because the delegates-at-large
were usually considered the leaders of the intra-state delegation. Bryant, who began the resolutions, failed to get a post
as either delegate or delegate-at-large.

Even with this lion's share of representation on the
state delegation, Blacks still sought more control and advantage. They next turned their attention to the state chairmanship and the state central committee, electing William
Pledger, the young Black publisher of the Athens Blade, to
serve as state chairman. This was a signal honor for
Pledger: he was the first Black to serve in this capacity.
Having elected a Black state chairman, Blacks then named
twenty-four Blacks to a thirty-two-member new states central
committee. Once again, Bryant and most other white leaders
of the party were omitted. When the convention adjourned,
Blacks were in full control of the Republican party apparatus.

Concomitant with this take-over by Blacks was the
emergence of several new and younger Black leaders like
Pledger. There was also Edwin Belcher, the sharp and ar-
ticulate Black orator from Augusta, and other new Black party
wheelhorses included T. M. Dent of Rome, Monroe "Pink"
Morton of Athens, J. H. Deveaux and R. R. Wright[11] of Savannah, C. C. Wimbish, Jackson McHenry, and Henry A.
Rucker of Atlanta. These men replaced the old Black party
leaders and legislators such as Jefferson Long, H. M. Turner,
Aaron Alpeoria Bradley, and Tunis C. Campbell.

Long was the only Black in the United States Congress
and the first Black to speak on the floor of Congress. Born
a slave, he was self-educated and worked as a tailor-merch-
ant in Macon. After losing his seat in the U. S. House of
Representatives he remained active in Georgia politics for
only a short time. H. M. Turner, who was among the earlier Black organizers of the party, was one of the Black
members of the Georgia House who were expelled in 1868.
After being expelled, he organized a protest convention and
went to Washington to effect a change in the state legislature's
behavior. Later he became a missionary and then a bishop
in the African Movement. Aaron Bradley, a runaway slave,
found freedom in the North and pursued the legal profession.
Returning to Georgia after the Civil War, he set up practice,
built up a considerable following in and around Savannah, and
united himself with the Republican Party. He quickly rose
through the ranks and was elected to the Georgia House several times. After twice being expelled, he was disbarred in
1880 from the legal profession, and the state the same year.

Tunis C. Campbell was born in Bound Brook, New
Jersey and came to Georgia in 1865. Working as an agent
of the Freedom Bureau, he acquired a large following and
was elected to the State Senate in 1868. Although expelled
he was reseated in 1870 and held the seat until 1872.

Even with this new, young and better educated Blacks
in control of the party apparatus, whites were not happy with
the outcome. Immediately after the close of the convention,
white Republicans set their plan in motion. They ran a call
in all the Atlanta newspapers the day after the convention,
urging whites to assemble at the City Hall on April 27th to
make plans for a separate, lily-white, party organization.

When the white Republicans convened on April 27th,
Jonathan Norcross, a wealthy leading citizen of Atlanta and
a former mayor of the city (elected in 1850), gave the keynote address. He declared that this movement wasn't a bolt
but a move to strengthen the party by attracting to it the
thousands of whites who had not joined because that would
have officially brought them in contact with Blacks. Following Norcross' remarks, a committee was established to write
to those whites who had withdrawn from the party because of
its association with the Blacks, tell them of the plan for a
"lily-white" organization, and urge them to become once again
Republican members. Having made this decision to contact
latent and potential white party members, the lily-white meeting adjourned.

On May 15, 1880, this lily-white committee issued a
notice in the Atlanta Republican asking white Republicans to
attend a state meeting in Atlanta on June 22nd for further
consultation and action.   The call also urged the regular Republican organization--the one which Blacks dominated--to
hold simultaneously a similar but separate meeting, and suggested that the two groups could cooperate through conference
committee.   The call reiterated that this movement was not
intended to divide the party but to rebuild it.   It also indicated that both chambers of the state house had been reserv-
ed; one side for Blacks and the other for whites.

The scheduled June 22nd meeting didn't get underway
until July 6th and only a small number of white Republicans
attended.   When it convened Norcross was designated as chairman, W. L. Clark, editor of the Atlanta Republican, was
named secretary and a number of committees were named.

Pledger, the Black state chairman, came to the white
meeting and told the Norcross group that the white movement
was antagonistic to the interests of the state party.   Sharp
words were exchanged between Pledger and Norcross, and
Pledger finally left the meeting.

After the meeting, the Norcross movement disappeared,
unable to get the support of the white officeholders "who composed the real power bloc in the party."   The white officeholders refused to join Norcross' lily-white movement because
they were busy making plans of their own to recapture control
of the regular (Black-dominated) organization at the next state
convention in 1882.   The white officeholders behind this strategy were A. E. Buck (clerk of the United States District
Court) and General James Longstreet (a United States Marshal
in Atlanta).   Moreover, they organized a clique among the
white officeholders, dubbed by the newspaper as the "syndicate
to dispose the federal offices in the state, keeping the best
ones for themselves."   The syndicate members entertained
the notion of a coalition with the independent movement, if
necessary, to remove Blacks from control of the party organization.[12]

On July 31st the executive committee of the Party
(composed of Blacks and a few white officeholders) met to
make plans for a state convention on August 2nd.   Little was
accomplished and the meeting was adjourned.

On August 3rd, the Black and Tans held a caucus in
the printing office of the Weekly Defiance in Atlanta, a meet-

ing was headed up by Pledger and T. H. Brown, the Black editor of the Defiance. At the same time the Pledger-Brown meeting was going on, General Longstreet was holding a meeting of the white federal officeholders at the post office building. When the Defiance meeting adjourned, Pledger, Brown and several other Black and Tans went over to the post office and tried to gain entrance. Although the door-keeper temporarily barred them, the Black and Tans forced their way in. A ruckus ensued and Pledger and Brown were arrested. Later they posted bond and were released. 13

The next morning the Longstreet faction held a caucus before the scheduled 10 o'clock convening of the state convention and issued a call for a convention to take place at noon at the United States courtroom. To make this new convention appear authentic, the Longstreet faction issued and distributed circulars and dodgers containing the names of two Blacks, John H. Deveaux and James Few, and two whites endorsing the rescheduled meeting. Three of these men were also members of the regular state executive committee--which made the circulars appear all the more official.

The Pledger-led group convened at ten o'clock sharp and waited until eleven before they started party business, hoping party members would realize they had been duped and return to the fold. With the Pledger group (composed primarily of Blacks and a few whites--i. e., the Black and Tans) starting at eleven, Longstreet's group (mostly whites and a few Blacks--i. e., the lily-whites) began their separate convention at noon.

The first order of business at each convention was the establishment of a conference committee to work out the differences between the two factions and seek some means of grounds for reconciliation. But each attempt at reconciliation failed. With all hope of conciliation "cut off, each convention proceeded with its own business and drew up its own slate of candidates for state office, " and both groups endorsed the candidacy of the Independent, General L. J. Gartrell, for Governor.

Each faction evenly divided its slate so that it would appear to the public that it represented the real Republican organization in the state. The tickets were as follows [p. 55]:

After naming their respective tickets, each faction named its own state central committee and state party chairman.

Pledger Ticket

Congressman-at-Large	R. D. Locke (W)
Secretary of State	R. R. Wright (B)
Attorney General	George S. Thomas (W)
Comptroller General	W. A. Pledger (B)
Treasurer	F. F. Putney (W)

Longstreet Ticket

Congressman-at-Large	James Longstreet (W)
Secretary of State	W. J. White (B)
Attorney General	J. D. Cunningham (W)
Comptroller General	Floyd Snelson (B)
Treasurer	William F. Bowers (W)

After these developments the Longstreet faction made an appeal to President Arthur (who had adopted a southern strategy of supporting the white Independent movement in the South as a way of building upon the Republican party) for help. The first appeal went unanswered, but a second appeal to Arthur and his political advisor on Southern matters, William E. Chandler, resulted in a deal. The Pledger-led Black and Tans were promised minor public offices in the state and national party positions if they would give up their control over the party machinery, let whites run the party and support the Independent candidate for governor. The deal was accepted and A. E. Buck, a white man, emerged just before the state election as chairman of a united party. A coalition slate of candidates was offered to the voters on election day, headed by the Independent General Gartrell, who was running for Governor. The new coalition had the following candidates:

Coalition Ticket

Independent Governor	Lucius J. Gartrell (W)
Independent Congressman- Ninth District	Emory Speer (W)
Independent Congressman- Seventh District	W. H. Felton (W)
Republican Secretary of State	William A. Pledger (B)
Republican Attorney General	S. A. Darnell (W)
Republican Comptroller General	Floyd Snelson (B)
Treasurer	W. F. Bowers (W)

Prior to election day, "Black Gartrell Clubs" began organizing in the Black communities "in every county of Georgia. "

Moreover, as the ticket indicates, there was an attempt to one balanced among the lily-whites (Snelson and Bowers were of the Longstreet group), Black and Tans (Pledger and S. A. Darnell), and the Independents. Despite its balance, its white leadership and its appeal to the best whites in the state, the entire ticket was defeated by the Bourbon Democrats. A. E. Buck, nevertheless, arose as undisputed "boss of the Republican Party in Georgia and held unbroken tenure as its chairman ... [from] 1882 until his departure for Tokyo in 1897. " In addition, he was a delegate to every national convention from 1880 through 1896. [14] Pledger, the new Black and Tan leader, who had agreed to give whites control over the organization, was appointed Surveyor of Customs at Atlanta. James Deveaux was appointed national committeeman and several other Black Republicans received minor positions in Savannah, Augusta and other places. [15]

Jonathan Norcross played no part in the 1882 fight for party control. In 1884, however, he made another futile attempt to establish a lily-white party. He held two poorly attended conventions, delivered a series of "addresses" to white Republicans and, at the first convention meeting on April 8th, even adopted the name, the "Whig Republican Party. " Although General Longstreet joined Norcross' movement because he had lost power to Buck in the regular party organization, the lily-whites, or Whig Republican Party, never got much support. In fact, Norcross merged with the regular party to become a presidential elector by August of 1884.

After 1884 the lily-white group remained dominant and the Black and Tan wing declined to a position of subservience in the party organization. That arrangement remained intact until 1920. In fact, racial matters subsided in the party and for the next decade intra-party clashes arose mainly over the question of fusion with the agrarian and Populist movements that arose in Georgia in the 1890's until nearly 1900.

Populism, being a movement on the part of farmers to gain a political hearing for some of their economic and agricultural problems, invariably involved Blacks. When state elections came up, the Republican chairman, Buck, urged his organization to fuse with the Populists and support them. This caused dissension in the ranks and some Republicans, Black and white, disagreeing with Buck, bolted the party. At the same time, the Populist movement had a strong appeal to Black voters. In fact, during state elections from 1890 to

1900, some Black Republicans voted with the Democrats, others merged with the Populists and supported their organization. In the 1894 state election "there was a great deal more fusion between the two parties" (Republican and Populist) than there had been in 1892, and this trend continued until 1896 when the Populist movement collapsed on the national level and steadily declined thereafter in most Southern states, especially Georgia. [16]

By 1896 the Republicans turned their attention to the presidential campaign, having lived for four years under a Democratic President, Grover Cleveland. Republicans were also interested in state elections and congressional races, and supported the Populists for state offices while the Populists supported Republican congressional candidates. When the Republican meeting that year selected an all-white ticket of presidential electors, however, the Black wing of the party began to bolt.

Led by new Black leaders like C. C. Wimbish of Atlanta and Henry L. Johnson, an attorney and law partner of W. A. Pledger, Blacks sought their share of possible national patronage. Knowing that the Populists wanted "their votes but not their company, " the majority of Blacks at the state central committee meeting on April 17th refused to fuse again with the Populists. One Black leader, H. L. Johnson, stated that "the intelligent Negroes of Georgia know that there is far more hate and spleen against the Negroes in the Populist camp than in the Democrats. " With this understood, Black leaders who had conferred with Republican Presidential hopeful William McKinley in his tour through Georgia in 1895 began taking steps to be included among the delegates to the National Convention.

McKinley's southern tours set the stage for another party division on racial lines. Here was the advent of a new tactic for Republican Presidential hopefuls. Since the Civil War, there had been numerous candidates at every Republican National Convention seeking the Presidential nomination. These individuals would bargain and dicker with nearly every state delegation to attain their support. Generally, the bargaining and persuasion took place chiefly during the convention.

However, in 1895, one year before the National Convention, McKinley's political advisor, Mark Hanna, a wealthy Ohioan industrialist, decided to apply his business principles to politics: that is, he planned to secure the support of state

delegations prior to the convention.   As Hanna envisioned it,
the best possible region in which to employ this pre-convention strategy was the South, since in most states there existed
two distinct and competing factions.   Each faction could be
polled as to the candidates it planned to endorse and at least
one of the factions could be persuaded before hand to support
a particular candidate.

With such a plan in mind, Hanna, in January, 1895,
rented a large house in Thomasville, Georgia, "where he and
McKinley met and entertained federal officeholders, whites
and Negroes, from the entire South. "   "All winter, " says
Professor Shadgett, "a steady stream of Southern politicians
flowed through the House on Dawson Avenue, " and his political strategy assured McKinley "of a large majority of delegates from the deep South. "

Although Hanna and McKinley saw both Blacks and
whites at their Thomasville retreat, McKinley held a special
meeting with Black Republican leaders in Georgia (the Black
and Tan faction) to insure their support for his candidacy in
case the white McKinley clubs should change their minds at
the convention.   Before the meeting McKinley visited several
local Black churches and then proceeded to a meeting at the
State Industrial College for Blacks, presided over by the college President, a leader among Georgia Republicans.

At the meeting, Reverend E. K. Love gave the main
address to some "fifty colored preachers, teachers, lawyers,
and politicians. "   After Love's address, McKinley spoke of
the advancement that Blacks were making in education and in
agriculture, and of the pleasant reception given him.   Then
he advanced patronage promises to the group if they would
support his Presidential bid, and quickly left for a tour of
Florida, where, again, the majority of Republican voters were
Blacks.   His political advisor, Hanna, knew that it was wise
not to antagonize the Black community, at least before the
Convention.

McKinley wasn't the only candidate playing up to the
two southern Republican factions.   Others were Thomas B.
Reed, Speaker of the House of Representatives, Senator W.
B. Allison of Iowa, Senator Shelby M. Cullom of Illinois,
Senator Matthew Quay of Pennsylvania, and Levi P. Morton,
the New York Governor and former Vice President under
Benjamin Harrison.

At the state convention on April 29th, a tremendous
fight took place. Each district had contesting delegations who
issued charges of political deals. At first the fight centered
mainly on candidates, but later the division was along racial
lines, since the majority of both whites and Blacks were for
McKinley. To add sparks to the fire, each presidential candidate opened a headquarters across from the state convention and openly and lavishly courted the prospective delegates.
Shadgett says, "a special feature of the McKinley headquarters was a large room where only delegates were admitted, "
fitted with tables fairly groaning with eatables and drinkables,
sandwiches and cakes, and a hogshead of lemonade.   "Cigars
were passed out with a free hand; a bootblack dispensed free
shines. " The other presidential hopefuls, not having the
financial backing of McKinley, had a "combined" headquarters
in the Imperial Opera house, next to McKinley's.   "The
headquarters of the 'combine' presented a lively appearance
alone with the Atlanta Dixie Band as the star attraction. "
Both groups had people to meet the delegates coming to the
state convention and take them to the reception rooms of their
respective candidates.

This sharpened the competition between the two groups
and no harmony could be ascertained.   The A. E. Buck and
Pledger-led lily-whites named their delegates amidst the confusion and left the convention hall.   Upon their departure, the
Wright-Love (Rev. E. K. Love, president of the First African
Baptist Church in Savannah, the oldest Black church in
America, founded in 1789) Black and Tans named their own
delegates, a state central committee, and a platform endorsing McKinley.

The two contesting delegations went to the National
Convention and the dispute was settled by the convention committee.   Twenty-two of Georgia's twenty-eight votes eventually went to McKinley, two to Quay, and two to Reed.

After the convention white Republican leaders made a
bid to attract more white businessmen on the issue of protection and to drop Black members.   Black party leaders were
persuaded to go along with this move by offers of patronage
favors in exchange for their agreeing to only whites being
presidential electors and electors-at-large.   Even after the
November national elections, the all-white trend continued,
with Blacks acceding because of the many positions McKinley
gave Blacks in the state, ranging from paymaster to United
States Marshal.

In spite of McKinley's wooing of white Republicans, writes Professor Bacote, Blacks "regarded McKinley as the best friend they ever had, pointing out that he had appointed more Negroes to responsible positions in Georgia than all earlier Presidents combined, including posts not held before by the race. " For instance, on the state level he appointed Blacks to the Internal Revenue Collectorship, Collectorship of the Port of Savannah, Postmasterships at Athens and Hogansville, and the superintendency of the stamp division. On the national level, he appointed a Black as Consul at Asuncion, Paraguay, and R. R. Wright as paymaster in the U. S. Army with a rank of major.

When McKinley visited Georgia on December 18, 1898, he stopped off at the Industrial College for Blacks (Savannah State College) and delivered an address to over one thousand people, urging Blacks to "be patient, be progressive, be determined, be honest. . . . " Although he didn't during his tour, condemn race restrictions or lynching, which was on the rise, criticism or independent action were not forthcoming from Blacks so long as he continued his policy of giving them recognition as officeholders. Black Republicans were thus content to let whites run the party, and the Black and Tan revolt was once again undermined by patronage.

If Blacks did little to stop the new move toward an all-white leadership of the Republican party, with Black subordinates in the background, the Democrats, recognizing that such a party could break their hegemony over the state, took action. McKinley had polled more votes in Georgia in the 1896 election than any other Republican candidate since 1872. Thus, the Democratic state executive committee adopted a statewide primary system in 1898 and made it mandatory for all counties. This shifted the focus from the general election to the Democratic "primary. " In 1900 the primary was made a white primary--that is, it was limited to white voters only. Southern states had earlier disfranchised Blacks, the main supporters of the Republican party in the South, and this new move decreased even further what limited powers the Republican party had and reduced it to a small coterie or "a small closed corporation" of a few Blacks "and white men who kept up just enough organization to send themselves as delegates to Republican National Conventions and to keep themselves in office. " In fact, the party was deliberately kept small because the "fewer there are to divide the pie, the more there is to go around. " The party failed to put up candidates for state and local elections or to conduct all-out campaigns for

new voters. The primary function of party members became
that of controlling the state party machinery and nominating
delegates to the national convention every four years. The
entire party became primarily "Presidential Republicans, "
acting every four years, then falling back into oblivion until
the next national convention.

To be sure, from 1900 until 1932, when Hoover capitulated to lily-whiteism (we shall discuss this in detail in the
next chapter), there was some dispute in the Georgia delegation. For example, when the few remaining Blacks--like
newcomers A. T. Walden, a Black attorney in Atlanta, John
W. Dobbs, a Black insurance executive, and Ben Davis of
Atlanta--felt that they were not getting their fair share of
patronage, they sent rival delegations to the national conventions in 1920, 1924, 1928, and even 1952. But while they
gained seats based on the Presidential hopefuls' control of the
Credentials Committee, the Black and Tans' day had long
since faded, as the party had faded in the Southern states.

The final blow to the limited Black and Tanism that
existed after 1928 came after Hoover was elected in 1928.
The President-elect removed all Black Republican officeholders and party officials and placed whites in their place. For
instance, he used Ben Davis' delegation to secure his nomination and after the election removed Davis from his post of
National Committeeman from Georgia. Democratic control of
the Presidency from 1932 to 1952 and the attraction of the
New Deal in Georgia gradually drew Blacks into the Democratic fold. Black and Tanism in Georgia ended, essentially,
in 1928. Although in any meaningful sense it had faded much
earlier, even its limited expression after 1900 ended with
Herbert Hoover's election and the coming of the New Deal.

In sum, then, Black and Tan Republicanism in Georgia
was primarily a matter of coalition. Each time the Black
wing of the party revolted against white hegemony and sought
to control the party, it was eventually bought back with patronage and national power. Desirous of public office and
patronage handouts, the Black and Tans generally acceded to
white control over the party in order to obtain their ends.
Thus, each revolt ended in a return to the same organization
they had bolted from. The only real revolt occurred in 1880.
Although it lasted only until 1882, this was probably the longest period in which Blacks dominated the organization. In the
final analysis, coalition was the principal ingredient of Black
and Tan politics in Georgia.

TEXAS

On July 4, 1867, Unionists, Radicals, and Freedmen converged in Houston and held the first state Republican convention in Texas. "This convention came about as a result of several mass meetings held throughout the state" by the Union Loyal League during the first half of 1867. In Texas, as in the other southern states, the Loyal League aligned Blacks and the Black vote with the fledging Republican Party. Professor Casdorph states that in Texas, the "Radicals through the League lost little time in enlisting the colored voters on their side. "

Consequently, when the convention met at Houston in July, it was "overwhelmingly African in composition; the white delegates did not exceed twenty in number while the colored numbered about one-hundred and fifty. "[17] A state Republican organization was formally established and the outlook of the party was clearly delineated.

On July 19th, fifteen days after the convention, the second Reconstruction Act was passed by Congress and a call went out in Texas for a constitutional convention to be held in February, 1868. In that election, the Republicans were overwhelmingly victorious, receiving 44, 689 votes for and 11, 440 against the calling of a new convention.

Nine of the ninety delegates elected to the constitutional convention were Blacks. A new constitution, which took the convention more than a year to draw up, gave Blacks full voting rights in Texas. Before adjourning, the convention set November 30th as the date for state election of officials to serve under the new document.

However, the final document as drawn up caused a split in the Republican party ranks. This split occurred over the so-called ab initio question, which asserted "that all laws passed in Texas during the Confederate regime were null and void from the very beginning. " When the party members failed to write the ab initio doctrine into the state constitution and state party platform, a section of the Republican party under the leadership of two whites--E. J. Davis and J. P. Newcomb--bolted the party. It was at this point that the Texas Republican party became solidly divided into two distinct factions: the Radical wing led by Davis and Newcomb, the other considered the Conservative element in the party. Most Blacks supported the Davis-led wing.

Although the two wings sought reconciliation, even
sending delegations to the Grant Administration to discuss the
matter and ask for the President's help, no progress was
made.   Each group, therefore, prepared in its own fashion
for the new upcoming election.

The Radicals (or predominately Black group) held their
first pre-election convention in Galveston on May 10th.   A
Black, C. T. Ruby, who had been a delegate at the 1868 National Convention in Chicago, was made president of the convention.   A tentative platform was adopted at a second meeting held in Houston on June 7, 1869, and named a state ticket
with E. J. Davis as their choice for Governor.   The Conservative wing of the Republican party nominated a well-known
white Unionist, A. J. Hamilton, and numerous Democrats
promised to support his bid for election.

In the election, the Radical Republicans captured control of both houses of the state legislature.   Eleven Black
Republicans were elected in the party's landslide victory.

After taking power in 1870, the Republicans in Texas,
already badly split and competing with each other, came under
severe attack from the Democrats.   The national split in the
Republican ranks in 1872, with the appearance of the Liberal
Republican third-party movement, furthered the Radical-Con-
servative schism within the state party, the Conservative wing
strongly supporting the new Liberal party movement.   As a
result, the Democrats captured both houses of the state legislature in 1872.   Since the governor was elected for four
years, however, Davis didn't lose his seat to a Democratic
candidate until 1874.   That was the year when the Democrats
supposedly restored home rule.   In any event, the crushing
defeat handed the Republicans in the 1874 gubernatorial election relegated the party to one of token opposition in Texas.

Even after the defeat of E. J. Davis and his Reconstruction government, though, Blacks continued to play a
prominent part in Texas Republican politics.   A sizable number of Black delegates were sent to the national convention
in 1876 and several Blacks were in the state legislature during this period: for example, in the Twelfth state legislature
(1871) there were eleven; in the Thirteenth (1873), eight; in
the Fourteenth (1874), seven; and in the Fifteenth (1876),
four. [18]

In 1876, at the party's state convention in Houston in

January, Blacks dominated the convention proceedings and even changed the method of electing delegates to the national convention from a vote by acclamation to a vote by counties. After the delegates had returned from the national convention, the Radical wing launched its state campaign. By 1876 the Conservative wing had coalesced with the Democrats and what little support the Republicans got in 1876 came from the area of high Black concentration in East Texas. The Republican vote in 1876 was only 45, 013.

Having made such a poor showing, the Davis-led, predominately Black party allied with the Greenback party in 1878 to support an "independent" ticket for state offices. Other Republicans, who didn't go along with Davis, put up a separate Republican ticket with a Black, Richard Allen, running for the lieutenant governorship. Both the Independent and the mixed Republican tickets lost.

By 1880 the Republican party in Texas, which was rapidly losing its potency in the state, began to play primarily national convention politics and to support the proper individuals for the Presidency so that state patronage would be restored to them. Thus, at the Republican National Convention the mixed Texas delegation switched to the winner, James A. Garfield, on the thirty-sixth and final ballot. Up to that point the Texas delegation had supported Grant on twelve ballots, John Sherman on one, Elihu Washborne on one, Garfield on three and E. J. Davis on one. The other ballots were mixed.

After the Convention, the state Executive Committee named a state ticket headed by the perennial E. J. Davis. In the general election, Davis polled 64, 000 votes, while Garfield received 57, 225 votes from the so-called Black Belt counties.

In 1882 the Republicans held a state convention in Austin on August 23rd, with over 400 delegates from all over the state (one-half of whom were Blacks). At the convention, the delegates, at the suggestion of E. J. Davis, agreed not to put up a slate of candidates but to support the Greenbackers-Independent ticket. This fusion move proved futile because the Independent ticket was well beaten by the Democrats, receiving only 102, 501 votes to the Democrats' 180, 809. E. J. Davis lost his bid for Congress on the Independent ticket.

Governor E. J. Davis, the perennial state Republican

leader, died on February 7, 1883, and Norris Wright Cuney,
a Black, emerged as the new state party leader. [19] The first
test of Cuney's leadership came when the state convention
convened on April 29, 1884 to select delegates for the 1884
National Convention.   In-fighting developed over whom to support, President Arthur or James C. Blaine.   Generally
speaking, the Blacks led by Cuney supported Blaine, while the
whites led by A. C. Malloy favored Chester A. Arthur.   The
conflict was not resolved at the state convention, "the old
animosities of officeholders versus non-officeholders and
Blacks versus whites were carried over to Chicago, and the
Credentials committee" there fell heir to the task of resolving
the internal conflict.

        After the national convention, Texas Republicans held
another state convention on September 2, 1884 to nominate a
slate of officers for the upcoming state elections.   When the
Blacks in the convention voted to support a fusion ticket with
Independents, the white Republicans bolted, held their own
convention and placed their own ticket in the field.   The animosities and jealousies between the blacks and the whites
continued at the 1886 state nominating convention, the two
groups resorting to fisticuffs.

        Two years later, warfare broke out between white and
Black Republicans in Fort Bend and Wharton counties.   In
Fort Bend, the struggle between Black and white Republicans
for control of the government resulted in the Jaybird-Wood-
pecker war which lasted two years.

        Elsewhere in Texas, whites began early in 1888 to or-
ganize "white Republican clubs" for the purpose of controlling
the county conventions, "that they might elect their delegates
for the state conventions. "   At the state convention another
in-fight developed over party control.   The members of the
white Republican Clubs opposed Cuney's Black leadership, for
reasons of prejudice and ambition, and it was during this
struggle that Cuney coined the phrase "Lily-White. "   Later
the newspapers dubbed the Cuney-led faction the "Black and
Tans. "   From that point on, in fact in every election thereafter, a bitter rivalry ensued between the Lily-whites and
Black and Tans.   Beginning in 1892, each faction held its own
convention thereafter.   There were attempts at various times
to reunite the two groups, but they all failed.

        Cuney continued his leadership of the party until his
death in 1897.   Just prior to his death, however, his control

had begun to wane. Early in 1896, for example, he supported
William B. Allison for the presidency at the national convention, while the Lily-whites supported McKinley, as did another group. Both Cuney's Black and Tans and the "Lily-
whites" lost and white man, Dr. John Grant, was named
Texas national committeeman for the next four years. In the
regular party convention of the Black and Tans, held after
the national convention, Cuney lost his state chairmanship,
being defeated by another Black, H. C. Ferguson, who assumed the temporary chairmanship of the convention.

After Cuney's death, W. M. "Gooseneck" McDonald,
became leader of the Black and Tan Republican Party in the
state and continued the struggle against the Lily-Whites from
1898 until 1912. In 1912, the Lily-White Republicans became
the National Progressive Party, which excluded Blacks and
was sanctioned by Theodore Roosevelt. The Black and Tans
continued to support the regular Republican candidate, Taft,
and the rivalry between the Black and Tan and the Lily-white
parties went into abeyance for a period. The rivalry was
rekindled in the 1920 election and continued in varying degree until 1928 when the Lily-white faction throughout the
South had the support of Presidential candidate Herbert Hoover.
The state of Texas was no exception. The Credentials Committee at the 1928 convention voted to seat the Lily-White
group led by R. B. Creager, and thereafter Creager ruled
unchallenged. Black and Tan Republicanism came to an end
in Texas in 1928.

The politics of the Black and Tans in Texas revolved
around electioneering. Prior to every election after 1888,
the Black and Tan group put up or endorsed a separate slate
from the Lily-White, in hopes that the national convention
would readily see which group controlled the majority of the
votes and therefore would give their faction seats at the convention, appoint one of their members as state chairman for
the next four years and pass on to them the right to disperse
whatever federal patronage was available. In almost every
election, the candidate backed by the Black and Tans received
the most votes.

In 1920, however, the Lily-White delegation was seated
because it backed the nomination of Warren G. Harding, while
the Black and Tan group backed the nomination of Leonard
Wood. After the national convention the Black and Tans held
their own convention, nominated their own electors for president, and cast some 27,000 votes for them. This show of

strength didn't help.   The Black and Tan faction was again
not seated in 1924.

During the period after disenfranchisement the Texas
legislature passed a law which declared that "any political
party desiring to elect delegates to a national convention shall
hold a state convention at such place as shall be designated
by the executive committee of said party on the fourth Tuesday in May, 1928, and every four years thereafter. "   This
law greatly aided the Lily-white faction because, from 1920
onward, only the Lily-White faction received national recognition and state chairmanships.   But the Black and Tans fought
back, holding district conventions and electing delegates, both
at-large and district-wide.   In addition, they hoped that the
credentials committee would agree with their view that no
state law could be held binding upon the Republican national
convention.   Arguments to the contrary, the credentials committee rejected the Black and Tans.

Black and Tan politics in Texas in summary, were
principally concerned with electioneering and innovation.

LOUISIANA

In Louisiana, Blacks had been associated with Republicanism from 1865. [20]   Although Republican rule came to an
end in the state with the disputed election of 1876, Black Republican leaders continued their association with the party, [21]
and between 1877 and 1892 "a full Republican ticket was presented for every state election. "   Numerous Republican state
and parish officials of both races were elected during this
period, and four Republicans were sent to Congress.   But
each year the party's power declined, political offices became
scarce and patronage control grew in significance.   It was
over the control of patronage that an intra-party conflict developed.

In 1894, a group of white sugar planters and businessmen, who were sympathetic to the Republican tariff policy,
bolted from the Democratic party of Louisiana and formed the
National Republican Party.   They made no attempt to associate
themselves with the regular Republicans.   However, in 1896,
the National Republicans fused with the white faction of the
regular party and this union became known as the "Lily-White
faction. "   At the national convention in 1896, though, McKinley
recognized the Black Republican group, but appointed a white,

A. T. Wimberly as National Committeeman. Walter L.
Cohen, a Black, was appointed state chairman.

Two years later, Louisiana ratified a new constitution
containing a literacy clause which reduced Black registration
by ninety-five per cent. [22] Although this weakened the Black
and Tan faction, they still dominated the state convention
which was held on March 5, 1900 in New Orleans. The Black
and Tans nominated their own slate of offices for the state
election; it polled only 3.18 per cent of the vote. The Lily-
White faction also received only 12.06 per cent, but they were
victorious at the national convention in 1900. The Black and
Tans achieved some success in 1904, 1908, and 1916, but
compromise giving half the votes to each delegation denied
complete victory to either side.

From 1920 to 1928 the Black and Tans ruled the Louisiana Republican Party. Prior to this period the politics of
the Black and Tans had been primarily a matter of electioneering and persuasion. But when the Black and Tans left the
1920 national convention with a Blacks' appointed as secretaries of the party's state central committee and in complete
control of federal patronage, things began to change.

For instance, one of the Black secretaries, Walter
Cohen, was appointed by President Harding to the position of
comptroller of customs in New Orleans. Congress refused
to affirm the appointment but President Coolidge resubmitted
his name for the same post. Approval was finally granted on
March 17, 1924. [23] During the entire period, the white politicians of Louisiana fought the appointment, but numerous
national Republicans came to Cohen's aid. And W. E. B. Du-
Bois, then director of publicity and research for the NAACP,
wrote letters to various newspapers editors supporting him.
Finally the Postmaster General used his power to pressure
Republican senators into voting for Cohen's confirmation.

When this made his appointment almost certain, a
white Washington, D. C. attorney, H. Edwin Bolte, filed suit
against Cohen, challenging his right to hold a federal position
on the ground that "he is a person of African blood and descent and therefore cannot be a citizen of the United States."
In addition, Bolte claimed that the 14th Amendment, which
gave Blacks citizenship, had never been legally enacted. The
case, which was tried in the U. S. District Court in New Orleans, was dismissed on November 24, 1924. [24] Bolte refused
to give up: he charged Cohen with impersonating a federal

officer on the grounds that no person of African blood can be a federal officeholder.   This motion was also dismissed.

Later, after Cohen assumed his post, he was arrested on August 17, 1925 and charged "with being a member of a gigantic rum ring" which was smuggling liquor into New Orleans from Havana, Cuba in violation of the Volstead Act. Another federal trial ensued, this one being declared a mistrial due to lack of evidence. [25]

Another suit was filed against Cohen in February, 1928 by the Lily-white faction because Black and Tans won eleven of the thirteen positions on the state central committee, in the primary election held on January 17, 1928. [26]   The Lily-Whites wanted control of the committee before the 1928 national convention and their suit asked the court to issue an injunction restraining the Blacks from serving as members of the State Central Committee.   The Court issued a temporary restraining order.   Later, a permanent injunction was issued but the decision was appealed. [27]   The final decision gave only two seats to the Black and Tans out of the contested eleven.

Prior to the National Convention, the Lily-Whites, spurred on by their first legal success, filed another suit against Cohen. [28]   This one asked for a restraining order to prevent him from calling a convention to select delegates to the National Convention.   The injunction did not halt the Black and Tan convention, and two delegations from Louisiana went to the Republican National Convention.   At the convention, however, Presidential candidate Hoover capitulated to Lily-Whiteism, recognized the Lily-White Faction, and after the convention the Black and Tan party was out of power--forever.

Thus, the politics of the Black and Tan Republican Party in Louisiana were primarily legalistic.   The party fought numerous law suits in order to maintain its viability and existence.   Although electioneering was used, it was, in the final analysis, of less importance than legalism.

ALABAMA

Republicanism emerged very slowly in Alabama.   There was no major coalition of Scalawags, Carpetbaggers, and Blacks immediately after the Civil War, as in other southern states, and it was some time before limited Republican and Unionist sentiments in Alabama were welded into a formal political structure.

The passage by Congress of the second Reconstruction
Act in March, 1867 and the establishment of military districts
led to the emergence of several small Republican coteries.
For instance, Blacks from twelve counties met in a convention at Mobile on May 5, 1867, drew up a resolution and proclaimed themselves a part of both the national and the emerging state Republican Party. [29] But even with this declaration
and all of the political maneuvering prior to the election on
October 1-5, 1867, no coalition or unification took place between the numerous coteries of Blacks, Scalawags, Carpetbaggers, and disgruntled Democrats.   At best, only a spirit-
ual name or union held the diverse groups together (they competed with the conservative party) during the October election
of delegates to the constitutional convention.

When the constitutional convention convened in Montgomery on November 5, 1867, twenty Blacks calling themselves Republicans took their seats. [30] One Black delegate,
Moses B. Avery, was elected assistant secretary to the convention.   James T. Rapier (one of the Blacks elected to the
House of Representatives from Alabama) became titular head
of the Black delegation and urged moderation on their part.
He was opposed by another of the Black delegates, Thomas
Lee of Dallas County, who urged that Blacks should press
with some immediacy for their rights.   In spite of this minor
internal disagreement, the convention issued a constitution extending suffrage rights to every male person twenty-one years
or older who had lived in the state for six months, regardless
of his race, color, or creed.

Even though the Republican sympathizers and supporters in the convention were not formally united, they got the
kind of new constitution they desired.   When the convention
adjourned and submitted the constitution to the people for ratification, the Republican backers of the constitution met strong
opposition, however, from the Conservative party, which had
not had enough strength to alter the document at the convention.

James Hold Clanton, head of the Conservative party,
presented two addresses to the people of Alabama, one to
Blacks and one to whites, immediately after the adjournment
of the convention.   The Black address called upon the "intelligent" Black people not to support the new constitution because
it would work to their disadvantage.   The address to whites
asked them not to go out, pointed out that 84,000 votes were
needed for the document to be ratified, and said that any white

man who supported the "unclean Negro minority constitution,"
was a traitor and non-believer in white supremacy. [31]

   The Conservative's address succeeded: the vote for the
constitution was 70, 812 for and 1, 005 against, but the new
constitution was lost because the needed 84, 000 favorable votes
were not attained.   Among Blacks, 62, 089 of the 95, 000 registered voters voted for the constitution and only 104 against.

   Shortly after the defeat of the constitution, Congress
changed the law to make a majority of the votes cast sufficient for ratification and on June 25, 1868, Alabama's constitution was declared adopted.   At this point the disorganized
and disgruntled Republican coteries finally coalesced and uni-
fied for the upcoming general election.   A major role in the
consolidation effort was carried out by the Freedman's Bureau
and its political arm, the Union League.   These agencies
trained the Black voter, kept him in the party and safeguarded
his voting rights as much as possible.   When friendly tactics
didn't work, the Bureau used more drastic means, such as
ostracism and economic pressure, to keep the Black voter in
line.   As usual, the consolidation movement in Alabama ended
up with the "leading roles in the party ... assigned to the
whites and supporting roles to Blacks. "

   However, with the party consolidated, thirty-five Blacks
went to the state legislature.   Again, though, they held the
minor offices, such as assistant clerk, engrossing clerk,
assistant engrossing clerk, enrolling clerk and page.   This
legislature, however, passed an election law designed to protect electors (Black) from fraud, bribery and deceit at the
polls.

   The 1870 election saw thirty Blacks returned to the
state legislature but, due to a conflict over election returns
and a subsequent compromise, only fourteen of the thirty were
allowed to retain their seats.   Each year thereafter, Black
representation declined in the state legislature, until it came
to a complete end in 1876. [32]

   Generally speaking, Black participation in lawmaking
and politics before 1870 did not encounter any large-scale organized resistance from white Alabamians.   "Many whites, "
Professor Brittain says, "maintained and worked toward securing for Blacks justice before the law, equal protection of
property, some education, and the granting of the ballot to
those intelligent enough to use it ... Black state officeholders

were generally resented but such resentment was not so
openly shown toward Black federal officeholders. "

    After 1870, the situation changed drastically. The
Democratic party adopted the slogan of "white supremacy"
and set out to recapture the state government from Republican
and Black control. To help them regain control, the Ku Klux
Klan emerged in Northern Alabama, while in the South and
West its associates--the White Camelia, the White League,
the White Cape, and the Regulators--arose. These secret
societies pledged "never to vote at an election in which colored
opposed white. " Silence and non-violence, also among the
original pledges of these secret societies, did not remain in
practice very long. By 1874 new pledges were made declaring death on "Nigger equality, " and any and every method
possible was to be employed in winning the 1874 election. In
that election Republicans lost control of the state government
in Alabama, never again (thus far) to regain it.

    If the secret societies assisted the Democrats extra-
legally, the Democrats did all they could politically and legally.
On July 30, 1874, at the Democratic convention in Montgomery, the Democrats chose "White supremacy" as its
theme and selected a "no-middle-ground" candidate to be the
party's gubernational candidate. The convention drew up a
platform which denied Blacks the right to hold office, denied
them social equality and the right to civil legislation. The
convention also endorsed a resolution which denied suffrage
rights to all Blacks and which would ostracize or treat as
enemies all whites sympathetic to Black rights. Before adjourning, the convention added a slogan to their party platform: "State first, myself last; don't sacrifice the state. "[33]

    The "lily-white" activity of the Democrats stimulated
already existing negative feelings about Blacks in the Republican organization. Republicans had already relegated Blacks
to the lowest positions in the party, and the white supremacy
movement of the Democrats led the Republicans to further
suppress Black political aspirations and demands for a greater
share of the spoils and offices. Despite the treatment of
Blacks by both parties, the two organizations made every
effort to secure the Black man's vote. In the vigorous contest the side which received the Black vote had a good chance
of carrying the election. Both parties in 1874 made a strong
appeal to the 80,000 Black voters in the state before the general elections. Republicans told Blacks that they were obli-
gated to the party for their emancipation, political rights, and

basic civil liberties, and that if the Democrats regained
power, Blacks would be put back into slavery.   In short, the
Republican pleas were based on obligation and fear.   On the
other hand, the Democrats urged Blacks to "stand shoulder to
shoulder with their white friends" because the Republicans
were "opportunists" who used Blacks badly for their own
ends;   the Republicans, they said, would soon abandon the
Black man when trouble came.   The Democrats tried to por-
tray themselves as the "true" friend of the Black man, and
represented the Republicans as incapable deceivers who provoked violence in the state.

The irony here is that both parties could play up white
supremacy, denounce Blacks and commit numerous outrages
against him, then, without any recognition in consistency,
make a complete about-face, as they did in 1874, and appeal
in a forthright and friendly manner for help and support from
Black voters.

Beyond these appeals, numerous other tactics were
employed to obtain the Black man's vote.   Economic pressures were applied by both parties.   Since the Democrats
employed more than seven-tenths of the Blacks in the state,
they sent their workers to the polls with Democratic ballots.
Both parties dispensed whiskey freely to Black voters and poll
attendants: "It was the practice to give the Freedman all
they could drink and when they were drunk to cheat them out
of their ballots. "   Another effective method was to set barrels
of whiskey before Blacks the night before election and en-
courage them to drink all they could hold, then, the next day,
the polls would be closed before the drunks could sober up
enough to cast their ballots.

Other subterfuges were invented to deceive the ignorant
Black voter.   Democrats, disguised as Republicans, and vice
versa, persuaded Blacks to vote for Republicans who had sold
out to the Democrats, or changed the labels on the ballots,
and the polls were quickly closed if a number of Blacks began
to protest over the various patterns of deceit.   However, "the
method preferred by both parties over all others was ballot
box stuffing. "   Usually, the box would be stuffed the night before election or while it was being taken from the polling place
to the office of the probate judge.

Blacks, cornered, bewildered, exploited and sometimes
leaderless, fought back to the best of their ability, and being
aware of the inconsistencies of the Republican and Democratic

parties, formed their own political organizations. Known as
the "Equal Rights Union, " it came into being early in 1874 as
an opposition wing in the Republican party, with the avowed
purpose of protecting and furthering Black rights. [34]   Although
the Equal Rights Association began on the state level, in a
short time it had trickled down to Republican county and pre-
cinct conventions.   In these conventions, Blacks urged the
delegates present to endorse civil rights and advocated the
right of Blacks to serve on juries.   The Equal Rights Association went on, after the Republican local convention, to petition and memorialize state and national officials.   One memorial sent to the President of the United States and Congress
in December, 1874, stated that "for three or four months
past, especially, our lives and the lives of nearly all Republicans in this state have had no protection ... hundreds of the
active and earnest Republicans of this state ... have been
assassinated (and) many our race were shot down and killed
at the polls on the 3rd day of November last only because they
chose to exercise their right to vote.... "[35]   The memorial
concluded, "We present these facts for the consideration of
the government of the United States and ask its immediate interference in the terrible situation that it has left us after
solemnly promising to guard us in the enjoyment of the privileges that it has given to us--namely, all the rights of citizenship. "

Beyond these memorials, pleas, and petitions, Blacks
of the Equal Rights Union also "set in motion a 6, 000-man
militia, to protect their property and person. "   Minor skirm-
ishes took place at Huntsville, Eutaw, Eufauls, Belmont, Tuscaloosa, Mobile, and Lowndesboro.   Despite these self-defense
measures, Blacks still were unable to retain their power and
property.

Self-defense and political separation did not exhaust all
of the Black Man's efforts in Alabama in 1874.   A number of
Blacks joined the Democratic party, despite its declared position as the party of white supremacy.   Some of these Blacks
joined the Democratic ranks to spite the Republicans and register a protest against their inaction and white supremacy
practice; others viewed politics as did the Democratic Bourbons, that is, as the only profession for a gentleman.   Some
Black Democrats, viewing themselves as aristocrats of their
race, felt that the masses of their race were "unprepared to
assume the duties of citizenship and enfranchisement. "   Fearing that the franchise might be lost because of the unreliable
support of the "opportune" party (the Republicans), which

sought to use Blacks for selfish motives, the aristocratic
Black became a turncoat, an opportunist himself.

Thus, Black Democratic leaders like Caesar Shorter
and Levi Ford, at the behest of white Democratic party leaders, addressed the Democratic state convention as early as
1868 in an effort to attract more Black votes to the party.
During each election thereafter, the Democrats used Black
Democrats to help out Blacks faced with lawsuits and the
party from time to time even protected Blacks who went to
the polls with Democratic ballots, at the same time visiting
violence upon Black Republicans.

The Democratic courting of Blacks came to an end in
1876.   The Montgomery Democratic organization selected two
Black delegates, James A. Scott and John W. Allen, to attend
the state convention on May 30, 1878.   Some whites, however,
objected to the Black delegates and they were defeated by a
vote of 260 to 229.   Scott addressed the convention, then he
and Allen retired from the convention.   They were the last
two Blacks ever to be honored by a Democratic convention in
Alabama.

Thus, self-defense, political separation, joining the
Democratic Party, and withdrawal were among the options
taken by Blacks in 1874.   When the curtain fell in 1874,
Blacks found the Democrats in control of the state government.

Immediately upon coming to power, Democrats in 1875
sought to limit Black suffrage.   A constitutional convention
was called on September 6th at Montgomery.   Although the
Republicans opposed the convention, four Blacks were elected
to the convention.   Minor changes were made and Black disenfranchisement did not become the major issue, largely because of the fear of federal intervention.   Although a majority
of Blacks voted against the 1875 constitution, it was ratified
by a vote of 85, 662 to 29, 217.

The Democrats then moved quickly in the state legislature to courtail Black voting, passing several laws from 1875
to 1882 which put curbs on Black voting.   The Democrats'
effectiveness was evident in 1876 when, for the first time since
1868, Blacks were completely removed from the state legislature.

Prior to the 1876 election, a majority of Black leaders,

along with a few whites, broke away from the white officeholders and illiterate Black masses and formed the Smith-
Rice wing (Black and Tan) of the Republican party. The portion of the party that was left, the Spencer wing or lily-
whites, put up their own candidate for the governorship, as
did the Smith-Rice wing. But before the election, Alexander
Curtis, a Black Senator from Perry County, and others managed to heal the split and work out a compromise ticket. The
independent ticket, which the Democrats called a trick
"hatched in a den of thieves at a buzzard's feast, " lost. In
spite of intimidation by members of their own race and by
whites, five hundred Blacks in Sumner County alone voted the
Democratic ticket.

This defection in 1876 was still not enough to convey
to the Republican party caucuses the depths of Black dissatisfaction with their representation in the party's offices.   In
1878, when Blacks represented 1,400 of the 1,450 votes in
Elmore County, the county convention chose only white candidates to attend the state convention.   In Montgomery County,
7,000 Blacks were allowed only ten votes in the county convention.   Madison County gave all the patronage to whites,
even though the party vote was 2,000 Blacks to 300 whites.

Thus, in 1878 the party once again broke into Black
and white factions, with the Blacks holding their own convention and selecting a full Black slate, headed by a prominent
Black businessman, James K. P. Lucas.   In Selma, the
Blacks selected Jere Haralson to run for Congress again,
while the lily-white Republicans fused with the Greenbackers.

During the campaign Democrats made a tremendous
appeal to the Black electorate, also attracting the Greenbackers.   The all-Black Republican ticket did very badly, receiving only 105 votes in Montgomery county and even less in
other counties in the state.   In Jefferson County Blacks voted
solidly for the Greenbackers, while in the rest of Alabama the
Black voters went overwhelmingly for the Democratic ticket.
Chief credit for the Black switch went to Black leader James
Scott, who addressed the Democratic state convention that year
and used his newspaper, the Montgomery Advance, to lure the
Black voter into the Democratic camp.

In 1880 Blacks bolted the Republican state and county
conventions again and set up an all-Black ticket as well as
sending an anti-administration Republican delegation to the
National Convention at Chicago.   At the polls, however, Black

educator William H. Council, principal of the Black state college at Normal, Alabama, led Blacks into the democratic column. [36] The all-Black Republican ticket was once again defeated.

In 1882 Republicanism factionalism reemerged. The Lily-white Republicans held their own state convention, with one-third white officeholders and two-third Blacks. They endorsed the Greenbackers' ... platform of a free ballot and a fair count. The second Republican convention, composed of Blacks only, declared their independence of white party control and endorsed the Democratic ticket. Once again, Blacks voted overwhelmingly for the Democratic ticket, but after the election the Democrats refused to give Black supporters any of the spoils or to recognize them as jurors. Thus, Blacks returned en masse to the Republican party ranks, only to break away again in 1884. That year, the two factions sent separate delegations to the National Republican Convention, but neither put up a state ticket or endorsed any party.

In 1886 the two Republican factions united and put up their first joint state ticket in nearly ten years. The state election, which was held in August, proved to Blacks that Republicans were still trying to use them for their own purposes, so the Black and Tan faction put up its own Congressional slate of candidates in the national election held in November. Although the slate lost, Blacks maintained their independence, and in 1888 they won several local offices in Tuscaloosa and Birmingham. The Black and Tan Republicans' gubernatorial candidate, Q. William Harvey, and Congressional candidate, Frank H. Threat, lost, but they received full Black support.

Nationally, Benjamin Harrison was elected President and immediately adopted a southern strategy of supporting high tariff whites. In Alabama he appointed ranking lily-white high-tariff men to offices throughout the state. Blacks retaliated by sending an ultimatum and a delegation to Washington to see the President on April 20, 1889. The President ignored their pleas and officially recognized the lily-white Republican Party in June, 1889. It was founded on "April 10, 1889, when three hundred Republicans, Independents and Democrats from all parts of the state, met at Birmingham and organized a high tariff party from which colored men were excluded."[37] When Blacks protested, Charles Hendley, Black editor of the Huntsville Gazette, received the post of Receiver of Public Monies of the state. A few other minor offices were granted

to Blacks but officially the Lily-white Republican party was in
control of the state.   When the decade closed in 1890, Blacks
discovered that their twenty-five years of fealty to the Republicans had left the Black "still a hewer of wood, drawer of
water, a ward of the party who supposed to jump at the crack
of the party whip, and a pilgrim on an eternal pilgrimage
never reaching the shrine. "

In 1890, the Populist Party emerged in the state and
the Jeffersonian Democrats, the liberal wing of the Democratic
party, led by Reuben Kolb, was ready for a new alliance. The
lily-white Republican leaders, lacking a following, were also
looking for an alliance, with any political group except the
Black and Tans.   In 1890 the 1,600-member Black Farmer
Alliance merged with the Black Knights of Labor.   They also
invited the Kolb-led Jeffersonian Democrats to join, but Kolb
held out.

The Kolbites' action in 1890 did appeal to Blacks, so
the State Democratic Executive Committee, although it had
selected as its campaign theme, "white man's rule essential,"
sent Black speakers into the Black community.   The National
Afro-American Bureau of the Negro Democratic Congress organized Afro-American Leagues and "Colored" Democratic
clubs throughout the state in an effort to wrestle the Black
vote from the Black and Tan Republicans.   Said a white Democratic newspaper, the Wedowee Randolph Toiler, "Mr. Negro
is alright whenever he votes the Democratic ticket. "

In 1890 the Black and Tans held their own convention,
with some whites in attendance.   A platform was adopted
which called on Congress to regulate elections, grant equality
of citizenship and free ballots, and insure fair courts.   In
the state and national elections, however, Black Republican
candidates lost by a large margin, mainly due to Democratic
fraud and stealth in the Black Belt counties.   The election
resulted, though, in several Populists winning with the aid of
Black support.

Kolb officially left the Democratic ranks in 1891 and
allied his group with the Populists.   Kolb and his followers
retained their independence by calling themselves the Caucasian Democrats of Alabama, but the Kolbites nevertheless
appealed immediately to Black voters for support.   The Lily-
whites, led by Robert Mosely, tried deceptively to attract
Blacks by creating a Black Republican League.   Blacks were
not fooled and held their own convention in 1892, choosing a

Black, Bill Stevens, to lead them. The convention decided not
to offer a state ticket, condemned the Mosely-led lily-whites
and petitioned the Civil Service Commission to investigate
their practices, and sent a delegation to the Republican National Convention. But the Lily-white delegation, which had
one Black, Jere Bleven, was seated.

Thus, in the state and national elections, the Lily-
whites, the Black and Tans, the Kolbites (Caucasian Democrats) and the Populists, as well as the Regular Democrats,
all tried to attract the Black vote. The Lily-white faction
supported the Kolbites and Populists, while the Black and Tans
maintained their independence. But the Kolbites organized
Black clubs to offset the straight Republican ticket put forth
by the Black and Tans, led by Bill Stevens. This action split
the Black vote and the Democrats, with the aid of fraudulent
practices, won the day.

In 1894, the Kolbites tried to join the Democrats in
the state election and set up a white primary which would bar
Blacks. When the suggestion was rejected by the Democrats,
who felt they didn't need the Kolbites, the latter fused with
the Lily-whites and the Populists once again. The Fusionists
held their convention, elected Kolb to run once more, opposed
restrictions on the ballot, discouraged Black emigration, and
favored "the setting aside of a special territory (in the state)
for Blacks exclusively, whereby they alone would be entitled
to suffrage and citizenship. "

When Bill Stevens, leader of the Black and Tans, tried
to attend the Fusionist Convention, he was threatened and
hounded out of the convention. To retaliate, he tried once
again to put a Black ticket in the field, but he failed. He
then urged his Black and Tans to fuse with the Democrats in
the 1894 state election, which they did, to the dismay of the
Fusionists. The Afro-American Democratic League formed
colored Democratic clubs throughout the state and had Black
ministers cajole their parishioners to support the Democrats.
Moreover, Black newspaper editors were paid to have their
papers endorse the Democrats.

Even with all this urging, Black voters failed to support the Democrats (or any party) in large numbers. Nevertheless, the Democrats won, and Kolb promptly claimed
fraud. [38] In the tumult which followed, all the white party
leaders blamed Blacks for upsetting the so-called harmony in
the state. All year in 1895, cries of disenfranchisement were
heard throughout the state.

In January, 1896, the Democratic Executive Committee declared that Blacks should not participate in the Democratic primary.   The same opinion, plus the notion that a new constitution should be drawn up which would curtail Black political participation, was voiced at the Democratic State Convention shortly after.   Blacks immediately protested the Executive Committee's decision and the committee made a small concession by permitting each county to decide whether Blacks should vote or not.

Blacks also held their own Republican county and state conventions in 1896 and sent an acceptable Black delegation to the National Republican Convention.   At the convention, Bill Stevens was selected to serve on the State Republican executive committee.   Stevens' appointment drew a number of both Blacks and whites out of the Mosely-led Lily-whites into the Black and Tan Movement.   At the state convention of the Black and Tans a platform was drawn up which condemned Democratic violence, fraud, perjury, and denial of civil rights. The Black and Tans went it alone in the state election, rejecting a proposed merger with the Populists.   The Mosely-led Lily-whites did join the Kolb faction of the Populist party. All the Black and Tan state candidates lost.   The Democrats were once again victorious.

By 1898 the Democrats were more thoroughly united and aggressive than ever.   Kolb and his Caucasian Democrats, after having taken such a strong beating, were now defunct and inactive.   The Populist movement had also collapsed.

Bill Stevens and the Black and Tans, however, once again put up an all-Black state ticket.   Their platform called for fair elections, equal protection of the law and better schools, and denounced the Democratic political machine.   A Black minister, A. J. Warner, was elected to head the Black and Tan ticket.   The Populists put a limited ticket in the field themselves, but on the whole the 1898 electoral campaign was very mild.   Warner received a total of only 422 votes,   150 of them coming from one county, Etowah.   The reason for the Warner ticket's (Black and Tan) poor showing was that Blacks "voted for all tickets" rather than wholeheartedly supporting the Black one.   "This was the last important election," states Professor Brittain, "for the Negro ... a kind of apex of Negro Independent political efforts for the decade." Although Rev. Warner and A. N. Johnson, a Black politician from Mobile, ran for Congress in November in the national election, they were both defeated.

By 1900 the Democrats were without meaningful opposition. The Populist party collapsed after the 1898 elections
and the Republicans in 1900 were split four ways: the lily-
white, Lily-Black, and two mixed Black and Tan factions.
However, before April, 1900, the Lily-whites merged with
one of the other groups: during the county conventions, one
faction of the Black and Tans, led by Ad Wimbs, Black lawyer
from North Alabama, went along with the merger after he had
received satisfactory concessions in regard to the state organization. The two remaining factions, the all-Black one (by
now infiltrated with whites) and the regular Black and Tans,
met in separate halls, adopted platforms which guaranteed a
ballot free from fraud, and decided against a state ticket.
Out of this activity an all-white Republican slate appeared just
before the state election and was soundly defeated. Two
Black Republicans, E. H. Matthews and Jesse Ferguson, were
elected justices of the peace on the local level.

Since Booker T. Washington's influence, which urged
Blacks to stay out of politics, was so strong, only a few
Blacks took part in the 1900 election. Once again the Democrats were victorious, and after this election they set in motion plans to strip Blacks of any remaining political power
they had.

The Democratic state convention, meeting January 15,
1901, declared a constitutional convention which would disfranchise Black voters. Booker T. Washington agreed that
some restriction should be placed on the ballot. H. V. Cashin
disagreed with Washington and noted that "the white vote was
the menace, since the Black vote had been controlled since
1874, and that a convention based on race prejudice would
limit the franchise to white men and depress Negro voters."
The Republican Executive Committee vacillated on the issue,
but the Black and Tans were strongly opposed to it because the
Democratic move would deprive illiterate Blacks of the vote,
leave the Lily-whites in control and void the Fifteenth Amendment. The Black and Tan press, the Huntsville Republican,
further contended that 20,000 educated Blacks would also be
disenfranchised. Black newspapers elsewhere in the state told
Blacks that the convention would result in their disenfranchisement and that this might be their last chance to vote in
any election in Alabama. Blacks therefore went to the polls
in droves on April 23rd in an effort to defeat the referendum
for the constitutional convention, but all to no avail. "The
official state-wide count was 70,305 to 45,505 in favor of the
convention." Many counties recorded warped, deceptive re-

turns.   For instance, Lowndes, with a voting population of
5, 590 Blacks and 1, 000 whites in 1900, cast 3, 226 votes for
the convention and 338 against.   Another county, Dallas,
which had 9, 285 whites and 45, 371 Black voters in 1900, cast
5, 608 votes for the convention and 200 against.   States Professor Hackney, "the large majorities for the convention in
the Black Belt made it seem as if Blacks were voting for their
own disfranchisement, but nothing could be further from the
truth. "   White poll managers neutralized and circumvented
the Black electorate.

"It is good bye with poor white folks and Niggers
now, " wrote one Black editor, "for the train of disfranchisement is on the rail and will come thundering upon us like an
avalanche; there is no use crying, we have got to shut the
shute. "   The editorial was prophetic for the convention gath-
ering in Montgomery on May 21, 1901.   The president of the
convention, John B. Knox, let it be known in his keynote
speech that Black voters would be the prime issue.

Blacks as individuals and in groups petitioned the convention and its select committee on suffrage and elections.
Three Blacks, the Reverend A. F. Owens, former slave Dr.
Wille E. Stern, a leading North Alabama physician, and William H. T. Holtzolaw, a teacher and political leader, sent
individual petitions to the convention.   Owens told the convention that the interests of intelligent law-abiding citizens of
both races were identical.   Dr. Stern's petition warned the
convention that "might is not all times right" and that it was
unfair to judge the whole race by the criminals.   And Holtzolaw accused the convention of placing a premium on ignorance
for the young white man and barring the purposes of both
races.

Booker T. Washington and several other Blacks also
petitioned the convention.   They indicated that Blacks did not
seek to rule the white man; but "the Negro does ask, " the
petition continued, "that since he is taxed, works roads, is
punished for crime, is called upon to defend his country, that
he should have some humble share in choosing those who rule
over him.... "[39] The Huntsville Journal, a Black newspaper,
considered this petition a prayer of beggars which would pre-
vail little on a convention doing its work against color.

The Journal proved right.   The petitions were tabled
and forgotten about.   The majority report of the Suffrage
Committee required for the franchise that male voters be

twenty-one years of age; residents of the state for two years, of the county for one year and of the ward for three months; pay all present poll taxes and those accumulating after 1901; be of good character, able to read and write, and be gainfully employed and not guilty of certain crimes (many of the crimes listed were commonly committed by Blacks). Prospective voters had also to pass a court of registrars and swear to tell the truth. All veterans of all American wars since 1812 and their descendants, and veterans of the American Revolution were to become voters for life, if they registered prior to January 1, 1903.

The report was debated and then sent to the people for public ratification on November 11, 1901. Blacks took matters into their own hands and called a convention in Birmingham for the purpose of developing a strategy to defend their rights. H. N. Johnson, a Black newspaperman from Mobile, headed the convention and urged Blacks to raise money to carry a suit to the Supreme Court of the United States to defeat the Amendment. Blacks at the convention accepted Johnson's view but generally stayed away from the polls. On November 11, the constitution was ratified by a vote of 108, 613 to 81, 734. Only in one County, Lee, where 1, 214 Blacks cast 827 votes against ratification, did the Blacks dominate the vote.

In the 1902 election only twenty-five Blacks showed up at the Republican state convention, and they were turned away. The Lily-white faction drove Blacks completely from the party and put guards on the door to keep them out. The Lily-whites put forth an all-white ticket. The ousted Blacks organized their own party, passed resolutions condemning the Lily-whites, and sent a telegram congratulating President Theodore Roosevelt for putting old time Republicans in federal offices in the state. The Black and Tans then sent A. Wimbs to Washington to confer with the President. Roosevelt's political manager, K. C. Clarkson, told Wimbs that the President would crush the Lily-white rebellion in the state and restore Blacks to their rightful place in the party.

Shortly after Wimbs got back to Alabama, several of the Lily-whites were removed from office; other whites, who had quickly associated themselves with the Black and Tan organization, were elevated to power. The President made the Lily-white executive committee rescind their restrictive order and declared that the party would be open in the future to all qualified voters. But this move came too late. Disenfranchisement had already taken its toll.

A few Blacks did run in the November 1902 election. Dr. George H. Wilkerson of Birmingham ran for Congress, H. C. Burford and Daniel Brandon for aldermanic seats at Huntsville; Ad Wimbs received write-in votes for Governor, and four Blacks served on the election board. All Black candidates lost the election. This was no surprise because the size of the Black electorate had dropped significantly with the onset of disenfranchisement: in 1890 there had been 140,000 Black voters; in 1900, 100,000. Only 46 Blacks were registered in the entire state in 1906.

Understanding the limitations of the new disenfranchising constitution and their dwindling electorate, which was graphically revealed in the 1902 election, the Republicans, Blacks and whites, met in 1903 to discuss what could be done about their plight. Of the 300 delegates to the convention, one hundred and seven Blacks were seated in a segregated section and few of them were given important appointments in the convention. Lily-whites told Blacks that they would allow qualified Black voters to participate in their party affairs and that they had nothing against Black officeholding. Black delegates took exception but the Lily-whites quietly ignored them and adjourned.

At the 1904 state convention, however, the Lily-whites selected one Black, Dr. E. Scrugg of Huntsville, to be one of the delegates to the National Convention. This was an attempt by the Lily-whites to improve their relationship with the national party, but the gesture didn't help; a mixed Black and Tan delegation was seated at the National Convention in Chicago. In the November 1904 election, Eugene Stewart, a Black man, was elected Constable of Purtala.

After the Convention, President T. Roosevelt sent two referees (J. O. Thompson and Charles G. Scott) to Alabama for the purpose of uniting the various factions of the party. However, the referees made matters worse by siding with one faction against the other. They supported the Black and Tans and denied the Lily-whites the right to use the party's emblem in the 1906 and 1908 state elections. In each election, both the Black and Tans and the Lily-whites lost.

In 1908 the two factions once again sent separate delegations to the national convention. The Julius Davis-led Lily-whites were rejected and the J. O. Thompson-led Black and Tans were seated because they favored the nomination of William Howard Taft.[40] Booker T. Washington was perhaps the only

Black in the state, however, who was pleased with Taft's nomination. Other Blacks were resentful of Taft's handling of the Brownsville, Texas incident in which a number of Black soldiers were dishonorably discharged for defending themselves. The majority of Black registered voters, therefore, cast their ballots for the Democrats in the November election. Black leaders argued that "it was far better to vote an avowed enemy rather than a false friend."

For the next four years after 1908, Taft gave a few Black Republicans minor federal positions in the state. This was viewed by most Blacks as window dressing, and the election year of 1912 found Blacks organizing a Bull Moose Progressive Party and sending a separate delegation to the Party's convention in Chicago. However, Theodore Roosevelt denied them seats and emphasized that in the South his Progressive party would be Lily-whites. [41] By 1912 Black and Tan Republicanism in Alabama came to an end. The lily-whites were officially recognized from 1916 on, although they had no aid and little help from the national office. The Democrats were now in national power.

From 1912 on, Blacks dropped practical politics and tried other ways to re-enter the political arena. Black suffrage leagues were formed and several test cases were instituted, but little money could be raised to take these cases to appeal court. From 1912 to 1930 little progress was made; in fact, the number of Black voters declined from 3,742 in 1908 to 1,500 in 1930.

Numerous campaigns for raising Black registration were led by individuals like Mrs. Indiana Little. Civic Leagues such as the Tuskegee Civic Association and the Macon County Democratic Club were established. Finally, in the early 1940's, Blacks formed their own wing of the Democratic party, the Alabama Progressive Democratic Association (APDA). Other organizations carried such names as the Right to Vote Clubs, United Registration Committee, Metropolitan Council of Negro Women, Abraham Lincoln Suffrage League of Alabama, National Negro Prayer Associations, etc.

Through their efforts, Supreme Court decisions such as Smith v Allwright and Gomillion v Lightfoot, and Martin Luther King's Selma drive, Blacks reemerged in the late sixties as a force once again in Alabama politics, this time as Democrats.

NORTH CAROLINA

In North Carolina, as in the other eleven states of the old Confederacy, emancipation in 1865 was not enfranchisement: "Freedom from bondage ... did not mean elevation to political power. "[42] Blacks had to organize for political equality, and in North Carolina a meeting took place in Raleigh in September, 1865, four months after Appomattox. Heading the all-Black meeting was a Black minister, J. W. Hood, from Connecticut, and James H. Harris, a native of the state who had received his education in Ohio. Two other prominent Blacks in the assemblage were A. H. Calloway and Isham Sweat. Several resolutions were adopted, among them one calling for suffrage rights, but the meeting did little else.

The demands for suffrage rights were met when the new Reconstruction Acts were passed. In November, 1867 some 73, 000 Blacks registered as voters to choose delegates for a state constitutional convention. They sent fifteen Black delegates to a convention of one hundred and seven people. Among the fifteen Black delegates were Harris, Hood and Calloway. After the convention in 1868 three Blacks were elected to the State Senate and sixteen to the House of Representatives.

Blacks figured prominently in other political developments. According to Professor Mabry, "the launching of the Republican Party in North Carolina practically coincided in point of time with the enfranchisement of the Negro. " When the first initial organizational meeting of the party was held in Raleigh on March 23, 1867, Blacks participated actively. "Proceedings were opened by a colored minister, and the president was escorted to the chair by a white delegate and a colored delegate. Representatives of both races spoke, the white speakers joining with the Negroes in expressing satisfaction at the admission of the ex-slaves to the electorate. "[43]

After the initial meeting, Republicans sought to perpetuate Black support of their party by employing their secret societies in the state--the Heroes of America and the Union League--to indoctrinate and propagandize almost exclusively among the Black populace. The Union League, argues Professor Mabry, "instructed the Negroes in the principles of the Republican party and dictated the candidates for which they were to vote. "

Despite the backing of their Black allies, the Republi-

cans lost control of both houses of the legislature to the Conservatives in 1870, only two years after they had taken control.   The Republicans remained strong enough, however, to
elect their gubernatorial candidate to office until 1876.   Afterwards, the party, as in other southern states, went downhill.

The Republican coalition in North Carolina came under
increasing attack from the Democrats immediately after the
restoration of "home rule, " and the coalition began to break
up under the pressure of white-supremacist Democrats and
the policies of various Republican Presidents.

Although the coalition rapidly deteriorated, the emergence of Black and Tan and Lily-white politics in North Carolina was decidely uneven before 1900.   "True enough, " says
Professor Mabry, "the Carpetbaggers, in the main, had fled,
the Scalawags were politically ostracized, and the Negroes
commonly lacked able leadership, " but the Republicans "by no
means ceased to be a factor in North Carolina politics after
the Democratic triumph, " in spite of their internal problems.

Political impotency did not prevent racial flare-ups
within the Republican ranks.   The first Black and Tan Lily-
white separation came early, as a result of President Chester
A. Arthur's policy of supporting white Independent movements
in the South as the first step toward rejuvenating the Republican party in that region.   White Republicans in North Carolina, seeing Arthur's policies take effect all around them in
neighboring states such as Virginia, Georgia, Mississippi,
etc., launched a movement of their own in late 1882.   It included numerous white Democrats and the majority of white
Republicans.   In its attempt to gain adherents, the new movement lashed out at the Democrats' slogan of "Negro dominance, " claiming it to be a "scarecrow to frighten whites"
into voting for the party.   "Surely two million whites, " the
Liberal Republican leadership argued, "with all the guns, can
withstand one million poverty stricken, defenseless Negroes,
and if not, they deserve defeat. "[44]   The Democrats immediately retorted by connecting the new movement's party name
with Blacks.   The Democratic Executive committee lampooned
the new movement in 1884, its campaign literature asserting
that "North Carolinians will ever know the Radical party ...
the party of the Carpetbaggers ... the party of Negro equality ... Radical eggs hatch nothing but Radical chickens. Strip
a Liberal and a naked Radical stands before you every
time. "[45]   Democratic newspapers ran cartoons showing Liberal Republicans and Blacks riding together in the same car-

riage.   Before long, the damage was done.   "The Liberal Republicans were handicapped by the party's name and by the
inevitable connection with Negroes. " In addition to being outmaneuvered by the Democrats and acquiring a discredited
public image, the Liberal Republicans lost their main backer
and sponsor, President Arthur, when Democrat Grover Cleveland captured the Presidency in 1884.   Shortly after the national election, the movement dissipated.

If this brief Black and Tan/Lily-white clash died out,
another, on a limited scale, occurred in the same year.
Democrats not satisfied to discredit just the Liberal Republicans (Lily-Whites), tried to further weaken the regular Republican Party (Black and Tans) by creating dissension among
Blacks and the few whites who remained.   In Grannville
County, in particular, the Democrats convinced Blacks that
they had not been allotted a fair share of places on the Republican county ticket, and urged them to put their own ticket
in the field.   Two influential Blacks in the county, Tom Lewis
and Banky Gee, called a rump Republican convention and
nominated their own Black candidates for office.   Their candidates consisted of a Black school teacher, Walter Patillo,
for Register of the Deeds, and W. K. "Spotted Bull" Jenkins,
"a large powerful, freckled-face who raised cattle for the
home market" for the state Senate.   During the campaign the
Black candidates proved very popular until the Democrats gave
their support to the Republicans (Lily-whites) in the final days
of the campaign, even providing money to defeat the Black
candidates whom they had spurred on initially.

The party usually returned to its old precarious unity
after the election, at least for a while.   The emergence of
the Populist Party in 1891 as another political challenger in
the state helped the Black-white Republicans to put a momen-
tary halt to their internal differences and present a united
front in the 1892 election.   The majority of the Blacks voted
the Republican ticket in the election but both the Republicans
and the Populists lost to the Democrats, who took strong
measures in the legislature of 1893 to restrict the activities
of the Populist Party.

This caused the Populist leadership to effect a fusion
agreement with the Republicans for the 1894 election. [46] The
agreement held that separate party organizations were to be
maintained but only one ticket, partly Republican and partly
Populist, was to be put in the field.   Although expediency was
the main binding force in the agreement, the arrangement

proved victorious and the fusionists gained control of the state
legislature.   Some Black Republicans questioned whether the
Populists were worth supporting because of their seeming
opposition to Black officeholding, but the actions of the Populists proved otherwise: the number of Black officeholders
more than tripled.   It was under this fusion arrangement, in
fact, that the last Black Congressmen from the South was able
to obtain and hold office.   The man was George White.

Once in office, the Fusionists repealed the Democrats'
restrictive electoral law, re-gerrymandered the city and
municipal governments in their favor, and urged Blacks to
vote.   Having proven politically successful in 1894, the Populists and Republicans decided to try the same technique again
in 1896.   Just before the campaign got under way, however,
a third breakaway of Black and Tan Republicans occurred.
Both parties (Populists and Republicans) had agreed to enter
their own gubernatorial candidate in the field but to divide up
the remaining elective offices.   The Republicans named a
Judge, Daniel L. Russell, as their gubernatorial candidate.
During his earlier political career Russell had been disre-
spectful to Blacks.   In several campaigns prior to 1896, he
was reported to have characterized Blacks as "savages who
stole all the week and prayed it off on Sunday, " and who were
"no more fit to govern or to have a share in governing than
their brethren in the swamps of Africa. "   Although in his
speech accepting the Republican nomination he made a concerted bid to capture Black support, many Black Republicans
were unhappy about the nomination and withdrew from the regular Republican convention.   These Black Republicans held
their own convention in Raleigh in July.   They endorsed the
Populist candidate for Governor, William A. Guthrie, who
appeared well disposed to Black people, rather than nominating a candidate of their own.   The bolt proved abortive: Russell won in September and the fusion victory of 1896 placed
an estimated one thousand Blacks in office.

Having lost twice, the Democrats began preparing immediately for the 1898 election with their one sure weapon,
the call for white supremacy and the end of Negro domination.
All during 1897, the Democratic executive committee used
every method to play up the issue.   Pro-Democratic editors,
Democratic White Supremacy Clubs, and Democratic speakers
kept the matter continually alive.   The Democrats were so
sure of themselves and the effects of their propaganda that
when the Populist sought fusion with them on May 26, 1898,
rather than with the "Nigger Republican Party, " they turned

the offer down flat, indicating that they wanted nothing to do
with supporters of Republican Negro-rule.

The Democrats were shrewd enough, though, to appeal
to individual Populists through the race issue and a platform
that included many of the reforms the Populists desired. Some
Populists and Republicans had joined forces solely for the
sake of expediency, but many of the Populists held negative
attitudes toward Black participation in politics, and they
moved over easily into the Democratic camp.

Just a few days prior to the election the North Carolina Democrats pulled out one additional technique to defeat
the predominately Black Republican organization.   They im-
ported the famed South Carolina demogogue, Ben "Pitchfork"
Tillman, who made several "Niggerbaiting" speeches throughout the State.   Tillman brought with him the "Red Shirts," a
new version of the Ku Klux Klan who employed violence and
intimidation to make sure that Blacks stayed at home on election day.   The Democratic technique worked; on November
8th the Democrats captured both houses.   Only seven fusionists were returned to the State Senate and twenty-six to the
House.   Black representation likewise declined.   The next
year, 1889, the legislature passed a new election law over
the protest of several Black lawmakers, completely disenfranchising Blacks in the State.   Since the law had a grandfather clause and didn't go into effect until 1902, the legislature in the interim appointed white members to local government boards to ensure white control at municipal and county
levels.

The Democrats launched a tremendous "White supremacy" campaign between 1900 and 1902, thereby arousing great
racial feelings.   The remaining whites in the Republican party
pulled out in 1904 and 1905 and formed a separate "lily-white
organization that in 1906, in the party's Handbook, officially
repudiated Blacks and their participation in politics.   By 1912
the lily-whites had become enough of a force that they put
their own political ticket in the field, but it made a "miser-
able and disappointing showing in the state election."[47] While
Black and Tan competition before 1906 was sporadic and uneven, there was continuous strife after 1906, both groups (the
Black and Tans and the Lily-whites) having set up permanent
operating organizations.

Fusionism in North Carolina during the 1890's had not
only helped revive the Republican Party and increase the

number of Republican political officials; it had also contributed
to the revival of the spector of Black domination and Negro-
phobia.   White supremacy Democrats were angered by the
new emergence of Black politicians and by their repeated
election losses to the fusion candidates.   Their resulting emphasis of the notion of "Nigger domination" eventually won
them many adherents and the fusion effort of the Republicans
and Populists collapsed.   By 1901 the collapse was final.[48]

It should be remembered that while "fusion was (fairly)
sound on the surface ... beneath were personalities and prejudices which constituted a problem." As Professor Helen
Edmonds puts it, "historians who uphold the idea that Blacks
voted the Republican ticket with a slavish fanaticism must not
overlook the fact that there was never complete harmony between [white] party leaders and Negro party followers during
the fusion period." While fusionism did give the party more
electoral successes, it did not remove Black-white antagon-
isms.   The factional fighting continued during the fusion
period and thereafter.   The Lily-white Republicans did little
to stop the disenfranchising amendment from passing and the
majority of Blacks had lost their right to vote when the year
1900 ended.   According to Professor Edmonds, "The Republican Party proved its disloyalty to the Negro group after the
election of 1900.   The Negro who could qualify to vote under
the disfranchisement amendment was forgotten and the party
marched thereafter under the banner of a Lily-white party."

However, "the national Republican administration's indifference to the disfranchisement of Negro Republicans in
North Carolina did not pass unnoticed.   A leading Black
paper, The AME Zion Quarterly, editorialized that 'our friends
(the national Republicans) are still in possession of the national government but they have not done as much for our
race as they had led us to hope'."[49]

After disenfranchisement the Black and Tan Republicans
did little challenging on the state level, concentrating more
upon the national conventions.   Patronage became the key
issue, not electoral or political power.   The Black and Tan
wing in North Carolina, although badly hampered by disenfranchisement, did lead several convention challenges against
the Lily-whites at the national convention (this will be discussed later).

VIRGINIA

Virginians sympathetic to the Republican party and its goals met in Alexandria on June 12, 1865. The "Union Association of Alexandria, " as this delegation named itself, adopted a resolution urging that the "constitution of Virginia should be amended so as to confer the right of suffrage upon, and restrict it to, loyal male citizens without regard to color. "50 The convention took additional steps to see that the Freedman's Bureau would be brought into the state. In fact, within three days after the convention, on June 15, 1865, the Freedman's Bureau was established in Virginia. The Bureau not only protected and cared for the freedmen but "also impressed upon their minds the debt which they owed the Republican party. "

The next year, on May 17, 1866, the Union Association met again in Alexandria and this time adopted a resolution that declared, "no reorganized state government of Virginia should be recognized by the government of the United States which does not exclude from suffrage and holding office at least for a term of years, all person who have voluntarily given moral or material support to rebellion against the United States and which does not, with such disfranchisement, provide for the immediate enfranchisement of all Union men without distinction of color. "

The convention sent several delegates to a meeting in Philadelphia called by President Andrew Johnson to see how much support he had among the Republicans in the North and the Unionists in the South in his fight with the Congressional Republican Radicals. After the September 2nd convention in Philadelphia, several members of the fledging Republican organization brought back with them the Union League organization to begin its work, late in 1866, in the Black community. In its secret and mysterious meetings, the organization taught Blacks that "their only friends were the Union Republicans, and that their chief enemies were their former masters, who were not of the Republican party. " When the Reconstruction Acts were passed in March, 1867, although several white Democrats tried to induce Blacks to join them rather than the Republicans, as registration of voters began in late March the Freedmen became more and more attached to the Republican party.

Prior to the October elections in 1867, the Republicans held meetings in numerous Black churches to reinforce Black

allegiance to the regular Republican organization.   At one
mass convention of Blacks and white Radicals in the Capital
Square in Richmond, there was a call for the confiscation of
"rebel lands, cheers for Thaddeus Stevens, condemnation of
President Johnson and of the rebel aristocracy." The Republicans, however, met some competition from the Conservative
Democrats in the State, who held several meetings with
Blacks and urged them to join with them instead of the Republicans.   While the Conservatives advocated Black suffrage,
however, they hoped to become the leaders of the newly freed
Blacks, and this hampered their appeal.

     The election results revealed that Blacks almost unani-
mously supported the Republicans' mixed slate of candidates.
In all, 91,869 of the 92,507 registered Black voters voted for
the Constitutional convention, while only 14,835 of the 76,084
white registered voters did so.   Of the 105 delegates elected,
35 were Conservatives, 65 were Radicals, and five could not
be classified in either group.   The Black delegates made up
25 of the Radical delegation, and it was with their backing
that the new constitution granted substantial rights, even the
elective franchise, to Black Virginians.   When the convention
came to a close on April 17, 1868, the vote for the adoption
of the constitution was 51 to 36, with only one Black and 11
Conservatives among those voting against.   The constitution
was debated back and forth for the rest of the year, and was
finally approved by the Virginia House of Representatives on
December 8, 1868.

     Immediately after adoption, both the Conservatives and
the Republicans began preparations for the forthcoming state
election, each group propagandizing among Blacks for their
support.   In one instance, "Conservative Negroes of Richmond,
at the risk of personal violence from the colonial Radicals,
arranged a barbecue for their men and invited a number of
prominent white conservatives."   The Republicans, playing
upon the superstitious strain in the Black community, declared that "the hand of God is to curse those who apostalize
and to bless and guide those who go faithfully to the polls
and vote the Republican ticket...."   Blacks voted for both
parties, the Republicans and the Conservatives, but the former
received the majority of their support and six Black Republicans were elected to the General Assembly.   Republican control of the state government did not last very long, the white
Conservatives (Democrats) recapturing the state government
in 1870.

With this resurgence of white conservatism, Black representation in the House dropped from twenty-one to fourteen in the 1871 election, and from six to three in the State Senate. Each year thereafter, Black representation declined steadily until 1879 when the Conservatives lost power to the emerging Readjuster movement that held power in the state from 1879 to 1883.[51] When the Readjusters began to come to power in Virginia in 1878, there were only seven Blacks left in the state legislature and the Republican party, in the period of Conservative control, had become almost a Black organization. In 1878, the Readjusters increased their number in the state legislature from six to twenty-three, a fact which attracted the attention of Republican President Hayes, whose aim was to rebuild the Republican party in the South.

As indicated in Chapter 2, the Readjuster movement in Virginia grew out of the inability or the refusal of the Conservatives to adopt a forthright economic policy which would enable payment of the state debt, while at the same time introducing new social legislation and reform programs. The Conservatives took a hard-line approach and insisted that the debt be paid off before any new programs could be initiated. The Readjusters disagreed, and they put their ideas into political action.

First, they made strong appeals to the Black community, particularly Black Republicans, who had at this time tremendous electoral power. Since the white registered voters numbered approximately 150,000 and Blacks 121,000, the budding movement needed Black voters if it were to wrest a substantial share of the power now held by the Conservative whites. Blacks, who were suffering under the repression of the conservatives and continual losses at the polls because of Black predominance in the Republican party, saw the great possibilities of such a political alliance.

Republican Presidents like Hayes and Garfield, looking for a way to revive the Republican party, supported the Readjusters in varying degree during their tenure in office. Arthur gave the Readjusters full recognition, and full support with Republican party patronage. In fact, William Mahone, who headed the Readjuster movement, became chief disperser of Republican patronage in the state. With such recognition and financial backing, the Readjusters drew many Blacks into their ranks.

When the 1879 election was over, the Readjusters, with

the aid of Blacks, had won control of both houses of the legislature.   They elected fifty-six out of one hundred delegates
and Black representation rose from seven to eleven in the
House and from zero in the Senate to two.   Mahone, again
with Black support, later went to the U. S. Senate.   But when
the Republicans lost on the national level, the Readjusters in
Virginia also lost control of the State government.   While they
were in power, however, they received so much Black support
that the Republican party itself achieved very little.   The first
major accomplishment for the predominantly Black Republican
party was the election of John Langston to Congress in 1889.
In that year, moreover, five of the twenty-four Republicans
within the general assembly were Black, and one Black Republican, N. M. Griggs, was elected to the State Senate.

     In 1891 no Black Republicans or Readjusters were
elected to the state legislature.   With only three Republicans
holding office in the legislature that year, the party coalesced
with the newly organized farmer party, the Populist Party in
1892.   The fusion sent thirty-six Populists to the state legislature and set off a wave of concern in the Democratic ranks.
When the Democrats regained sufficient power in the State
Assembly, in 1897, they put in motion plans for a new state
constitution, as Mississippi had in 1890, that would disenfranchise the Black voter.   The call in 1897 for a constitutional convention was defeated in a referendum by a vote of
183,483 to 38,326.   The Democratic-dominated general assembly tried again in 1900, calling for a vote for a constitutional convention on May 24th of that year.   In the election,
77,362 votes were cast for a convention and 60,375 against.
Professor Morton states, "Of the 35 counties in which there
was a majority of [Blacks], 18 voted for a convention and 17
against it. "   Many Blacks had apparently supported a convention which was bent on disenfranchising them.   But the reality
is that conservative whites, who had the economic and political
power, dominated and manipulated Black voters and forced
them to vote their way.   While the Republicans strongly opposed the convention and the proposed constitution, they were
too weak, with only twelve delegates out of one hundred and
eight-eight, to forestall the convention or its known purpose,
to disenfranchise Blacks.

     Professor Morton, commenting on the convention and
its purpose, said: "the [Black man] had been a failure and a
menace in politics.   As long as he was in politics the color
line was a line of friction and danger to both races.   Therefore, he must be removed, not only because he was for the

most part an ignorant and irresponsible voter who had usually
stood solidly behind the worst elements in state politics, but
also because he had been taught in the beginning to vote as a
Negro and must therefore be disenfranchised because he was
a Negro.   While Republicans in the convention voted against
the disenfranchisement of Blacks, the convention decided to
proclaim the document the law of the state rather than submit
it to the electorate for their consideration.   On May 29, 1902,
the new constitution was proclaimed to be in force.   And in
1902 and 1903, when voters re-registered under the conditions
of the new constitution, only 21,000 Blacks became voters.
Whereas 147,000 Blacks had been voters before the act, only
this marginal number remained to give support to the collapsing Republican party organization. "52

        In retrospect then, there was no major schism in the
Republican party in Virginia before 1900 which produced well
defined Black and Tan and Lily-white factional organizations.
Although there had been friction within the party between the
two races, the Readjusters and the Populists served as out-
lets for dissatisfied Blacks and whites and an alternative to
factionalizing the Republican party.   Black and Tan and Lily-
white Republicanism, however, did start developing after 1902.

        When the disenfranchising constitution went into effect
in 1902 many white Republicans saw it as an opportunity to
revive the Republican party in the state and "restore two-party
politics in Virginia as a process that enfranchised Negroes
hampered. "   Therefore, when the state GOP chairman, Park
Agnew, had the executive committee on June 17, 1902 issue
a resolution condemning the proclamation of the constitution
as illegal, Black Republicans, aware of past white actions,
viewed the matter as a facade.   This Black attitude toward
Republican announcement was justified in September, 1902 when
Blacks "in several areas of the state ... found themselves
excluded from Republican meetings and conventions. "   Black
participation in state Republican circles, in fact, declined
each year thereafter, as Lily-whiteism surged.   Black participation was so stymied that Black Republicans began offering
their own candidates for local and state offices.

        The first Black and Tan Republican candidate, J. B.
Johnson of Manchester, was nominated for the third congressional House seat in Richmond on October 11th, 1906.   Johnson, a Black man, was selected after the white nominee had
indicated to Blacks that they should take a "back seat" in
party affairs.   The Black and Tan candidate received only 196

votes, the Lily-white candidate 639.   The white Democrat who won the contest received 3,908 votes.

Political exclusion of the Negro continued in the Republican state convention at Lynchburg on April 8, 1908, and Blacks therefore held their own convention on May 14, in Richmond, selecting a slate of delegates to contest the Lily-whites at the Republican national convention in Chicago.   Although the Black and Tan delegation protested strongly to the Credentials Committee at the national convention that the Lily-white organization was illegal because it held closed city, county, and district conventions, the challenge failed and the lily-whites were seated.

Recognizing their weak electoral power, the Black and Tans forsook local and state politics, not reemerging again until 1912.   The Lily-whites pledged themselves that year for Taft, while the Black and Tans supported Theodore Roosevelt for the Republican nomination.   At the national convention the Taft forces prevailed and the Lily-white were again seated over the protests of the Black and Tans.

The Black and Tans didn't reemerge this time until 1920, when a new "Lily-Black" Republican movement was begun to counteract the ever-growing Lily-white movement. The new movement, started by the Black editor of the Richmond Planet and some influential Black leaders, nominated Joseph R. Pollard, a noted Black attorney, for the U.S. Senate. The Lily-whites didn't put up a candidate, so the race was a straight contest between a white Democrat and the Black Republican.   The Democrat, Carter Blass, received 184,646 votes to Pollard's 17,576 votes.   In Richmond, his home city, Pollard received 2,971 ballots; in Norfolk, 653; in Portsmouth, 469; in Lynchburg, 446; and in Newport News, 406.

Encouraged by Pollard's state-wide showing, Black editor Mitchell called for a Lily-Black Republican state convention in 1921 at the True Reformers' Hall in Richmond. When the convention convened on July 8th, forty-five delegates were elected to attend the Lily-white state convention and urge the Lily-whites to give Blacks meaningful representation in the party organization.   This request pointed to the number of votes--17,576--that Black Republicans had cast in 1920, indicated to the Lily-whites that if they hoped to win the 1921 state election, or any other, they would need these votes. The argument didn't previal; the Black delegation, except for three, was turned away.   The attempt at reconciliation had failed.

On September 6th, in Richmond, therefore, the Lily-
Black leadership nominated a full state ticket as a protest
against the Lily-whites' maltreatment. Editor John Mitchell,
Jr. was nominated for Governor, Theodore Nash for Lieutenant Governor, J. Thomas Newsome for Attorney General,
Thomas E. Jackson for Treasurer, J. Z. Baccus for Secretary of the Commonwealth, Mrs. Maggie L. Walker for
Superintendent of Public Instruction and J. L. Less for Commissioner of Agriculture.

During the election campaign dissension and personal
jealousy developed among the Black community. Opposing the
Lily-Black ticket was Black editor P. B. Young of the influential Norfolk Journal and Guide, who had declined the nomination for Lieutenant Governor. Jealous over the success of
Mitchell's paper, the Planet, Young strongly attacked the
ticket and advised Blacks not to vote for it because it was
ill-timed and unwise and it drew a color-line by excluding
whites from party plans. Young's opposition had an effect.

In the election the Democratic candidate polled 139,416
votes; the Lily-white Republican candidate, 65,933; and the
Lily-Black candidate, Mitchell, 5,046, nearly 12,000 votes
less than a Black candidate had polled a year earlier. In
Norfolk, out of 1,600 registered Black voters, Mitchell received only 90 votes. After such a dismal showing the Lily-
Black organization gave up the ghost. A few Black Republicans remained in the political arena after 1921, individually
or in conjunction with the Lily-whites, but organizationally,
Black Republicanism was defunct.

FLORIDA

Republicanism began in the Black community in Florida
"soon after the war--before freedmen were permitted to
vote."[53] This activity was begun by the Union League, which
began springing up "all over Florida in 1865."[54] It soon
started to fade, however, because prospects for Blacks getting
suffrage rights in Florida at that time seemed bleak. The
political organizing that the Union League started was continued by Thomas W. Osborn, an assistant to the head of the
Freedmen's Bureau.[55] Osborn had been the first head of the
Bureau but was replaced in 1866 and stayed on in a subordinate capacity. Some time in 1866, he invited a few influential
Blacks to a meeting at the home of another Black freedman in
Tallahassee. At this meeting, an organization, the Lincoln

Brotherhood, was formed with Osborn as president.   The
Tallahassee society became the parent lodge for the Lincoln
Brotherhood organization, which had lodges throughout the
state.   The "combination of elaborate ceremony, secret signs
and passwords, together with a promise of free land and civil
rights bills" by this secret society was "such a strong attraction for the freedmen [that] by late summer of 1867, it
claimed the fidelity of thousands of Negro voters. "[56]   The
oath of the Brotherhood read, in part: "I will not vote for
... any person for any office who is not a brother of this
league. "[57]

Osborn soon encountered competition in trying to organize the Freedmen politically.   Liberty Billings of New Hamp-
shire, a former Unitarian minister and army chaplain in a
Black regiment, spoke to an assembly of Blacks on February
8, 1866 in a Baptist church at Fernadina.   He condemned the
conservative state legislature and its Black codes, and had
the meeting pass a resolution commending Republicans in
Congress for trying to secure civil rights for all citizens.   In
the Spring of 1867, Billings was aided in his attempt to organize Freedmen by "Colonel" William V. Saunders, a Black
barber from Maryland, and Daniel Richards, a white man
from Sterling, Illinois "who claimed to be the representative
of the National Republican Committee. "   Richards had been in
Florida since early 1866, served for a short period of time
as a tax commissioner, and had been in constant contact with
northern Republicans, insisting that Black suffrage was imperative for the protection of the Freedman.

Billings, Richards and Saunders combined and in the
Spring of 1867 organized another secret society, the Loyal
League of America, effectively competing among Blacks with
the Osborn-led Lincoln Brotherhood.   Saunders, who had been
characterized as "one of the shrewdest, most influential and
dangerous Negroes in Reconstruction politics, " became president of the newly formed organization.   The League made their
rituals even more elaborate than the Brotherhood's, using
special hand grips, passwords and secret signs.   Billings
made numerous speeches throughout the state denouncing segregation and the Black codes, kissing Black babies and frequently lacing his speeches with shouts that "Jesus Christ was
a Republican. "

When asked by an inquiring reporter what participation
in Loyal League meetings was like, one Black described it
this way:

> Well sar, Ill tell you, you see one man he takes a
> piece of paper and tars it in little pieces and gives
> us all a piece, den another man, he comes round
> wiff a pencil and writes somefin on de paper, and
> gives it to us again, den de first man, he comes
> round with a hat and we puts em all in; den he
> takes en up dar, counts em all and sass unani-
> mously. [58]

The League was so successful that it replaced the Lincoln
Brotherhood and in November, 1867, Richards wrote, "...
Saunders, Billings, and myself have created the Republican
party and save not all cliques and factions before us. "[59]

At this point, however, the more than five percent of
white Floridans who had been "Union sympathizers during the
war and had held Union rallies in 1863 and 1864 under the
protection of federal soldiers," as well as a small convention
in May, 1864 (attended by John Hay, President Lincoln's private secretary), were unhappy with both the Osborn-led Lincoln Brotherhood and the Saunders-led Loyal League. A
meeting was held, therefore, on March 27, 1867 in a local
attorney's (Ossian B. Hart) office in Jacksonville to form the
Republican Club of Jacksonville. A later meeting was held on
April 1, to adopt a constitution and by-laws, and a committee
was formed to invite those who favored the organization to
join. An invitation was sent to Blacks and was answered: two
Blacks, William Bradwell, a local minister, and Jonathan
Gibbs, who later became the Secretary of State and then Superintendent of Public Institutions, became officers in the new
organization. Bradwell became one of the eight vice presidents and Gibbs served on the executive committee.

Thus, shortly after the announcement of the Reconstruction Act, there were three factions, each calling themselves the Republican party, in Florida. The three factions
met together on July 18, 1867 in the first state-wide convention of the Republican party in Florida, at Hart's request.
Differences were resolved and the factions were united in a
much more permanent organization.

Seeing the emergence of the new Republican organization and understanding the political muscle of the new freedmen, Democrats began preparing for the election (made possible by the Reconstruction Acts) to be held November 14-16
by reversing themselves and appealing to Blacks. They immediately won some Black adherents. One Black Democrat,

William Martin, speaking in Lake City, counseled Blacks to
join the Democrats because, as he saw it, such a coalition
was the only way to live happily in the South.   To break with
southern whites, he prophesied, would lead to racial strife.
Black spokesmen and nice overtures didn't win any large
number of Black Democratic converts, however.   On the
election days, out of 28,000 registered voters (15,434, or a
majority, were Blacks) only 14,503 ballots were cast.   Thirteen thousand two hundred eighty-three (13,283) Blacks voted,
and only 1,220 whites; 203 of the whites voted against the
constitutional convention.

        In late December, General Pope announced the results
of the election and designated January 20, 1868 as the date
for the convention to assemble.   "Of the forty six delegates
elected, eighteen were Blacks and they demonstrated in the
proceedings of the convention a surprising ability."   According to a reporter, Solon Robinson, who covered the convention
for the New York Tribune, several Blacks stood out.   Charles
H. Pearce and Jonathan C. Gibbs, both Black ministers, delivered excellent speeches during the convention.   Green
Davidson, a barber turned politician, made speeches on social
equality and political rights which many considered inflama-
tory.   Robert Meachum, another Black minister-politician who
made talks during the convention, was considered by some
whites to be a trouble-maker and by others as an honest and
respected man.   The most powerful speaker in the convention
was William U. Saunders, who was described as an orator
who could "tear the wind and scatter thunderbolts."   Despite
Blacks and their ability, the new cemented Republican organization came apart in the heated convention debates.   Osborn,
who had lost most of his Black support, opposed those Republicans like Billings, Richards, and Saunders who backed
the proposed new constitution, and urged their ouster on the
grounds that they were ineligible as delegates since they had
not been residents in the state one year.   Osborn was joined
by a group of conservative Republicans, and for two days
these factions fought each other.   Later, the conservative Republican factions withdrew, held their own convention, drafted
their own constitution, then rejoined the original convention
and reorganized it.   At this point the Osborn-led conservative
faction was composed of white federal officeholders, Scalawags, and three Blacks.   The Saunders-Billings-Richards
group had the support of all the other Black delegates, including influential Blacks like Pearce and Gibbs.   When bickering
continued after the conservative Republicans rejoined the convention, the military commander ordered a reorganization and

a new selection of officers.   The reformed convention ousted
Billings, Saunders, Richards, and Pearce, but drew up a
constitution that granted universal male suffrage and remained
in effect in the state until 1885.   Whites apportioned the state
in such a fashion, however, that legislative control would re-
side in white hands.   One outstanding feature of the new constitution was that it granted one seat in each house to the
Seminole Indians.

Although whites objected to the suffrage rights granted
to Blacks, the constitution was ratified in May, 1868 by a
vote of 14, 520 to 9, 491.   In addition to the ratification of the
constitution, nineteen of the seventy-six delegates elected to
the state legislature were Blacks, and three of these nineteen
sat in the State Senate.   Five Blacks sat in Florida's senate
in 1869-70, three in 1871-72, five in 1873-74 and six in
1875-1876.   In the House the number never rose above thirteen after 1868.

In 1868, Governor Harrison Reed appointed Jonathan
Gibbs as Secretary of State, a post he held until Reed was
succeeded in January, 1873 by Ossian B. Hart.   Hart, due to
Black pressure, appointed Gibbs as Superintendent of Public
Instruction, a post which he held until his untimely death on
August 14, 1874.

In 1870 Josiah T. Walls was elected to the House of
Representatives.   However, the result was contested and a
white man, Silas L. Niblack, was declared the winner by 137
votes.   Walls was "renominated and reelected in 1872, " serving in the 43rd Congress.   He presented credentials to the
44th Congress and served from March 4, 1875 until April 19,
1876, at which time he was succeeded by Jesse T. Finley, a
white who successfully contested his election.   Walls had the
unhappy distinction of being thrice elected and twice unseated.
Numerous other Blacks represented the Republican party during Reconstruction but Gibbs and Walls held the highest elective posts.

The split which occurred during the convention became
a permanent factor in the Republican organization thereafter:
the Black and Tan group, being the Billings-Saunders-Richards
faction, and the Lily-white conservatives led by Osborn.   From
the outset, the Black and Tan group dominated state politics
and held state patronage, while the Osborn Lily-whites held
federal patronage.   The latter had an advantage because federal posts carried cash salaries, while state salaries were

paid in depreciated scrip because the state was bankrupt.
This factor of money, as well as the fact that Osborn was
elected to the U. S. Senate in 1868 and had national connections, caused the Lily-white faction, which has been in the
minority at first, to soon become a force equal in political
power to the Black and Tans in 1875 and gaining in ascendancy
each year thereafter.

The Black and Tan wing received its major setback in
the election of 1876 when the Democrats recaptured the state
government and embarked upon a program of white supremacy
which opposed Black suffrage (already opposed by the Lily-
white Republicans). Thus, when reconstruction ended with the
state redemption, the Black and Tans found themselves under
violent attack by Democratic organizations such as the Ku
Klux Klan and the Young Men's Democratic Clubs. The Republican cleavage was further aggravated by the Democrats of
the state who made available to either Republican faction the
opportunity to criticize the other. Newspapers offered full
pages for such criticisms, paid for by Democrats. Black
officeholders dropped in numbers each year thereafter, while
the shifty southern policy of Republican Presidents pushed the
Black and Tan faction further and further back from view and
real political power. Even minor appointments were given
grudgingly.

Things became so hard for Black Republicans after
Democrats captured the state in 1876 that a few Blacks
"joined conservative clubs and worked openly for Democrats."
During the 1876 election many Black women "threatened to
abandon their husbands if they voted Democratic. " To help
these Black husbands, a Democratic paper, the Monticello
Constitution, wrote that a prominent attorney had directed the
legal fraternity in the state to grant divorces to Black men so
threatened. "Thus honest Democratic Negroes, " the paper
added, "can get rid of their old, ugly, and crazy hags, and
be placed in a condition to marry young, sensible, and pretty
mulatto girls. " Democrats won the day and carried the election. Fraud was so prevalent in the election, by both Republican and Democrats, that the result for the presidential election was thrown out. Later, a special commission awarded
the election to Hayes, but the Democrats held power on the
state level.

While a few Black politicians held on thereafter, Democrats held a new constitutional convention in 1885 and instituted several devices including the multiple ballot box law and

a poll tax to disenfranchise Black voters. These moves
proved successful because the number of Black Republicans
in 1888 (26, 485) had shrunk to 8, 861 by 1892. Fusion with
the Populists temporarily increased the number by 13, 560,
but violence, intimidation, Populist failures and resurging
white supremacy caused the number of Black Republicans to
drop to 6, 869 in 1900. Black and Tanism was slowly fading
into oblivion.

After the white primary was established in the state in
1902, Black voters were forced to register as Republicans because the Democratic party would not accept them. But the
Democratic primaries were, in effect, the elections. "In
practice a few Blacks of the right opinion were permitted to
vote in Democratic primaries, sometimes in states with a
state-wide primary rule. "[60]

The majority of Blacks who desired to register continued to do so as Republicans and fought the Lily-white Republicans "who occasionally sought to impose Republican
white primaries for the control of the state party organization
and for possible federal patronage. " The disenfranchised
Black voters fought back through determined Black leaders,
and sundry Black community organizations, which led occasional registration drives, raised the number of Black Republicans in the state from 6, 869 in 1900 to 15, 877 in 1946. [61]

Generally speaking, "between 1902 and 1937, a politically conscious Black in Florida ... found his way to effective
participation in politics cut off by any one of the three legal
barriers"[62] set up during the era of disfranchisement (1889-
1902) in the state. These legal barriers, "the poll tax, the
multiple ballot box, and the white primary, " as well as the
Australian Ballot, "contributed greatly to the destruction of
the Republican party (especially the Black and Tan supporters)
as a significant force in state and local politics. " As one
student of Florida politics put it, "the party having become a
nullity, Blacks lost what had been the traditional vehicle for
the expression of their political demands, and general elections became ritualistic formalities. "

Black and Tan Republicanism in Florida came to an
end in state and local politics as in almost all other southern
states, shortly after disenfranchisement was institutionalized.
But Black and Tans, as in other southern states, became an
occasional force to be reckoned with at the national convention, as we shall see in the next chapter.

The politics of the Black and Tan Republicans in
Florida assumed no clearcut pattern; they had no character-
istic political style.

SOUTH CAROLINA

Black Republicanism began in some areas of South
Carolina before the War ended, but not until after the War in
certain other sections.   For instance, Blacks living in the
liberated Sea Islands off the coast of South Carolina began to
express an interest in the politics of the Republican Party as
early as 1862. [63]   They hailed their "Yankees" and "Massa
Lincoln" as God-sent and promised to be their loyal supporters and followers.

For Blacks on the mainland, Republicanism came only
after the War.   Before the War ended Free Blacks in Charleston were calling for civil and political rights, and in 1865
a "Colored Peoples' Convention of the State of South Carolina" met in Charleston November 20-25 and issued a document to the "white inhabitants of South Carolina" asking that
Blacks be granted their civil and political rights.   This appeal supplied the Radical Republicans in Congress "with highly
potent ammunition for their coming attack" upon the Presidential policies for Reconstruction.   Blacks continued their
protest for suffrage rights intermittently and sent a delegate,
William Beverly Nash, to the National Freedmen's Convention
in Washington early in 1867.   Nash "strove vigorously to have
the convention endorse Nego suffrage without educational or
property qualifications. "   After the convention, Nash visited
the House of Representatives and sat in the gallery as that
body overrode President Johnson's veto of the First Reconstruction Acts.   Returning home, Nash called an assembly to
thank God for having "seen fit to cause this great nation to
release them from the disadvantages and deprivation that they
labored under as a people. "

By March, 1867, the Republican Party held its first
state convention in Charleston and endorsed the Reconstruction
Act which enabled Blacks and loyal whites to register and vote
for delegates for a new constitution.   The factions which
coalesced into the Republican organization in South Carolina
included Blacks, Scalawags, and Carpetbaggers.   The nominal
preparatory work among the Freedmen had been done by the
Freedmen's Bureau and the Union League. [64]   But in the case
of South Carolina, Black themselves had gained some political

consciousness and strongly endorsed the Republican Party on their own.

Following the structuring of a formal party organization in March, 1867 at the Charleston meeting, another meeting concerned with principles and platform was held in July, 1867 in Columbia.   There, 45 of the 69 delegates were Blacks and they helped to draw up a platform calling for universal suffrage and equal rights for Blacks, and including a broad program of economic reform.   Specifically, the platform called for a system of free public education, "internal improvement, public support for the poor and destitute, those aged and infirm people, houseless and homeless, the revision and reorganization of the judicial system, and the division and sale of unoccupied lands among the poorer classes. "

After the convention, the Republican Party began campaigning for its newly developed platform.   In the meantime, registration of Blacks had begun and continued through the summer.   Black Republicans apprised the Black masses of their new potential, and were aided by the Freedmen Bureau and governmental agents.   In the election in November, 1867 "nearly 69, 000 of a possible 81, 000 Negroes--roughly 85 per cent--participated and voted for the convention. "   When the delegates to the convention assembled at Charleston in January, 1868, there were 76 Black Republican delegates and 48 whites.   As in other states, the convention of South Carolina debated the major issue of suffrage, the structure of the new government and the proper role for Black Americans within the new political structure. [65]   After meeting for fifty-three consecutive days, the convention adjourned, having drafted a new constitution, on March 17, 1868.

The document was submitted to the electorate for ratification on April 14-16.   In the period between the convention and submission of the constitution to the public, the Republicans and Democrats actively propagandized.   White Democrats objected to the idea of Black voters and Black participation in the new state government, and were so angered that they submitted a petition entitled "Respectful Remonstrance on the Behalf of White People of South Carolina Against the Constitution of the Late Convention of that State, Now Submitted to Congress for Ratification, " to the House of Representatives. Later, another white appeal was sent to the United States Senate.   Despite this protest, 67, 000 of the eligible 81, 000 Blacks went to the polls, ratified the new constitution and returned Republicans to all major offices.   The vote was 70, 758 for ratification and 27, 288 against it.

The constitution having been ratified and accepted by
Congress, the first legislature of South Carolina under the
new constitution assembled at Columbia in July of 1868. When
the Senate convened in late July, it had 11 Blacks among the
31 Senators; the House had 71 Black Representatives out of
124.   The legislature's first action after organizing was the
ratification of the Fourteenth Amendment.   With some opposition from the Democrats, the state legislature also ratified
the Fifteenth Amendment before it adjourned.

By 1870 the white Republicans so respected the strength
of the Black Republicans that they placed a Black, A. J. Ransier, on their ticket for the post of Lieutenant Governor. The
Republicans won with no trouble and Ransier received 85, 071
votes.   However, these continual Republican successes spurred
Democratic hatred that culminated in the organization and beginning of Ku Klux Klan terrorism in 1871.   Although several
Klansmen were put on trial between 1871-72, this limited
public exposure did not slow the organization's terrorist tactics against the Black community. [66]

If the Democrats used threats to intimidate Blacks,
though, they also employed other tactics to attract them into
the party.   As early as the Spring of 1868 White Democrats
had succeeded in several areas of the state in organizing
Black Democratic Clubs.   "In Columbia, for instance, a Democratic association of Colored citizens was formed in mid-
April with about forty charter members.   By mid-June it re-
portedly mustered one hundred Blacks on its rolls. "   In 1870
the Democrats had two Blacks of questionable background
speaking for the party throughout the state.   One, Jonas Byrd,
described as "a respectable Negro of Charleston, " who declined the Democratic party's nomination for the lieutenant
governor's post that year, spoke in Edgefield, Lauren and
many other counties, urging Blacks to support their trusted
friends, the Democrats.   The other Black, Richard Gayle,
echoed these sentiments and said he was certain whites were
going to win the struggle: white men "had conquered the Indians and the forest, had built cities, telegraphs, railroads and
steamboats, " and therefore would surely regain power in the
South.   These overtures failed because of vigorous Republican
responses and Black awareness of the Democrats' past relationship to the slavocracy.   Thus, shortly after 1871, the
Democrats dropped or greatly slowed their efforts to attract
Black voters and began to rely more and more on political
intimidation and terrorism to force Blacks from the political
arena.

By 1872, Democratic pressure on the Blacks within the
coalition was not the only force working against the Republican
party. From the outset the party had had some internal difficulties arising from its coalition of whites and Blacks. According to Professor Williamson, "the most striking facet of
the political behavior of Negroes in South Carolina during Reconstruction was their tendency to dissociate themselves from
white persons." This was abundantly apparent, suggested
Williamson, "within the Republican party itself." Williamson
holds that "the segregation of Negroes and whites into Republican factions was the result of the prejudices each entertained toward the other." The white Republicans in the state
consisted primarily of officeholders and their immediate fam-
ilies.   While the number of white Republicans voters fluctuated
in the state, with whites entering and leaving the party from
time to time for various reasons, it generally stayed between
three and four thousand. The Black wing or faction, the
largest group, remained loyal and constantly tried to get more
Blacks to join or to accept the party's ideas and platform.

Although these two factions existed in the Republican
party ranks in South Carolina from the outset, ideology had
not at this point separated them; the basic separation or segregation was on the basis of color.   But real factionalism
came soon in 1872, spurred initially by the issue of party reform.   Several conservative white Republicans began an attempt to rid the party of internal corruption, and of dishon-
esty, incompetent and bad men in office.   These conservatives
also tried to commit the party to reducing the state's debt
before it began any expensive program of social welfare.

At the state Republican convention in 1872 the supposedly corrupt wing or faction of the party--the Black and
Tans--nominated a white man, F. J. Moses, for the Governorship and four Blacks for state office, including R. H.
Gleaves for Lieutenant Governor.   Other Blacks were given
the posts of Secretary of State, State Treasurer and Adjutant
and Inspector General.   The Black and Tans also drew up a
platform endorsing the national Republican party's suspension
of interest payments on suspicious bonds, guaranteeing the
payment of interest on the legal debt, and pledging the party
to place safeguards on the treasury.

These assurances were not enough to satisfy the majority of white Republicans, and they and a few Blacks bolted the
convention and held their own.   The defection was led by a
leading Democrat now turned conservative Republican, James

Orr, who had been Governor just prior to the establishment of the new government by the Reconstruction Act of 1867. The newly-formed group, calling themselves the Reform Republican Party (in reality the Lily-whites or their forerunner), nominated a white man, Reuben Tomlinson, for Governor and James W. Haynes, a Black, for Lieutenant Governor. Blacks were also nominated for the post of Secretary of State, Adjutant and Inspector General and Superintendant of Education. These reform or "Lily-white" Republicans endorsed the national Republican party platform, repudiated previous Republican administrations in the state and declared themselves in favor of an ad valorem system of taxation.

During the campaign, several key and leading Black political figures in the state urged other Blacks to vote for the Reform or Lily-white party. The Moses-Gleaves ticket-- i.e., the regular party (Black & Tans)--won the election by more than a 33,000-vote majority. During their tenure in office, however, much corruption took place, and it wasn't long before criticism arose in all sections of the state and other leaders of the Black community began calling for reforms. At the 1874 Republican State convention, the Reform (lily-white) Republicans failed to make any meaningful impact on the Regular party (Black and Tan) nomination and platform. The Regulars nominated another white man, D. H. Chamberlain, instead of Moses for Governor, and R. H. Gleaves, the Negro, was renominated for Lieutenant Governor.

The Reform (Lily-whites), having failed to influence the convention, again bolted and held their own convention. Naming themselves the Independent Republican Party, the Reformers nominated a white man, John T. Green, and a Black man, Martin R. Delany, for Governor and Lieutenant Governor respectively. The party adopted a platform which called for "reform, retrenchment, and honest government." Before and after Green's nomination, supporters of the reform movement organized Blacks into groups known as the Honest Government League of South Carolina, to work for securing Green's nomination and election in the Black community. Further help came to the Independent Republicans from the Democrats who once again, as they had in 1872, fused with the Reformers.[68] Despite this new support the Independents lost the election. Chamberlain received 80,403 popular votes and Green, 68,818. R. H. Gleaves defeated Martin R. Delany, the Reform Black candidate, who is considered the father of Black Nationalism, by a majority of eighty-six (86) votes for the Lieutenant Governor's post.

In 1876, the Democrats spurned all fusion overtures from the Reform Republicans and launched their re-entry into state politics under the leadership of their folk hero, Wade Hampton. To facilitate their political resurgence the Democrats once again began a campaign to attract Black voters. "Hampton, " the Democratic gubernatorial nominee, "devoted much energy to winning the confidence of Black voters. " He declared, states Professor Taylor, that the "rights of all would be respected and furthermore, to the colored man, he promised more work and better schools. " In addition to Hampton's efforts, several Democratic Clubs throughout the state initiated good will campaigns in the Black community. For instance, "the white Richland Democratic Club in Columbia brought Negro members into the club and held weekly meetings to convert others. "

The Democrats' efforts were so strenuous that one Black, Martin Delany, declared himself in favor of Hampton, "whom he considered a just, true, dependable man, " and in October 1876, the New York Times indicated that between 1500 and 2000 Blacks would vote for the Democratic ticket. Prior to election day, the Democrats held a Hampton Day Celebration and Negro Democratic Clubs rode in the parade. Meanwhile, the Hampton Red Shirts, a para-military organization similar to the KKK, suppressed and intimidated those Blacks who had not declared themselves in favor of the Democrats. Economic pressures were applied to Black Republicans--but not to Black Democrats.

To inducement and intimidation the Democrats added fraud: Georgians and North Carolinians were brought over the border to vote. Confusion and chaos abounded on election day and the Republicans reacted timidly to the Democratic threat. Several Black Republicans, also, couldn't support the Republican nominee Chamberlain for a second term and simply refrained from voting. At first both sides claimed victory and both men--Hampton and Chamberlain--went to Washington to discuss the matter with President elect Hayes. Hayes removed the federal troops from the state and supported Hampton. The future of Republicanism in the state was sealed.

Following the Democratic takeover in April 1877 there was an increase in intimidation designed to destroy the Republican party. At first, minor corruption which supposedly occurred during the Republican administration was exposed to justify the intimidation but later, intimidation became standard practice when it was realized that Republican President Hayes

would not interfere.   Prior to the 1878 election, the Democrats passed a new election law aimed at further repressing
the Republican party.   Ballot boxes were labeled for each
office and any ticket in the wrong box would be declared void.

       At the Republican convention in 1878 a new split oc-
curred along policy lines.   Some Republicans urged fusion
with the new party, the Greenbackers; others urged party
members to concentrate on only county and legislative offices;
still others wanted a full state slate.   The arguments were
not resolved, but the majority of the Republicans did concentrate on county and legislative offices.   The divisions in the
Republican ranks were reflected at the polls and permitted
several Black Democrats to get elected to state offices. Each
year after 1876, indeed, policy matters split the Republicans
into several factions.   Almost every leading political personality had his own political clique.   No one individual arose
with enough charisma to unite the numerous factions behind a
single program or candidate.   One of the largest factions
within the Republican Party, a predominantly Black group led
by Robert Smalls, a leading Black Republican officeholder and
wheelhorse, electioneered on the local and legislative levels
to maintain themselves in power. [69]   Other factions within the
party were groups headed by Christopher C. Bowen, Dr.
A. C. Mackey, W. N. Taft, Ellery M. Brayton, E. A. Webster, and R. W. Memminger, among others.   All these men
were white but some had Black followers.   The majority of
Blacks, however, stayed in the Smalls organization.

       In the 1878 election six Black Republicans were elected
to the General Assembly (six Black Democrats were also
elected to the same body).   Three Blacks were elected to the
State Senate but Robert Smalls, the titular head of the group,
was defeated for Congress.

       In 1880 several of the white Republican factions fused
with the Greenbacker Party, which nominated W. R. Blair for
Governor.   The Smalls-led Black Republican faction put up
candidates for the General Assembly, county offices and Congress.   "The election of that year returned one hundred forty-
two Democrats and six Republicans to the General Assembly."
The latter included two Black Senators from Beaufort and
Georgetown, respectively, and four members of the House
from Beaufort and Georgetown.   One Black Democrat was
elected to the House from Charleston.   In addition, Robert
Smalls this time was seated in Congress.

Growing fearful of the alliance of Greenbackers and
Black Republicans, the Democrats enacted in 1881 the "Eight
Ballot Box Law" which "confused the less intelligent voters.
According to the Republican state convention in 1882, this law
contemplated the disfranchisement of four-fifths of the Republicans in the state. " Fearful of the new election law and the
Democrats' repressive measures, the Republicans partly
closed their ranks and a majority of the Republicans fused
with the Greenbackers. As a result, "the Republicans sent
twelve Blacks to the General Assembly. Three of the twelve
were Senators, from Beaufort, Berkeley, and Georgetown,
respectively. " In the House, in addition to the nine Black Republicans, there were also three Black Democrats. Robert
Smalls that year returned to Congress to serve out the term
of white Republican E. W. M. Mackey.

By 1884, however, the new registration law had led to
a decline in Black Republican political strength in the state.
Republican factionalism was at a minimum but the Greenbackers were almost defunct due to continual election losses
and anti-Black prejudices, so no fusion took place. Only six
Blacks were elected to the General Assembly; one Black Democrat was also elected to the House.

Virtually the same conditions prevailed in 1886, eight
Blacks being elected this time to the General Assembly. "Six
of these were Republicans, two of whom sat in the Senate and
four in the House. " The other two Blacks, Marshal Jones of
Orangeburg and George M. Meas of Charleston, were Democrats.

When the General Assembly convened in 1888, there
were only three Black Republicans and two Black Democrats
in the House. However, one Black Republican, Thomas E.
Miller, was elected to Congress. The basic reasons for the
decline in Black Republican power were the lack of any other
political group with whom to coalesce and the impact of the
Eight Ballot Box Law which required the illiterate Black
voters to guess the right box or have his ballot thrown out.
Democratic invasions into the Black community and intimida-
tions of Black Republicans placed further burdens on the slowly
collapsing Republican party.

On February 4, 1889 a group of Independents and old-
line Union men held a convention in Pickens, South Carolina
and officially formed the first Lily-white Republican party in
the state. After some years the party died, but it was re-

vived again on October 28, 1930.   The Pickens County Sentinel
carried the following announcement:

> Fourteen Republicans from Pickens County attended
> the organizational meeting of a new white Republican
> party in South Carolina held at Columbia October
> 28.   Total attendance was 700 to 800 and every
> county in the state was represented except Dor-
> chester.   No Negroes were allowed.   J. C. Ham-
> bright, businessman of Rock Hill, was named state
> chairman of the new party. [70]

Although the Black Republicans fought back and tried
to revitalize themselves, they were only able to elect six
Black Republicans to the State House in 1890.   This slight increase was due in part to the fact that the Black Republicans
fused with the Haskellite movement or Independent Democrats
who bolted in protest against the Democratic party leader,
Benjamin "Pitchfork" Tillman, who had deposed Wade Hampton, N. C. Butler, and A. C. Haskell, "respectable" white
Democratic Bourbons. Tillmanites were poor white farmers--
i.e., Populists.

Black Republicans and the Haskellites fused again in
the 1892 election and three Blacks were sent to the State
House and one Black, George W. Murray, was elected to
Congress.   By 1894, however, there were only two Black Republicans in the House and Murray, although reelected to
Congress, was seated only after a dispute with his white Democratic opponent.

The fraudulent character of the 1894 election--in part
attested to by the difficulty the Tillman Democrats had in
winning--the dislike that Tillmanites had for the aristocratic
Bourbon whites as well as the anti-Black prejudices they harbored, led the Democrats to call for the convening of a constitutional convention on September 10, 1895.   The purpose of
this convention was to "obviate the remote possibilities of a
fusion of the white minority (Haskellites) and the Black Republicans which might have brought such a ticket success in subsequent elections. "   In the general election of 1894, the state
electorate had decided in favor of the proposed convention.

When the convention did convene, six Black Republicans
were in attendance but their presence didn't prevent the disenfranchisement of a considerable number of their race.   Benjamin "Pitchfork" Tillman, the chairman of the Committee on

Suffrage, moved the suffrage article through the convention
and got it approved by a decisive vote of seventy-seven to
forty-one.   Later in 1895, the new constitution went into
effect.   The new document embodied an "understanding clause,"
a Tillmanite device which he described as "the most charming
piece of mechanism ever invented. "   He even explained on the
floor of the U. S. Senate in 1900 (he was elected to it in 1895)
how Black voters were rejected through difficult questions and
illiterate whites accepted through easy ones. [71]   He further
explained on the Senate floor how he had helped drive Blacks
in the state from political power: "We [the white South Caro-
linians] took the government away.   We stuffed ballot boxes.
We shot them [Blacks].   We are not ashamed of it.   We have
done our best ... We have scratched our heads to find out
how we could eliminate the last one of them. "

     In such an atmosphere and with the aid of the new dis-
enfranchising constitution, Black Republicanism, at least on
the state level, died in 1896.   In that year the last Black Republican, R. B. Anderson of Georgetown, went to the state
legislature.   After 1896 the Black Republicans had to abandon
their party because disenfranchisement had removed their chief
supporters, Black voters, and they had no way to get new
supporters.   Moreover, with people like Ben "Pitchfork" Tillman, in control of the state government participation in politics was a dangerous undertaking.   The Black Republican
leaders in the state either resigned from politics, took federal positions elsewhere, or moved out of the state.

     However, in 1900, a white man, Joseph W. Tolbert
(nicknamed Tireless Joe or Fighting Joe--because he was a
delegate or a contestant for a seat at every Republican national convention from 1900 to 1944) rebuilt the Republican
Party in the state, organizing it into a unit which "consisted
of himself, a few other whites and several handpicked Negroes
over the state. "   The purpose of the Tolbert organization was
to choose delegates to the national convention and to distribute
patronage to its members, particularly to Tolbert.   Tolbert
added several Blacks to ensure his group a seat at the national Republican convention; racial composition was a major
argument at credentials hearings and a mixed delegation usually fared better than a Lily-white one.   Tireless Joe's group
of Republicans soon became known as the Black and Tans.
The group made only minor attempts to enter state or local
politics but emerged every four years to go to the national
convention, get seated and acquire patronage, the latter being
its chief objective.

Tolbert's Black and Tan Republicans didn't go unchallenged. Another white South Carolinian, seeing the benefits that were accruing to Tolbert's Black and Tans and understanding that occasionally the national convention seated lily-white delegations, organized such a group for his own enrichment. This man, Joe Hambright of Rock Hill, in October, 1930, organized his Republican group along lines similar to Tolbert's, with only one exception--Hambright excluded Blacks. Hambright's lily-whites, like Tolbert's Black and Tans, made no effort to attract supporters or participate in state politics. They only challenged the Black and Tans at the national conventions.[72]

The efforts of Tireless Joe and Hambright made the South Carolina Republican party a national joke and, in 1938, J. Bates Gerald, a wealthy lumberman, formed another Republican group to challenge the old Black and Tan and lily white groups. Gerald, understanding the importance of delegation composition, got three white-"approved" and well-known Blacks and two unknown Blacks, all from the middle class, to dispose of Tolbert's main argument at the national convention --that of racial composition. Moreover, while Tolbert's Blacks were handpicked and considered safe and loyal to him, the Gerald-led Republicans selected their Blacks in a convention or executive convention fashion. This strengthened their case and in 1940 the convention seated the Gerald-led Republicans in preferance to old Tireless Joe's group. By 1952, however, the Gerald-led Republicans, now feeling sure of being seated, formally ousted the three prominent Negro Republican leaders, who had helped boost the faction from its inception, for alleged disciplinary reasons. Once in power, the Gerald group reverted back to lily-white Republicanism.

Although no longer recognized as the Republican group in the state, the Tolbert group challenged the Gerald group at every national convention until 1956, intermittently electioneering and putting up presidential electors to strengthen their arguments before the credentials committee, but with no success (see Table II on the Appendix). When Tolbert died in the forties, another white man, B. L. Hendrix, a lumberman of Estill, and I. S. Leevy, a Black undertaker of Columbia, assumed control and began organizing "Lincoln Emancipation Clubs" throughout the state in anticipation of a Republican victory in 1948 that never came.

In the main, Black Republicans in South Carolina from 1900 to 1944 never numbered more than 500, at the peak there were never more than 1200 white members.

Blacks established their own party, the South Carolina
Progressive Democratic Party, in 1944 and supported it
through three convention challenges until 1956.   Other Blacks
simply remained outside the political arena: the mere 63
votes for the Black and Tans in 1944 reveals something of the
disgust and contempt of the Black community for a white-led
Black group.   It was, in fact, chiefly the sinister tactic of
Tolbert and Gerald which led to the emergence of the all-
Black political party in 1944.

TENNESSEE

In November, 1864, a group of Black Republican sympathizers conducted mock elections in the Black community in
Nashville, Tennessee; Lincoln received 3,193 votes and Mc-
Clellan, the Democratic candidate, only one vote. [73]   While
this was indicative of political opinion in the Black community,
Blacks in Tennessee had not yet acquired the right to vote
and thus could not fully support their political friends.   Assisted by visiting workers from the north and Freedmen Bureau agents, however, Black leaders "sought voting privileges
from the end of the fighting. "[74]   Even before 1865, Blacks,
under the protection of the Freedman Bureau "were able to
hold meetings and forward resolutions and petitions to the
legislature and governor's office" asking for the right to vote.

Finally, in 1865, Blacks held a state-wide convention
in Nashville that was addressed by the Tennessee chief officer
of the Freedmen's Bureau, Clinton B. Fisk.   The convention
drew up a petition and sent it to Congress, "praying for the
exclusion of Tennessee Representatives unless the Tennessee
Legislature acted on a petition for Black Suffrage before December, 1865 assembly. "   Congress, however, gave the petition only minor consideration.

On the state level, Black protests for suffrage rights
also fell on deaf ears.   One basic reason for this lack of attention to Black protest was the manner in which Tennessee
was reorganized after the War.   Unlike the other southern
states, Tennessee did not go through a period of Reconstruction per se.   "Attempts to restore civil government in Tennessee under federal authority began in the spring of 1862
when confederate forces evacuated most of middle and west
Tennessee. "   President Lincoln sent Andrew Johnson back to
his native state that year to become military governor and
restore loyal civil government.   Continued strife and internal

dissension slowed Johnson's efforts at first but he finally succeeded in creating a loyal government by the spring of 1865.

Before the spring of 1865 had ended a new constitution had been adopted, a new government restructed and a new governor named to head the state. The new governor, William C. Brownlow, had been a Unionist Whig before secession and had strongly opposed the disunionist sentiment in the state. When the state finally seceded the confederates had him imprisoned but he was later released. Upon his release he went North, all the while denouncing the act of southern secession. In many ways he became a symbol of martyr of Southern Unionism. [75] After the federal forces captured his state he returned and was received as a hero by many in the state who held like Unionist sentiments.

Assuming power on April 5, 1865, Brownlow supported Johnson's Reconstruction policy until a serious breach developed between the President and the Congressional Radical Republicans. At that point Brownlow formally broke with Johnson and supported the Congressional Radicals. Describing the situation, Professor Alexander states that "after Johnson and the Radical Republicans were openly at war, and after Johnson's backers promoted the Philadelphia National Union Convention of August, 1866 to seek coalescence around the President's Reconstruction policies, Brownlow with all of his antebellum and war-time gusto led a large Tennessee delegation to the Radical's counterattack at the Southern Loyalist Convention in Philadelphia in September of 1866. " Brownlow's bold action against Johnson, especially since he was from the same state as Johnson, and his call at the convention for the extension of suffrage to Blacks brought him great admiration among the Congressional Radical ranks. Brownlow had personally forced the 14th Amendment, through the Tennessee legislature, calling a special session and fraudulently obtaining a quorum to ratify it.

This had not been Brownlow's position on Black suffrage at first. In January, 1856, Brownlow went along with the major position of the convention that was reorganizing the state. One delegate, Harvey M. Watterson, succinctly captured the convention's disposition in a major speech. He said to the delegates:

> This brings me to the everlasting Nigger--that dark
> fountain from which has flowed all our woes ... I
> have always thought if the people of Tennessee,

Kentucky, Maryland, Virginia, and Missouri were
paid a fair price for their slave property and the
colored population removed beyond their limits, it
would be a good operation for the whites. ... Will
the people of Tennessee permit the valueless Negro
to stand between them and the establishment of
civil government. I cannot, I do not believe it...
I would not give one year of virtuous civil rule for
all the darkies in America. 76

Brownlow made no criticism of this speech at the convention;
he accepted it. Later in 1865 Brownlow, addressing the state
assembly, urged them to entice immigrants rather than admit
Blacks to the ballot. He further advised them "against enfranchising Negro men, offering the usual arguments concern-
ing incompetence and adding mention of his fear that rural
Negroes would be influenced by landowners, most of whom
were former confederate sympathizers, in the counties where
Negroes were most numerous. "

          Brownlow's conversion to a positive position on the
Black Suffrage question in 1866, stemmed, he claimed, from
two things: first, each new election indicated that the conservative Democrats in the State were about to regain power,
and secondly, "the drift of national opinion on the subject of
Negro voting" was in a positive direction there was a greater
aptitude among Blacks than he had earlier anticipated. Whether
from motives of political self-preservation or because of outside pressure, Brownlow began prodding his legislature to
pass the measure in 1866. Finally, on February 25th, 1867,
after much political maneuvering on Brownlow's part, the
Tennessee House passed the measure, five days after Congress
had passed its Reconstruction plan. While the other ten southern states were about to embark on Reconstruction, however,
Tennessee for the most part was concluding hers.

          Once Blacks had been given the right to vote in 1867,
the Union League stepped in and began the arduous task of
marshalling the new Black voters into the Republican party.
The League, which came to Tennessee in the early 1860's,
had become a Radical-controlled organization by 1867, and
employed all the regalia and secrecy it could muster to
channel Black voters toward the Republican organization.
Later in 1867 Tennessee voters went to the polls to select a
governor, legislature, and representatives to Congress. In
the contest, Black voters were also sought by the conservative
(Democratic) party but the campaign failed for the Democrats

had little to offer the newly enfranchised Freedmen.   When
the results were in, Republicans had made virtually a clean
sweep of all positions and had completely routed the Democrats.

The Democrats retaliated for their overwhelming electoral defeat by renewing the Ku Klux Klan on a state-wide
basis.   "The Tennessee Klan, " asserts Professor William
Gillette, "was first organized in middle Tennessee at Pulaski
as a social club of ex-confederates, in December, 1865, during the first year of Radical rule, but it did not become a
major political force until 1867, when Radical rule became
firmly entrenched ... by enfranchising Negroes so as to align
them with East Tennessee Republican whites. "[77]

"The first general test of Radical Republican strength
under duress from Ku Kluxism in Tennessee came in November, 1868 during the Presidential election and the Congressional elections. "[78]   Although the state was carried for the
Republican Presidential nominee, General Ulysses S. Grant,
his total popular vote was barely one-half of that received the
previous year by Brownlow.   The effect of Klan intimidation
in 1868 was clearly stated by Professor Gillette: "Many
Negro voters were scared away from the polls during the
federal elections of 1868.   The Negro vote dropped off in West
Tennessee and was cut in half in middle Tennessee. " (East
Tennessee had few Blacks).   The following year, 1869, the
Republicans, still under pressure from Democratic violence
and intimidation, lost the state elections.   The new Democratic government tightened their control and power in the
state by disbanding the state militia (which protected Black
Republican voters), lifting martial law, reenfranchising the
conservative confederates, and putting into effect a poll tax
which further reduced the Black vote.   The new governor,
himself once a Klan member, used the Klan to complete his
democratic restoration.   "Then, after 1870, Klan violence
began to decline, but it did not disappear. "

Another factor which figures prominently in the Republican electoral defeat was the low enthusiasm among Blacks
for the Republican party.   Under Brownlow's tutelage, "officeholding at the state level was totally denied Negroes" in practice, even after legal prohibition had been ungraciously aban-
doned.   Rarely did county or town offices fall to Negroes,
even where they were the majority among the voters.   In
short, Blacks found little to motivate them toward participation in the party.   For them, voting only meant keeping white

Republicans in power, with no visible rewards for their
efforts.   Many just abstained both from voting and from participation in party affairs.

          After losing the 1869 election, the Republican Party in
Tennessee began to suffer from intra-party friction and factionalism arising out of personal ambitions and jealousies.
During this internal upheaval, one group of white Republicans,
in order to regain power in the organization or a substantial
number of backers and supporters, began advocating nomination for Blacks and declaring their right to seek offices.
Such comments drew Blacks into their camp.   The alienated
white Republican officers then formed a faction of their own.
The former group, the Black and Tan wing, now geared up
for the 1872 election, heartened by the fact that the Democrats were embroiled in factional infighting themselves.

          The lily-white faction--i. e. the white Republican office-
holders--supported Horace Greeley in the 1872 electoral canvass, as did many Democrats, and the result was a significant comeback for the Black and Tan Republicans.   Although
the Black and Tans were led by whites and six white Republicans were elected to Congress, the first Black, Sampson
Keeble from Memphis, was sent to the State House.   The Republicans, having reassembled, coalesced with numerous independents in the State House and repealed the poll tax re-
quirement for voting.   This repeal gave the Republicans a
potentially larger Black vote for the 1874 state and federal
election and drew more Blacks to the party.   However, the
contest for power in 1874 became the most heated and the
bloodiest one in Tennessee's history after secession.   The
Democrats revived their Klan organization and resorted to
mob rule.   Many Blacks were lynched, murdered, fired upon,
intimidated or frightened away from the polls on election day.
The result was a disaster for Tennessee Republicans--only
one Republican was returned to Washington and the state elections went just as badly.   The Democrats had once again regained control.

          Despite the Democrats' return to power and the great
outbursts of racism during the 1874, 1876, 1890, and 1898
campaigns, Republicans sent ten Blacks to the State House
until 1897. [79]   Moreover, Black Republican aldermen sat on
the city councils in Chattanooga, Knoxville, Memphis, and
Nashville into the first and second decades of the Twentieth
Century.   In Chattanooga, for example, a Black alderman,
representing the Black section of the city, sat in the city

council until 1920.   That year the city instituted city-wide
representation and Blacks were outvoted.

On the state, local and national levels, Black and white
Republicans did not openly clash.   In fact, there is no record
of these two groups formally contesting each other until 1924
and 1928.   In 1924 there was a mild Black and Tan/Lily-
white clash in the tenth Congressional district in Memphis.
The two Black delegates, W. Wilkerson and F. T. Taylor,
were seated when they agreed to elect only white delegates
thereafter.   The next contest came in 1928, from the same
Congressional district in Memphis, this time between a lily-
white group led by "Jim" Quinn, World War I veteran, and a
Black and Tan group led by R. R. Church, a wealthy Black
businessman in the city.   Each man had held his own Congressional convention and received the nomination as the delegate from the district.

The Black vote in Memphis had been nurtured by the
E. H. Crump machine ever since Crump became mayor in
1911.   He knew that the "Negro vote was an important element in winning elections and that successful candidates traditionally had Negro support, and he tried extremely hard to
maintain and keep up the vote for his organization. "   In the
words of Professor V. O. Key, "Crump sees that Memphis
Negroes get a fairer break than usual in public services. His
organization, of course, follows through and takes specific
measures to hold Negro leaders in line. "   In one or another
Crump ensured control over the Black community.   One means
of control was to create a Black political boss with his own
machine.   One of Crump's Black bosses was Robert Church,
who although a Republican, worked for Crump and dispensed
numerous favors for him in the Black community.   "He do-
nated a public park in the midst of valuable urban property to
Blacks and his people credited him with colored appointments
to Federal offices, with acts of charity, and ... with invin-
cible political cleverness. "   Even Senator Heflin of Alabama
paid tribute to Church by reading a poem into the hearing of
a patronage investigation:

> Offices up a 'simmon tree
> Bob Church on de ground
> Bob Church said to de 'pointing power:
> 'Shake dem 'pointments down. '

Professor Lewinson states: "Church could in short deliver
the Negro vote of Memphis and influence it elsewhere. "   By

1928 Church's sub-machine, which had over 3, 500 Black voters, swung the mayoralty election for the Democrats and later
broke with the Crump machine.

Given this type of political power, the Credentials
Committee was informed that unless Church was seated the
Black vote in Tennessee would be lost.   The Lily-whites contended that Tennessee would be lost to the Democrats no
matter who was seated, but the convention finally seated
Church.   This clash was the last major Black and Tan factional fight at the national level.

Black and Tan Republicanism in Tennessee never really
materialized to any meaningful degree, unlike in other southern states.   Although there were two clashes in the 1920's,
both arose from the same city and area--west Tennessee.
Even if one goes back as far as Reconstruction, Black and
Tan Republicans never had much of a chance, although some
factionalism along racial lines did occur, dealing primarily
with whether Blacks should hold offices or not.   But even this
limited schism fizzled out.

Even if one turns to East Tennessee, with few Blacks
and white Republicans with a history going back before the
War and intense anti-Black prejudices, no such formation of
Black and Tans and Lily-whites took place.   Even in Knoxville, the major city in East Tennessee, Black Republicans
were permitted to flourish and carry on their political maneuvering undisturbed.   One Black colonel, Joseph M. Trigg, who
served as an alderman from the Negro ward in that city,
wrote numerous editorials for the Black owned pro-Republican
newspaper, The East Tennessee News.   In most of them he
simply told how the national party neglected Blacks, but there
was never mention of any local lily-white organizations or
efforts by local or regional groups to curtail Black political
action in the city. [80]

Black and Tan Republicanism, then, except for perhaps
two instances, didn't really materialize in Tennessee.   One
reason for this was that the Negro community itself was rife
with factionalism.   Blacks, thus played only minor roles in
state politics.   Professor Key suggests also that the absence
of Black state-wide organizations for political action stems
from the fact that there were no serious threat of a disenfranchising constitution nor a statewide Democratic primary
which eliminated Blacks as in other Southern states.   Devices
like the poll tax were passed and felt to be effective enough,
and harsher methods were never instituted. [81]

ARKANSAS

Arkansas came under federal military control in 1863.
That year "a group of Union sympathizers determined to re-
organize the state sought Lincoln's cooperation.   He cautiously
gave it under his military power, but the group went ahead
boldly, held a convention in January, 1864, adopted a constitution and elected Isaac Murphy governor. "[82]

When the two Senators elected by the new government
reached Congress, they were denied their seats and sent back
to Arkansas.   Upon returning, the new government, dominated
by ex-confederates, sent a commission in 1866 back to Washington to confer with federal authorities about the future of the
state.   The commission let it be known that the state's new
constitution abolished slavery and prohibited Black indentured
servitude, but that this was as far as they were willing to go.
Washington at this time was embroiled in a Presidential-
Congressional fight and the Arkansas group was sent home
with no definite commitment from federal authorities.   Early
the next year Congressional Reconstruction began and registration for the right to vote for delegates to a new state convention was scheduled for May, 1867.   A few whites told
Blacks that "registration was for the purpose of enrolling them
for taxes but the Freedmen's Bureau sent out agents to in-
struct them in the purpose of voting. "

After registration was complete, people in Arkansas
went to the polls and cast 27, 756 votes for and 13, 558 against
holding a constitutional convention.   The military commander,
General Ard, named the delegates who had been selected and
set January 7, 1868 as the date for the convention in Little
Rock.   When the convention convened there were eight Black
delegates present: J. W. Mason, Richard Samuels, William
Murphy, Monroe Hawkins, William Grey, James T. White,
Henry Rector, and Thomas P. Johnson.   These delegates
came from Hempstead, Jefferson, Lafayette, Phillips, and
Pulaski counties--counties in the heavily populated Black sec-
tions of the state, i. e. , middle and lower Arkansas.

In the convention white conservatives strongly opposed
Black suffrage.   General Albert Pike remarked, just prior to
the convention, that Black suffrage would make "a hell on
earth, a hideous, horrid pandemonium filled with all the devils
of vice, crime, pauperism, corruption, violence, political de-
bauchery, and social anarchy. "   During the convention proceedings, a white conservative, Mr. Cypert, who had been a

Freedmen's Bureau agent, claimed that "he knew the Negro
in all his attributes; that their people were now being misled." He then went on to say that "he could never consent to
see them [Blacks] entrusted with the elective franchise, and
made the ruler of white men."

The eight Black delegates effectively challenged Mr.
Cypert's remarks. For instance, Mr. Gray of Phillips County,
responding to the white conservative, said: "He took no objection to the appellation; his race was closely allied to the
race which built the great pyramids of Egypt, where slept the
remains of those whose learning had taught Solon and Lycur-
gus to frame the systems of their laws, and to whom the present ages are indebted for the hints of art and knowledge."
Numerous white radical Republicans also took issue with Mr.
Cypert. The leader of the Radicals declared: "We, the great
Republican party, hold that they [Blacks] should have the ballot; and we intend that they should have it, and we will sus-
tain the government based upon the principle of universal
franchise and universal equality." Blacks and the Radical Republicans carried the day. The vote on the suffrage amendment was 45 to 21 in favor of adoption.

"The Arkansas delegates adjourned in February after a
short session of 31 days ... with fifteen whites refusing to
sign the new document." Despite their objection, "on April
1st, it was announced that the constitution had been ratified
by a vote of 30,380 to 41. On May 7, a bill for the readmission of Arkansas was presented in Congress by Thaddeus
Stevens. It was finally passed in both Houses and over the
President's veto on June 22, 1868. Before the bill was presented to Congress, however, the state legislature had met on
April 2, 1868 and adopted the Fourteenth Amendment which
was one of the prerequisites to her admission."

Following the ratification of the constitution, the date
was set for the state-wide election that fall. In the meantime, the Republican party held a convention in April, 1867,
at Little Rock and nominated a state ticket with Powell Clayton heading it for governor. At the party's convention only
one Black, John Payton, had any official status: he served on
the Committee of Resolutions.

Although Governor Clayton ruled Arkansas with an iron
hand from 1868 to 1873, the Ku Klux Klan practically carried
on a civil war. The Klan, operating as an arm of the Democrats, sought in Arkansas, as elsewhere in the South, to
intimidate and suppress Black voters and Republicans.

Blacks nevertheless held a number of posts and continued to vote in varying degrees of strength. Arkansas Blacks held three state cabinet offices as well as positions in the state legislature. W. H. Grey became Commissioner of Immigration; J. C. Corbin, Superintendent of Education; and J. T. White, Commissioner of Public Works. In 1873 Mifflin W. Gibbs was elected city judge in Little Rock. Moreover, due to Black political influence, "an anti-Ku Klux Klan law of great severity was passed which prevented all secret political organizations and declared their members public enemies. Even the possession of a Ku Klux Klan costume was a criminal offense. The law was sternly enforced and the Klan disbanded after a season of martial law. " The bill was passed in 1869.

Four years later, in 1873, Arkansas passed a stringent civil rights law "which compelled hotels and places of public amusement to admit colored people and insured them equal school facilities in separate schools. Fines of $200 to $1000 or imprisonment of 3 to 12 months was provided. " Commenting on the toughness of the law, journalist and social historian Lerone Bennett states: "Arkansas passed a civil rights bill of such severity that it would not be possible to pass it today in either New York City or New York State. "

The Democrats recaptured the state in 1874. In the spring of that year the predominately Black militia of Arkansas fought "pitched battles in the streets of Little Rock and a naval engagement on the Arkansas River. The military struggle was a stand-off, but the Democrats triumphed by fraud and internal subversion and Washington refused to intervene." When President Grant and Congress refused to act, the Democrats finally secured complete control of the state by late fall.

Another signal event of that year was a schism in the Republican party ranks. One group of Republicans calling themselves Reformers (composed mostly of white conservatives, disgruntled Democrats and the supporters of the 1872 Liberal Republican movement) clashed with the regular Republicans (composed of the Carpetbaggers, the Scalawags, and the Blacks). At the state Republican convention neither group was able to force the other to bow out, and they went to the electorate with separate tickets. After the election both groups claimed to be the winner. The Regular group gained control of the legislature, or at least was recognized by it, but the Reform group took possession of the state building by force.

Later, the Reform group retreated and fused with the Democrats who toward the end of the year took the government by
force.

        Black Republicans were pivotal in the intra-party clash,
mostly siding with the Regular Republicans. Thus, a schism
that began over policies ended up again involving racial division, and this provided the basis for a rudimentary emergence
of Black and Tan and Lily-white factions, with several of the
Reform Republicans returning to the Regular party. Neither
side, though, was able to exercise any meaningful advantage
and Black Republicans continued occasionally to run for office
and participated in state and local politics until the Democrats
passed a poll tax measure in 1893 to curtail their activities.
During the first decade of the twentieth century Arkansas
further curtailed Black voters or disenfranchised them by
adopting the white primary.

        Although they were excluded from state and local poli-
tics Black Republicans could still participate in national politics, and this is what many did. In Arkansas the lily-white
opposition was extremely limited; it never got past district or
county conventions. There is hardly anything on record that
reveals great clashes between the Black and Tans and Lily-
white factions. There were numerous clashes between Black
Republicans and white Republicans but formally structured
factions did not emerge in Arkansas after Reconstruction to
any meaningful degree. Even on the national level there is
only one clash on record between two formally structured factions.

        Blacks appeared in the Arkansas delegation to the na-
tional convention from time to time, [83] and there were several
internal delegate disputes but no Black and Tan/Lily-white
factional fight took place until 1920. The Republican state
convention on April 28, 1920 seated the Lily-white delegation
over the Black and Tan group for predominantly Black Pulaski
County (which sent two Black representatives to the constitutional convention in 1868). When the convention voted to seat
the Lily-white delegation from Pulaski rather than the Black
and Tans, the Black delegates from Phillips County walked
out of the convention, and other Blacks present also bolted
the convention. The Little Rock Arkansas Gazette, described
it thusly: "As the Blacks from Phillips County swept majes-
tically out of the hall ... [the group] was followed by all the
sons of Ham, about 50 in number, and all the Negro specta-
tors in the galleries. "[84]

One white delegate urged the convention to seat the Lily-white delegates because Blacks had failed to support his gubernatorial bid in 1911. He remarked: "When two races undertake to ride the elephant one must ride behind. " The pro-Democratic Gazette endorsed the white supremacy action of the convention, opining that the Republican "Committee on Credentials performed [a] patriotic and congenial business by throwing out the Negro contestants from Pulaski and Hempstead counties and thus barred the Black brethren from the possibility of holding fat offices under a Republican administration, unless they can get a helping hand at the national convention. "

After bolting the white convention Black delegates from Pulaski, Hempstead and Phillips counties held their own Black and Tan convention (some whites joined them) at the Mosaic Temple on the corner of Ninth Street and Broadway. They chose delegates for the national convention, raised $6,000 for group expenses and nominated a complete state ticket headed up by a Black, J. H. Blount, as their gubernatorial candidate. In the 1920 election Blount received 15,627 votes, the Democratic candidates 123,604, and the Republican candidate 46,339. Blount, who was principal of a Black school in Helena, became the first of his race to seek the governor's post in the state.

At the national convention in Chicago the Black and Tan delegates lost in their fight with the Lily-whites before the Credentials Committee. The latter group was seated. The Black and Tans carried their fight to the convention floor, but lost again, the entire convention voting against them. [85]

Following that loss the Black and Tans evidently disbanded. There is no record of their continued existence on the national, state or local levels, or of their again contesting the lily-whites. It must be remembered that the dispute in Arkansas at first involved only one county, other Blacks retained their seats because they were unopposed. Had they been opposed also, they would probably have been denied seats at the state convention too. Thus, it is probable that the rebel group rejoined the regular party. The record does indicate that one of the Black and Tans, R. C. Samuels, who had been attending state Republican conventions since 1880, left the Black and Tan convention and returned to the regular one, and was laughed at as he tried to make a speech.

In sum, the story of Black and Tan Republican politics

in Arkansas was an abortive one.   The group quickly faded
from the political horizon.   In fact, Black and Tanism was
so short lived in Arkansas, in Tennessee, that it had virtually
no meaningful impact on state politics.   Part of the reason
for this is that Blacks made up a very small portion of the
population in the state and Black leadership in Arkansas never
really approximated the quality of that which prevailed in some
other southern states.   Thus, Black and Tanism in Arkansas
died in its beginnings.

MISSISSIPPI

Black Republicanism began to emerge in Mississippi in
June, 1865, just prior to a convening of a state constitutional
convention under the provisional governor, William L. Sharkey
(former chief justice of the state).   A few freedmen with the
aid of a white northern soldier held a mass meeting at Vicksburg and "drew up resolutions condemning the exclusion of
'loyal citizens' from the [convention] and appealed to Congress
to refuse readmission to Mississippi until she voluntarily enfranchised the freedmen. "[86]   "President Johnson, " responding
to the resolutions, "wrote Governor Sharkey suggesting that
Negroes of educational and property be given the right to vote
so as to forestall the Radicals in the North. "   Johnson indicated to the Governor that such a grant--i. e. , a limited fran-
chise--would completely disarm his adversaries, the Radical
Republicans in Congress.   Neither Johnson's letter nor the
Black resolution received much attention from the convention.
In fact, the convention denied the petition in short order by
arguing that "this is a white man's government, " and that "in
the sight of God and the light of reason a Negro suffrage was
impossible. "

The convention drew up a new state constitution and set
the date of the election as October 2, 1865.   A former confederate, B. G. Humphreys, was elected governor and his
election was accepted by President Johnson in November, 1865.
Once in office, Humphreys proceeded to disband the Black
federal troops and had the state legislature pass the infamous
Black Codes.   His actions precipitated the coming of Congressional Reconstruction and in March, 1867, General E. C. Ard
was appointed the military commander in charge of the state.
By April 15th, he began to register the new electorate, colored
and white, in preparation for a new state constitutional convention.   The result of registration was that 60, 137 Blacks
and 46, 636 whites signed the books.   The election was set for
the first Tuesday in November, 1867.

Seeing that Black enfranchisement was imminent, white
conservatives began, early in 1867, "an immediate and almost frantic campaign to bring the Negro voters under the
control of the Southern whites." White conservatives coalesced and mapped out and instituted their strategies. The
result was a series of state-wide bi-racial meetings in which
white and Blacks participated on an equal basis; but at each
meeting it was impressed upon Blacks "that the whites were
to furnish the supplies and the Blacks were to prepare them."

The entire movement was a "failure, utter and universal." The maneuvering clashed with the Black man's new
sense of freedom and his newly gained political rights. Even
whites, especially poor whites, in the cooperationists' camp
revolted. They didn't like the idea of their top politicians
"tranversing the state, making Negro speeches, getting up
Negro meetings and playing second fiddle to Sambo...." Seeing that their strategy would not work, and hearing that the
state of Ohio had rejected Black suffrage, white conservative
cooperationists decided to wait for a national Democratic victory in 1868.

In the meantime, Blacks were enthusiastically entering
political activity in the state. They gathered in Vicksburg in
July to set up a Black Republican organization. The regular
Republican party, seeing this move and noting its future potential, immediately absorbed the Black group at its convention on September 10th and 11th, over the cries and objections
of the lily-whites. The regular Republican party from its inception had failed to organize Blacks, due to its racial prejudice; now, expediency drove the party to do so. On election day 70,016 voters cast ballots in favor of the convention
while 6,277 voted against it. On January 8, 1868 the convention convened to write a new state constitution which would
accord Blacks equal justice in the state. To this convention
--designated by newspaper writers as a Black and Tan convention because of the color of the delegates--went seventeen
Black delegates out of the 100 selected.

From the outset the convention delegates began to
quarrel over proper rights for Blacks and the question of suffrage. The debates were deliberately prolonged because the
conservatives wanted to wait to see if a Democratic victory
could be achieved in November on the national level. Thus,
the convention continued for 115 days, not ending until June.
Then the constitution was submitted to the people for adoption.

Since the new state elections would take place at the same time as the vote on the constitution, conservative Democrats went all out, not only to win the election but to defeat the constitution. Organizing as the Democratic White Men's party of Mississippi, the party openly and scornfully attacked Black aspirations and those Republicans who were willing to support them, grant them the franchise, and solicit their votes. Finally, the Democrats resorted to intimidation and violence to carry the day. Their tactics succeeded: 56,231 votes were cast for the proposed constitution and 63,860 against. And the Democratic candidate Humphrey was re-elected governor. However, the elections were invalidated by the rejection of the constitution, thus ensuring a continuation of rule by the federal government. The whites were satisfied with this because they still hoped for a national Democratic victory in November.

In November of 1868, however, the Republicans were overwhelmingly victorious and when President Grant was inaugurated, he placed a new military man in charge of Mississippi. This killed the hopes of the Mississippi conservatives and hard-line Democrats. The new military provisional governor, A. Ames, removed all Democrats, appointed Blacks to office, and set the date for new elections.

The Democrats prepared for the election by reorganizing their party and naming it the National Union Republican Party. President Grant's brother-in-law, Louis Dent, was selected to head it up. The NURP also placed one Black on the ticket, Tom Sinclair, to run for Secretary of State.

The Republican regulars placed one Black, James D. Lynch, on their ticket for the same post. Lynch's appointment proved to be a master stroke because Lynch was the best known Black in the state and a powerful orator who drew crowds of two to three thousands Blacks at a time. The Regular Republican ticket, including Lynch, won and the constitution was ratified. [87]

It is not necessary here to discuss the long list of Black Republican officeholders in Mississippi because they are dealt with in nearly every book on Black history in the U.S. Suffice it to say that Mississippi had perhaps the largest contingent of Black officeholders of any southern state. It is the only southern state, even up to the present day, to have had two Black U.S. Senators, a Black lieutenant governor, and a host of Black cabinet officers, legislators, mayors, etc.

The results of this tremendous number of Black Republican officeholders were predictable: the regular Republican party was branded as a Black party, white party members were stigmatized as "Nigger Lovers, " and Democrats
were determined to regain power at any price.   And this the
Democrats did in 1875: "By blood, murder, intimidation,
stealth, race war, fraud, deceit, and repression, the Democrats regained political power in Mississippi. "

     For Black Republicans, the Democratic revolution in
1875 had even greater implications.   Professor Wharton illuminated this point well when he stated that "once the general policy had been adopted that Negro and Republican control
of the state government was to be broken at any cost, a number of methods were followed for its accomplishment.   One
of these involved the intimidation of those whites who still
worked for the Republican party.   Since the Democrats let it
be widely known that 'Carpetbaggers would be the first to be
killed, ' Black Republicans, as time went by, found fewer and
fewer white leaders at their meetings. "   The party, still
partly factionalized, was now becoming completely Black.   The
election of Hayes, Garfield and Arthur, and Democratic pressures led to a general white withdrawal to form their own
Lily-white Republican organization.   Color factionalism was
prevalent in the Mississippi Republican Party from the beginning, however.   Blacks and whites had their own Republican
organizations from the outset, and they only fused temporarily
from about 1868 to 1870.

     A new factional upheaval began in Natchez about 1873
when John R. Lynch, B. K. Bruce, and Jonas Hill seized
control of the party in the sixth Congressional district. These
Black leaders were determined to advance men of their own
race to public positions denied them by white Republican leaders.   The struggle between the Black and white factions in
Natchez "threatened to disrupt the Republican party throughout
the river counties. "   "The factions assumed the names of
'Warm Springs Indians' [Blacks] and "Modocs' [whites] in their
political battle with each other. "   The Blacks won because
Senator Ames "placed the influence of his patronage at the
disposal of Congressman-elect Lynch. "[88]   The rise of Lynch's
faction was checked when the Democrats recaptured the state
in 1875.

     The next major Black-white faction upheaval in Missis-
sippi came shortly after 1880.   The Black wing of the party
fused with the Greenbackers, then with the Democrats, while

the white Republicans, encouraged by President Arthur, set
up their own independent or white Republican movement in
1882-1883. 89   From the early 1880's on, the Mississippi Republican party had two distinct factions.   Although the Lily-
white faction nearly collapsed after Arthur lost his election
bid in 1884, they were rejuvenated by the Lily-white policies
of President Harrison in 1889.   The passage of the Mississippi disenfranchising constitution aided them even more because it removed most of the support of the party's Black
wing and made politics in the state a very risky business for
Blacks.   The absence of Black leadership and internal rifts
were also factors in the eventual Lily-white take-over.

Professor Harris says, "... during the mid-1890's a
rift developed between Lynch's aide, James Hill [Black Secretary of State during Reconstruction], which resulted ulti-
mately in the establishment of Lily-White control of the party.
Lynch's miscalculation in influencing the party to fuse with
the Populist party in 1892 and his lengthy absences from the
state were important reasons for the development of this factionalism within ... the party. "

In terms of chronology, Lynch left Mississippi in 1889
to serve as Fourth Auditor of the U. S. Treasury, an appointment given to him by President Benjamin Harrison as a re-
ward for his long devotion to the party.   He retired from the
post in 1893 when the Democrats returned to power.   Although
Lynch opened a law firm and a bank in Washington, he occasionally returned to his Natchez home for periods of three to
six months each year.   Then, in 1898, he joined the army,
received the rank of Major and stayed in until 1911.   When
he left he went to Los Angeles for a while and then permanently moved to Chicago in 1912.

Thus, from the mid-1890's the Black Republicans in
Mississippi were without one of their major leaders.   The
titular leadership position was assumed by James Hill, and
upon his death, about 1904, control of the Republican party
passed into the hands of a white man, L. T. Mosley, who
was elected national committeeman for the state.   Although he
was opposed by numerous Black Republicans within the party
ranks, he held that position until 1915, when he moved to
Chicago.

Following his exit from the state there was a scramble
for power between Blacks and whites.   (Most of the lily-whites
had returned to the party when Mosley assumed control.)

Whites sought to replace Mosley with another white man.
Blacks in the party, led by Black attorney Perry Howard and
Black dentist S. D. Redmond, fought the move. The whites
outmaneuvered the Blacks by holding a special meeting of the
state committee and electing another white, M. J. Muldihill
of Vicksburg, head of the state party and national committeeman. Ordinarily the selection was supposed to be made by
the state delegation to the national convention. Since attorney
Howard was a candidate for the national committeeman post,
which would have made him state party leader, he contested
Muldihill's election before the national committee when it convened in St. Louis in 1919. However, the national committee
ruled in favor of Muldihill.

The next year, 1920, at the national Republican convention in Chicago, and the contestants for President were
General Frank Lowden and General Leonard Wood. Mississippi sent two delegations: Perry Howard and Dr. S. D. Redmond leading the Black and Tans, and M. J. Muldihill the
Lily-whites. The Howard-Redmond group was supporting
Wood's nomination, who had been actively promoted before
the convention by Mr. Proctor, the P & G Soap man. The
Muldihill group supported General Lowden. As the convention
progressed, however, Dr. Redmond discovered that the Muldihill group was planning to switch and had even moved to the
Wood Hotel where the Black and Tans were staying. Redmond obtained a certified copy of the hotel register to use at
a later date as evidence against Muldihill's lily-whites.

Both delegations were seated at the convention, each
being given a half vote, but Muldihill was appointed as national
committeeman by the convention.

The convention was stalemated for three days because
neither Wood nor Lowden could get the nomination. On the
fourth day Warren G. Harding won the nomination after the
Lowden forces switched to his support. After Harding's inauguration on March 4, 1921, Dr. Redmond took his certified
copy of the hotel register and his information on the Muldihill
group's tactics to the Lowden people. Angered and seeking
vengeance, the Lowden forces supported Dr. Redmond's efforts
to get President Harding to give the Howard-Redmond faction
"one-third of all Mississippi patronage, one-third of all municipal, county and state committee memberships, and the
chairmanship of all committees. This agreement was quite
unusual and unique in its provision for the handling of Republican patronage because as a rule the national committee and

state chairman of the victorious faction is given full control
of patronage dispensation for respective states. "

     One-third of the patronage may not seem very signifi-
cant, but when Muldihill's two-thirds of the patronage was in-
sufficient to go around, dissatisfaction and a scramble for
patronage jobs occurred. In 1924 a meeting of the Muldihill
state committee and the Howard-Redmond state committee took
place; "at this meeting of the Mississippi Republican state
central committee, six of the members of the Muldihill committee deserted and voted with the Howard-Redmond (Black
and Tan) faction, giving them a majority. "

     Once this happened the Muldihill faction, now a min-
ority, called for a state convention. The Howard-Redmond
faction at this point also issued a call for a state convention.
Each group selected its own set of delegates to the national
Republican convention in Cleveland in 1924. At that convention
Calvin Coolidge was nominated for President, Perry W. Howard was elected national committeeman over Muldihill, and
Mrs. Mary Booze (a resident of the all-Black community,
Mound-Bayou) was elected national committeewoman. Dr.
Redmond was elected state chairman. In short, the Black
and Tans were given full control over state party matters in
1924, and they retained it through 1956. Although they were
contested strongly and vigorously every four years, the Howard-led Black and Tans were seated each year through 1956.
The task was not an easy one, however, and Howard came
close to defeat in 1928 and 1956.

     In 1928 Presidential hopeful Herbert Hoover used Black
and Tan factions in various southern states to secure his
nomination. After obtaining the nomination, he then "created,
under the chairmanship of a mysterious Colonel Horace A.
Mann, " a separate campaign committee "to drum up the white
southern vote independently of the regular Black and Tan state
organizations. " After his inauguration, Hoover praised the
existing lily-white Republican organizations in the South and
announced his full support for them. He removed such Black
and Tan leaders as Ben Davis of Georgia, William (Goose
Neck Bill) McDonald in Texas and Walter L. Cohen in Louisiana, turning their top state party positions over to whites.
He also launched an investigation of Perry Howard, the head
of the Mississippi Black and Tans, and Howard "was subse-
quently removed from his position and shorn of party power
while under charges of bribery and sale of federal offices. "

Later in 1928, "Howard, together with several other active Negro Republicans of Jackson, Mississippi, was indicted ... for the sale of federal offices and for levying political contributions on federal employees in violation of the civil service code.   He was given a jury trial in a federal court and the United States attorney in charge of the prosecution protested almost tearfully that the case against Howard was water tight and fool proof. " Following the Attorney General's announcement, the "Senatorial committee investigating the sale of federal offices in 1929-1930 condemned the Republican organization of Mississippi largely because of its opinion of Howard's activities. "   President Hoover, meanwhile, appointed a lily-white patronage committee to take over Howard's duties in the interim period until the trial.

The major driving force behind President Hoover's actions and support of the lily-whites was a desire "to successfully invade the South against the Democratic candidate Al Smith in 1928 because Smith was remarkably vulnerable, as Democratic candidates go. " He was Catholic, wet, and partial to Blacks, and Hoover saw this as an opportunity to resurrect the Republican party in the South, as past Presidents had, on a lily-white basis.   The strategy did not work. Howard, despite the massive evidence against him, was acquitted.

White Democrats in Mississippi came to Howard's aid and testified in his behalf.   The chief justice and associate justice and the clerk of the State Supreme Court, some of the major newspapers in the state wrote editorials and numerous Democratic politicians wrote glowing letters and made speeches in his behalf.   The basic reason for this support was that federal jobs obtained by Howard as patronage (or any other Black and Tan Leader) were often sold to white Democrats. Blacks could not hold positions like third and fourth class postmasterships in the South, so such positions and other jobs which could only be held by whites were sold to them by Black Republicans.   There were never enough "white Republicans to 'go around' for all the available federal jobs in the South, " so they went to the Democrats.   Hence, the gratitude and support for Howard. [90]   A second reason was that the new lily-white Republican movement, which threatened to supplant Howard, refused to deal with the Democrats or were friendly with other Democrats than those already holding patronage positions.   This threatened to upset the applecart, so whites whom Howard had favored now spoke out in his behalf. After his acquittal Howard returned to lead the Mississippi

Black and Tans (or Regular Republican Party).   Although he
lived and practiced law in Washington, D. C. , he was seated
as a Mississippi delegate at each subsequent national convention through 1956, despite serious challenges each year by a
lily-white group.   (see Table III in Appendix).

    The year 1956 was another rough one for the Howard-
led Black and Tans.   That year the Republican national committee's sub-committee on contests voted to seat both contending Mississippi delegations--i. e. , the Black and Tans and the
Lily-whites--splitting the state's fifteen convention votes un-
evenly between them.   The Howard delegation, consisting of
nine Blacks and six whites, received eight votes; E. O. Spencer's (a Jackson, Mississippi hotel operator) lily-whites,
comprised of all whites (nine) and six Black alternates, received seven convention votes.   E. O. Spencer's lily-whites
waged a tough battle, bringing with them signed claims from
several Mississippi courts recognizing them as the only party.
A suit that the lily-whites had initiated against the Black and
Tans was not accepted for review by the Supreme Court. [91]
After the 1956 election and Howard's death the reins of power
once again slipped back to the lily-whites.

    In sum, then, Black and Tan Republican politics in
Mississippi (they were known as the Mississippi Black and Tan
Grand Ole Party) were heavily dominated by individual personalities: Lynch and Hill, Howard and Redmond.   The politics of the faction reflected the policies or whims of these
leaders.   Moreover, each of these personalities established
friendly relationships with the Democrats.   In Lynch's time,
that relationship was with L. Q. C. Lamar; in Howard's day,
from 1920 to 1956, it was with the small job-seeking Democrats.   The Democrats supported their benefactors and were
in turn supported with patronage favors.   It is easy in this
kind of atmosphere to conclude that the faction was characterized by greed, desire for personal gain and corruption.   But
it was condoned by the national party, which looked to the
leader of the faction to keep the fences mended for the convention.   The state leader, whether Lynch or Howard, was
expected to be, and in the South could only be, a patronage
referee.   The Black chairman of the Warren County Republican
committee stated the reality succinctly:

            During the presidential campaigns, our committee
            performs its only cause for being.   We proselytize
            these few score Negroes to vote for Hoover or who-
            ever the Republicans' standard-bearer may be and,
            after pocketing the hand-outs from the party slush

fund, and this is the only real purpose of our organization, we put our committee back in mothballs
to await another Presidential election.   Hell naw.
He got no local program.   We are doctors and
preachers and barbers.   We make enough money to
buy enough liquor to wash the inconveniences of being a Nigger out of your brains. [92]

Black and Tan Republicanism died in Mississippi when its personalities died. In the early seventies, Black Civil Rights activist
and maverick James Meredith tried to resurrect Black support
for the Republican Party, but his success so far has been
marginal.

THE SOUTHERN STATES: SUMMARY

In this chapter the political history of the eleven states
of the old confederacy has been reviewed to pinpoint and trace
the rise, emergence, and decline of Black Republicanism. In
some states the Black and Tan organizations emerged long before 1900, in others they didn't appear until the 1920's.   In
some states the Black and Tans emerged, declined and then
reemerged before their final demise.   In Tennessee and
Arkansas the Black and Tan movement hardly got under way
at all.   In other states, such as South Carolina and Mississippi, Black and Tanism existed in one form or another from
Reconstruction until 1960.

No matter how different the factions may have been,
nor how different their political maneuvering, they all shared
one basic thing: they developed from and operated as a re-
version from racism in the regular state Republican parties.
All of the Black and Tan groups developed as a result of
deep-seated prejudices held and expressed by the Lily-white
Republican organizations.   In some states, whites deliberately
organized Lily-white factions or clubs as entities separate and
distinct from the regular Republican party.

In South Carolina whites founded such a group on February 4, 1889 and reorganized it again in a formal fashion in
the same county--Pickens--on October 28, 1930, indicating in
their convention call that no Blacks would be allowed.   In
Alabama the Lily-whites officially formed an organization on
April 10, 1889 at Birmingham.   Lily-white Republicans officially formed in Virginia in September, 1889.   In Georgia
such an organization was formed in the early 1880's; in Texas
in 1888, and in Mississippi in 1909.   In other states where
no official convention was called and no Lily-white organiza-

tion officially formed, similar groups were started on an in-
formal basis, eventually to arise as formal contending forces.

The date of the emergence of the Black and Tan factions, however, does not necessarily coincide with the official
formation of Lily-white organizations or the date of their
founding conventions.   These latter were often the culmination
of many years of grappling with the problem of what to do
with Blacks in the Republican party.   Prejudicial attitudes and
policies caused Blacks in states such as South Carolina, Mississippi and Georgia to bolt the regular conventions and back
their own slates of candidates.   Blacks, however, were not
always the ones to bolt.   White Republicans eager for more
control, more offices and more power also bolted the regular
party on occasion and held their own state convention, leaving
Blacks no alternative but to do the same.   These convention
bolts and factional actions often took place well before official
state conventions of Lily-white Republicans occurred.

Another influence on the beginning of the Black and
Tans was the consistent policy direction of successive Republican Presidents toward creating a "respectful party" in the
South that would appeal to whites.   Hayes, Garfield, Arthur
and Harrison began a move toward white control of the party
in the South by the late 1870's and 1880's, long before the
formal Lily-white Republican conventions took place.

Coupled with these forces were the pressures from the
Democrats, who by 1877 had captured the government of all
eleven states from the Republicans and their Black allies. A
consistent factor in the electoral battles nearly every state
was the promotion of the ideology of white supremacy and of
the Democratic party as the white man's party.   The corol-
lary in this propaganda was that the Republican party was the
Nigger party and whites who associated with it were traitors,
turncoats, Scalawags, or just plain ole "Nigger lovers."

Thus, white Republican officeholders saw a need to revitalize and give the party a face-lifting, and this, in the
final analysis, meant the removal of Blacks from the party
ranks.   Coinciding with this move among white Southern officeholders were the Presidential efforts to revive the party and
attract more whites.   These two factors reinforced each other
and created a mood, a spirit, a feeling that a lily-white organization had to be created.   Simultaneously, it created a
unifying mood amongst Black Republicans and a drive by some
of their leaders toward shaping a Black Republican organiza-

tion.   Yet rarely did the Black and Tans call formal conventions for this purpose.   Instead Black Republicans fused in
most instances with other groups: Populists, Greenbackers,
Democrats, or even the Lily-whites.

In the end, the lily-white movement, slowly or rapidly,
depending on the degree of pressure and criticism (internally
or externally), came to the forefront in each state.   After
1936 Lily-whiteism dominated in virtually every southern state.
The failure of the Black and Tans to see themselves as a
separate movement and to organize as such may have contributed more to their downfall than anything else.

Black and Tanism suffered from stops and starts, from
lack of motivation and a variety of setbacks.   In some states
its leaders were confused, unaware, or lacked political so-
phistication.   In some states they were self-seeking, maneuvering the faction in whatever direction seemed most profit-
able.   For instance, Presidential appointments and favoritism
quieted some Black and Tan leaders, moved some out of the
state, as in the case of Lynch, and caused others to acquiesce
to Presidential Lily-white policies.   This is why the Black
and Tanism was not a continuous phenomena in any of the
eleven southern states, nor was it as persistent as Lily-whit-
ism.

Lily-whites, in their desire to destroy the Black and
Tans, in many states openly assisted the move for disenfranchisement.   The white Republicans on more than one occasion
took passive roles and let the Democrats have their way, hoping in this manner to cleanse the Republican party of its
Black element.   Some white Republicans who belonged to the
Black and Tan faction objected, but white Republicans in general saw disenfranchisement as a means of saving or reviving
the party. [93]   By permitting the Democrats to disenfranchise
Blacks, however, the lily-whites aided in the removal of their
main party supporters.

When disenfranchisement was finally completed during
the first decade of the twentieth century, it left the Black and
Tan Republicans, in terms of voters, in a shambles.   Whereas Black and Tans could have expected some votes from at
least the majority of counties in each state, now they were
limited to a selected few, and sometimes to no more than one
county in a state.   In many states, like Tennessee, these
were the urban counties, the ones with large cities.   Such
Black and Tan revolts as occurred after disenfranchisement,

occurred only in Congressional districts where Blacks could
vote. In short, disenfranchisement forced Black and Tan Republicans to become basically a national rather than a state
and local movement. The party's voters having been eliminated, the Black and Tans could only look to Presidential elections and national conventions for state patronage.

OTHER STATES

There were rumblings of Black and Tan movements in
other states but for the most part they never came to be much
more. [94] In Louisville, Kentucky in 1929 Blacks found the
Lincoln Independent Party, "as a reaction on the part of Negro
Republicans to the rule of the Lily-whites who had assumed
power in Louisville in 1917. " During 1929 the Lincoln Independent Party (Black and Tans) put up a full Black slate for
the local election and waged a heated campaign. But it all
came to nothing. Commenting on the situation, one member
of the Lincoln Independent Party stated:

> We were met with violence on the part of their
> Negro Republicans and at the hands of white police
> ... tools of the lily-white Republicans' city admin-
> istration. My printing press was smashed, and I
> was beaten up along with several others.

The Lincoln Independent Party died the same year that it was
born. So it was with other independent Black Republican
movements and efforts in the border and upper south states.

In the northern states, numerous studies indicate that
a different situation prevailed. [95] Professors L. Fishel, G.
James Fleming, and J. E. Miller have indicated in their
studies that Blacks in the Republican party in the North suffered the same kind of racism which generally faced Blacks
in the south, but that they reacted differently to it. In general, Northern Blacks tried independent action only on the
local levels. On the state and national levels they generally
attempted unification with various third parties, and finally
moved to the Democratic Party via machine politics on the
national level in the mid 1930's.

In terms of today, a recent study by Professor Joyce
Gelb indicates that Black-dominated Republican organizations
in certain districts of northern cities are now moribund, after
years of neglect and unconcern by state and national leader-

ship. [96]   Gelb found that they had received no recognition
from the new Republican state and local leaders, much less
any patronage to keep their organization going.   Taking New
York as a case in point, she found that Republican Governor
Rockefeller and Mayor John Lindsay would appoint well-known
Black Republicans like the late Jackie Robinson or James
Farmer--outsiders--without even consulting the local Black
Republican organizations.   The governor and mayor, Gelb
says, paid little heed to the long-established Black Republican
leadership.   Rockefeller's and Lindsay's moves constitute an
attempt to build a new Black Republican organization from the
top down instead of from the grass roots up.

Notes

1.   Naud Cuney Hare, Norris Wright Cuney (New York: The
     Crisis Publishing Co., 1913), p. 93.   See also Paul
     Lewinson, Race, Class and Party (New York: Russell
     and Russell, Inc., 1963), pp. 110, 170.

2.   Joseph Dumas, "The Black and Tan Faction of the Re-
     publican Party in Louisiana 1908-1936." (Unpublished
     M.A. thesis, Xavier University, 1943), p. 22.

3.   Dumas, Black and Tans, p. 23.

4.   V. O. Key, Southern Politics (New York: Vintage Books,
     1949), p. 288.

5.   See H. Walton, Jr., "Blacks and Conservative Political
     Movements," Quarterly Review of Higher Education
     (October, 1969), pp. 177-183.

6.   Allen Chandler Smith, The Republican Party in Georgia
     (Unpublished M.A. thesis, Duke University, 1957),
     p. 1.

7.   E. Nathans, Losing the Peace, p. 41.

8.   In 1966, ninety years after the last Republican governor
     had run, another, Howard "Bo" Calloway, industrial-
     ist, ran and won a plurality of electoral votes.   How-
     ever, since Georgia law states that the winner must
     have a majority, the State House of Representatives,
     being Democratic, chose the Democratic candidate.

9.   Atlanta Constitution, May 4, 1876.

10. Shadgett, "Republican Party ... from Reconstruction
     ...," p. 151.

11. Richard R. Wright later became principal of the colored
     high school in Richmond County and then, in 1890,
     president of the Savannah State Industrial College for
     Negroes.

12. See John E. Talmadge, "The Death Blow to Independ-
     entism in Georgia," Southern Historical Quarterly
     (December, 1955), pp. 37-47.

13. Atlanta Constitution, August 5, 1882.   After the conven-
     tion Pledger and Brown were tried in police court
     and both cases were dismissed.   During the trial
     Longstreet claimed that as U. S. Marshal he had
     charge of the building, while Pledger insisted that as
     surveyor of the Atlanta Port, he was custodian of the
     building.

14. It is interesting to note that in the Union Army, Buck
     served as commanding officer to two regiments of
     "colored" troops.   Ibid., p. 165.

15. De Santis, "Negro Dissatisfaction with Republican Policy
     ...," op. cit., p. 152.   On this point see also C. A.
     Bacote, "Some Aspects of Negro Life in Georgia,
     1880-1908," Journal of Negro History (July, 1958),
     pp. 186-213; and his "Negro Officeholders in Georgia
     under President McKinley," Ibid. (July, 1959), pp.
     217-239.

16. See also A. M. Arnett, The Populist Movement in
     Georgia (New York: Columbia University Press,
     1922), and B. O. Quillian, "The Populist Challenge
     in Georgia in the Year 1896" (Unpublished thesis,
     University of Georgia, 1948).

17. Paul Casdorph, A History of the Republican Party in
     Texas 1865-1965 (Austin: The Pemberton Press,
     1965), p. 4.

18. See J. Mason Brewer, Negro Legislators in Texas
     (Dallas: Mathis Publishing Co., 1935).

19. Paul Casdorph, The Republican Party in Texas, p. 46.

20. L. D. Clepper, "Republican Politics in Louisiana from
     1900-1952" (unpublished M. A. thesis, LSU, 1950),
     p. 1.

21. P. D. Uzee, "Republican Party in Louisiana from 1877-
     1900" (Unpublished Ph. D. dissertation, LSU, 1950).

22. Perry H. Howard, Political Tendencies in Louisiana,
     1812-1952 (Baton Rouge: Louisiana State University
     Press, 1957), pp. 102-105.

23. Ibid., p. 42; New York Times, March 5, 1924; Con-
     gressional Record, 68 Cong., 1 Sess., 4325, 4330.

24. See H. Edwin Bolte vs. Walter L. Cohen, No. 17730,
     U. S. District Court, Eastern District of Louisiana--
     New Orleans Division.

25. Clepper, op. cit., p. 47. See also New York Times,
     August 28-30, 1925.

26. Dastugue vs. Cohen, Louisiana Civil District Court, Di-
     vision E, Case No. 173328-173338, Office of Records,
     New Orleans, La.

27. Dumas, op. cit., pp. 61-64.

28. See Coff vs. Borance, No. 3018, 19th Judicial District
     Court of Louisiana, Parish of E. Baton Rouge.

29. Joseph M. Brittain, "Negro Suffrage and Politics in
     Alabama Since 1870" (unpublished Ph. D. Thesis, In-
     diana University, 1957), p. 8.

30. For a list of names of these delegates, see Ibid., pp.
     10-11. Also see Monroe V. Work, "Some Negro
     Members of Reconstruction Conventions and Legisla-
     tures and of Congress," Journal of Negro History,
     V, pp. 63-125.

31. John T. Milner, White Men of Alabama Stand Together
     1860-1890 (Birmingham, 1890), p. 49.

32. Ibid., p. 48-49. In 1874, the State Legislature had
     twenty-five Blacks, twenty-four in the House and one
     in the Senate. See also Charles Brown, "Recon-
     struction Legislators in Alabama," Negro History
     Bulletin (March, 1963), pp. 198-201.

33. Ibid., p. 25. See also John B. Clark, Populism in
    Alabama, 1874-1896 (Auburn, 1927), p. 12.

34. The Alabama Equal Rights Union was a state branch of
    the National Equal Rights League founded by Blacks
    on November 24, 1864.

35. Executive Document No. 64, House of Representatives,
    43rd Cong., 3rd Sess., December 22, 1874.

36. Earle E. Thorpe, "William Hooper Council," The Negro
    History Bulletin, XIX (1956), p. 85-86.

37. Hirshson, op. cit., p. 179.

38. See Mary Tucker, "The Negro in the Populist Movement
    in Alabama, 1890-1896" (unpublished M.A. thesis,
    Atlanta University, 1957), and Sheldon Hackney, Pop-
    ulism to Progressivism in Alabama (Princeton:
    Princeton University Press, 1969), pp. 33-36.

39. Official Proceedings of the Constitutional Convention of
    the State of Alabama, 1901, I, II, pp. 189-192.

40. "Alabama Delegation," A pamphlet (contest over delega-
    tion from the State at large, Republican National Con-
    vention, 1900), pp. 2-4. In Alabama State Archives
    & History.

41. See Harvard Smith, "The Progressive Party and the
    Election of 1912 in Alabama," The Alabama Review,
    IX (1956), pp. 5-22.

42. William A. Mabry, The Negro in North Carolina Politics
    Since Reconstruction (Durham: Duke University Press,
    1940), p. 4.

43. Johnny W. Barnes, "The Political Activities of the Union
    League of America in North Carolina," Quarterly Re-
    view of Higher Education Among Negroes (October,
    1952), pp. 141-50.

44. Robert Winston, It's a Far Cry (New York, 1937), pp.
    165-167.

45. Democratic State Executive Committee, Democracy v
    Radicalism (Raleigh, 1884), p. 23.

46. James I. Moore (a former Union Whig) throughout his
     entire campaign castigated the Democrats for bring-
     ing on the Civil War and adopted the following speech
     for his Black audience. "Nigger, Nigger, Nigger,
     its [the Democratic Party's] only cry. The Nigger
     is the Democrats stalking horse. Down in Hell--and
     Hell's where Democrats belong--down in Hell you can
     tell a Democrat everytime. There he sits, holding
     some little skinny-headed Negro between him and the
     fire. " Winston, Far Cry, p. 104.

47. Monroe N. Work, ed. The Negro Yearbook, 1912 (Tus-
     kegee, Alabama, 1912), p. 31.

48. Helen Edmonds, The Negro and Fusion Politics in North
     Carolina (Chapel Hill: University of North Carolina
     Press, 1951), p. 218.

49. African Methodist Episcopal Zion Quarterly (December,
     1900), p. 52.

50. Richard L. Morton, The Negro in Virginia Politics
     (Charlottesville: The University of Virginia Press,
     1919), p. 17.

51. Eighty-seven Blacks were elected to the general as-
     sembly from 1869 to 1890, and one to Congress from
     1889 to 1891. Local officeholding continued until
     1895 and in some isolated counties as late as 1928.
     See L. P. Jackson, Negro Officeholders in Virginia,
     1865-1895 (Norfolk, Va: Quids Quality Press, 1945),
     p. vii.

52. Andrew Buni, The Negro in Virginia Politics, 1902-1965
     (Charlottesville: University Press of Virginia, 1967),
     p. 27-28.

53. Joe M. Richardson, The Negro in the Reconstruction of
     Florida, 1865-1877 (Tallahassee, Fla.: Florida State
     University Press, 1965), p. 141.

54. Ibid.

55. George Bentley, "Freedmen's Bureau in Florida, "
     Florida Historical Quarterly, XXVIII (July, 1949),
     p. 29.

56. Terrell H. Shafner, "The Presidential Elections of 1867 in Florida" (unpublished M. S. thesis, Fla, State University, 1961), p. 28.

57. John Wallace, Carpetbag Rule in Florida (Jacksonville: Da-Costa Printing & Pub. House, 1888), pp. 42-44. Wallace was a self-educated ex-slave who was active in Leon County politics as a Republican during Reconstruction and served both in the state senate and assembly. See also John T. Shaftner, A Colored Man's Exposition of the Acts and Doings of the Radical South from 1865 to Its Probable Overthrow by President Hayes' Southern Policy (Jacksonville: Gibson and Dennis, 1877), p. 8.

58. St. Augustine Examiner, November 2, 1867.

59. George C. Osborn, ed. "Letters of a Carpetbagger in Florida," Florida Historical Quarterly, XXXVI (January, 1958), p. 259.

60. H. D. Price, The Negro and Southern Politics: A Chapter of Florida History (New York: New York University Press, 1957), p. 22.

61. See Margie Hines, Negro Suffrage and the Florida Election Laws, 1860-1950. (Durham: North Carolina College, 1953).

62. Charles D. Farris, "The Re-Enfranchisement of Negroes in Florida," The Journal of Negro History (October, 1954), p. 264.

63. James M. McPherson, The Negro's Civil War (New York: Vintage Books, 1965), p. 57-60. See also Joel Williamson, After Slavery: The Negro in South Carolina During Reconstruction, 1861-1877 (Chapel Hill: University of North Carolina Press, 1965), pp. 335-36.

64. On this point see L. P. Jackson, "The Educational Efforts of the Freedmen's Bureau and Freedman's Aid Societies in South Carolina, 1862-1872," Journal of Negro History (January, 1923), p. 1-40; and Louis F. Post, "A Carpetbagger in South Carolina," Journal of Negro History (January, 1925), p. 20.

65. A. A. Taylor, "The Negro in South Carolina During Re-
     construction, " Journal of Negro History (October,
     1924), p. 384.

66. See Frances B. Simpkins, "The Ku Klux Klan in South
     Carolina, 1868-1871, " Journal of Negro History
     (October, 1927), pp. 621-647.

67. Taylor, op. cit., p. 464. It should be noted that the
     Democrats fused with the Reform Party ticket during
     the election.

68. See A. H. Gordon, Sketches of Negro Life and History
     in South Carolina (Columbia: University of South
     Carolina Press, 1971), pp. 55-79.

69. See James Welch Patton, "The Republican Party in South
     Carolina, 1876-1895" in F. W. Green, ed. Essays
     in Southern History (Chapel Hill: University of North
     Carolina Press, 1949), pp. 97-100.

70. Pickens County Sentinel (November 6, 1930).

71. Francis Butler Simpkins, Pitchfork Ben Tillman (Baton
     Rouge: Louisiana State University Press, 1967), p.
     400.

72. Letter from John McCray (Black politican, organizer
     and newspaperman in the state at that time) to the
     author, p. 2.

73. New Orleans Tribune, November 29, 1864.

74. Thomas B. Alexander, "Political Reconstruction in
     Tennessee, 1865-1870, " in R. O. Curry, ed. Radi-
     calism, Racism and Party Realignment (Baltimore:
     Johns Hopkins Press, 1969), p. 63.

75. E. Merton Coulter, William C. Brownlow--Fighting Par-
     son of the Southern Highlands (Chapel Hill: Univer-
     sity of North Carolina Press, 1937).

76. Nashville Dispatch, January 14, 1865.

77. William Gillette, "Anatomy of a Failure: Federal En-
     forcement of the Right to Vote in the Border States
     During Reconstruction, " in Curry, op. cit., p. 267.

78. See Thomas B. Alexander, "Ku Kluxism in Tennessee 1865-1869," Tennessee Historical Quarterly (September, 1949), pp. 195-219.

79. On this point see A. A. Taylor, The Negro in Tennessee 1865-1880 (Washington D. C.: Associated Publishers, 1941), pp. 102-110. See also V. M. Queener, "The Republican Party in East Tennessee, 1865-1900" (Ph. D. dissertation, Indiana University, 1940); R. E. Corlew, "The Negro in Tennessee 1870-1900" (Ph. D. dissertation: University of Alabama, 1954); and I. G. Snowden, "The Political Status of Negroes in the United States with Particular Reference to the Border States (Ph. D. dissertation, Indiana University, 1943).

80. Joseph N. Trigg, "Political Observation of Yesterday and Yesteryear," East Tennessee News (April 29, 1926), p. 1. See also Larry Dunn, "Knoxville Negro Voting and the Republican Revolution, 1928-1936," in G. Gaither & M. Peck, eds., The Negro in Tennessee, 1865-1965 (Forthcoming, University of Tennessee Press).

81. H. Walton, Jr., "Another Force for Disfranchisement: Blacks and the Prohibitionists in Tennessee," Journal of Human Relations (First Quarter, 1970), pp. 728-738.

82. W. E. B. Dubois, Black Reconstruction in America (New York: Russell & Russell, 1962), p. 547.

83. For a list of those delegates see Table I in the Appendix. The Black delegate Fred Harris in 1900 was a McKinley man.

84. "Negroes Bolt the G. O. P. Convention," Little Rock Arkansas Gazette, (April 29, 1920), p. 1.

85. "Negro Republicans Bolt in Three States," New York Times (April 29, 1920), p. 2.

86. Vernon L. Wharton, The Negro in Mississippi, 1865-1890 (New York: Harper Torchbooks, 1965), p. 140.

87. Sinclair, in comparison to Lynch, had no standing among Blacks.

88. William C. Harris, "Introduction" in J. R. Lynch, The
     Facts of Reconstruction (New York: Bobbs-Merrill
     Company, 1970), p. xxv.

89. See Willie D. Halsell, "Republican Factionalism in
     Mississippi 1882-1884, " Journal of Southern History
     (February, 1941), pp. 84-101. Also his "James R.
     Chalmers and Mahoneism in Mississippi, " Ibid. (Feb-
     ruary, 1944), 37-58.

90. The entire story is related in Lewinson's book. Lewin-
     son, op. cit. , pp. 185-93. See also, Ralph Bunche,
     "Political Status of the Negro" (Unpublished manu-
     script prepared for the Gunnar Mydral Study), 1176-
     1214.

91. "Racial Group Split Gap in Mississippi, " New York
     Times (May 6, 1956), p. 72, and "GOP Acts to Seat
     Mississippi Rival, " Ibid. , (August 15, 1956), p. 1.
     "GOP Backs Plan for Mississippi--National Commit-
     tee Favors Seating Rival, " Ibid. (August 16, 1956),
     p. 18.

92. Bunche, op. cit. , p. 1214.

93. See Hanes Walton, Jr. & James Taylor, "Blacks, The
     Prohibitionists and Disfranchisement, " Quarterly
     Review of Higher Education (April, 1969), pp. 66-
     69.

94. Curry, op. cit. , p. 1-219.

95. See L. Fishel, "The Negro in Northern Politics, 1870-
     1900," Mississippi Valley Historical Review (Decem-
     ber, 1955), pp. 466-489; his "Northern Prejudice
     and Negro Suffrage, 1865-1900, " Journal of Negro
     History (January, 1954), 8-26; and his "The North
     and the Negro, 1865-1900: A Study in Race Discrim-
     ination" (Unpublished Ph. D. dissertation, Harvard,
     1953). G. James Fleming "The Negro in American
     Politics: The Past, " in J. D. Davis, ed. , American
     Negro Reference Book (Englewood Cliffs; Prentice-
     Hall, 1966), pp. 414-430; and J. E. Miller, "The
     Negro in Present Day Politics with Special Reference
     to Philadelphia, " Journal of Negro History, (July,
     1948).

96. Joyce Gelb, "The Role of Negro Politicians in the Dem-
     ocratic, Republican and Liberal Party of New York
     City" (Unpublished Ph. D. dissertation, New York
     University, 1969).

Chapter 4

BLACK AND TAN REPUBLICANISM
NATIONALLY AND IN DECLINE

One might well wonder why the Black and Tan and
Lily-White factions did not disband after disenfranchisement.
They could no longer amass any meaningful vote for Republican Presidential candidates or for state and local candidates
in their respective Southern states, since the bulk of the
party's voters (Blacks) could no longer legally participate in
politics.   The reason for their continuance lay elsewhere.
During the era of disenfranchisement a new technique was developed by Presidential hopeful William McKinley and his political manager Mark Hanna.   This technique involved making
pre-convention tours of the South, talking to each delegation,
and buying up one or the other--Lily-whites or Black and
Tans--to support his nomination at the convention with their
delegate votes.   McKinley's technique proved successful and
other Republican Party presidential hopefuls after McKinley
began to scramble to buy up southern delegations.   In this
tug-of-war the Black and Tan factions became as important
as, if not more important than the Lily-whites.   From 1896
to at least 1956, the strategy of buying Black and Tan and/or
Lily-white delegations remained the chief tool of Republican
presidential hopefuls and convention power became the raison
d'être of the small Black and Tan and Lily-white factions.

Republican National Conventions

Professor Alexander Heard states that Republicans in
most of the South "do not win public office and the only posts
of significance they can hope to hold are party posts, mostly
as delegates and alternates to their own national conventions.
Year in and year out their eyes focus on the fight over the
Presidential nomination, where their votes count as much as
anybody else's. "[1]

Professor V. O. Key makes essentially the same point:
"No southern Republican leader entertains seriously the notion
that his party will during his lifetime gain control of his
state government. " This, says Key, is why Southern Republicans focus on the national party and the national convention.
"Presidential aspirants, invariably nonsoutherners, are interested in the control of state organizations primarily because of the votes they can deliver in national conventions. "
For this reason, Key insists, "those inside the states ...
[are] interested in control of the organizations because of
local federal patronage that they control when their party wins
the Presidency. "[2]

At the 1916 convention, the last one before state delegations were reapportioned on the basis of the number of
votes cast in the last election, "Southern delegates occupied
348 of 987 seats, or 36.3 per cent of the total number of
delegates. "[3] This had been generally the case since 1876,
the last year that Southern States gave any electoral votes to
a Republican Presidential candidate. Possessing one-third of
the delegates in almost all conventions until 1916, the Lily-
white and Black and Tan factions thus became crucial to any
Presidential aspirant.

Even after 1916, when the national convention moved
to reduce Southern representation because of its lack of vote-
getting power, Southern delegations still comprised nearly
one-fifth of each successive national convention,[4] and the two
factions continued to be much sought after. A presidential
aspirant arriving at the convention with 20 per cent of the
delegate votes already behind him was in a strong bargaining
position.

Prior to 1892 the claims of the contesting factions
which came to the national convention were basically resolved
on the basis of merit: the legality of the method of selection
of the delegation, or the amount of support that the contesting delegations had in the state, real or imaginary. Later,
when the importance of the Southern delegation's role in
nominating was apparent and the devastating effect which the
disenfranchisement era had had on the Republican party voters
in the South became clear, merit issues and technicalities became less important than "the attitudes of the competing delegations toward the presidential nomination. " Factional fights
between the Black and Tans and Lily-whites usually ended up
being decided on the basis of "what Presidential aspirant is
to get the states' votes. "

In the history of Republican convention proceedings or
accounts of Presidential nominations, the role of the Black
and Tan and Lily-white factions does not always come through
as a decisive factor.   But in three cases there seems to be
no dispute or disagreement in the record over how the Black
and Tans were used to secure a Presidential nomination.

The first presidential aspirant to buy up southern delegations to secure his nomination was William T. McKinley.
McKinley, as a Presidential hopeful in 1892, had lost the
nomination to Benjamin Harrison.   After that defeat his political manager, millionaire industrialist Mark Hanna, began
a campaign in 1893 to have McKinley nominated as the Republican candidate for President in 1896.   To achieve this
Hanna made a pre-convention tour of the South and bought
delegations in each state, either Black or white, which had
ever supported McKinley's nomination.   When the convention
convened in 1896, well over two-thirds of the delegates ar-
rived with instructions to vote for McKinely. [5]   Professor
Gerald Pomper writes: "the Republican convention was dominated by Mark Hanna who had lined up the Southern delegates
in favor of William McKinley. "[6]   McKinley received a first
ballot nomination.

The Black and Tan delegation from Texas supported
William B. Allison, while the Lily-whites supported McKinley.
The Lily-white group was seated.   Professor Paul Casdorph,
writing on the Texas situation, stated that "McKinley campaign manager Mark Hanna, who was attempting to line up
Southern delegations in support of McKinley, approached
Cuney in search of support of the Texas organization. " Cuney
remained true to the backers of Allison and Hanna eventually
"found it necessary to place the McKinley organization in
other hands. "   This same procedure was followed in all other
Black and Tan Lily-white factional disputes at the national
convention that year.

The 1900 Republican convention nomination for McKinley was won by acclamation.   That year, although there were
contesting delegations from Alabama, Georgia, Louisiana,
Mississippi, Tennessee, Texas and Virginia, the issues were
the regularity or otherwise of certain delegates, not their
attitudes toward the Presidential nominee. [7]

The drama of pre-convention tours and the purchasing
of entire state delegations, though, had now become common-
place and a major Republican stock in trade.   In fact, the

purchasing of Black and Tan and Lily-whites delegations became so widespread and deplorable that one Black leader expressed his distaste for the tactic in a major Black publication, the Crisis:

> Every four years the disgrace of buying up certain
> delegates for the Republican convention is repeated
> in the south... They are for sale to the highest
> bidder. Republican candidates begin their campaign
> by sending men into the South to buy the support of
> these delegates. [8]

However, effective use of the new technique developed by
Hanna for McKinley by other Republican hopefuls was initially
delayed by the course of human events. McKinley was assassinated in 1901, hardly six months after his inauguration, and
Theodore Roosevelt succeeded to the office. By the 1904 convention Roosevelt had gained tremendous popularity and Mark
Hanna was dead. There was little opposition to Roosevelt's
renomination, and he received every vote at the Chicago convention.

There were Black and Tan/Lilywhite contests at the
1904 convention, involving two states, Alabama and Louisiana. [9] The factional fight in Alabama occurred in the fourth
district over the desire for seats and patronage; the Black
and Tans were seated. In Louisiana, there were two opposing delegations, not a contest within a delegation as in Alabama. The Lily-whites led by ex-governor Warmouth and the
Black and Tans led by Black Walter Cohen each presented
lengthy and detailed legal briefs to the Credentials Committee, accusing each other of violations of the rules and regulations. Again, the Black and Tans were seated. The apparent favoritism toward the Black and Tan delegations
stemmed from Roosevelt's policy of recognition of Blacks.
During his first term he had invited Booker T. Washington
to the White House and had made Black appointments in the
Southern states that drew the ire of whites.

In 1908 the technique of using Black and Tan delegations to secure the nomination was continued. Although Roosevelt had declined to succeed himself, he tried to name his
successor, designating at one time or another three men:
Charles Evans Hughes, Elihu Root, and William Howard Taft.
Taft, in an effort to secure the nomination, actively sought
out the Black and Tans. At the convention all of the Taft
delegates from the South were seated. In all of the factional

fights between the Black and Tans and Lily-whites, the contests were resolved on the basis of which candidate the faction
supported. [10] Where both groups supported Taft, each was
seated and given half the votes.

The fight in Alabama and Arkansas was decided in
favor of the delegates committed to Secretary Taft, the Black
and Tans.   When the Louisiana Blacks agreed to cast their
votes for Taft (originally they were for Senator Foraker),
they were seated in addition to the Lily-whites, who from the
outset had been pro-Taft.   The national committee gave each
delegate a half-vote.   In the Tennessee and Texas contests,
the seating of each delegation was again decided on the basis
of whether or not they would support Taft.

The Virginia contest followed the same pattern.   The
regular Republican delegation (Black and Tans) was strongly
criticized by the Lily-white anti-Taft forces before the Credentials Committee as lacking in real voting support (Blacks
had been disenfranchised in the state in 1901).   When the
leader of the Lily-whites was questioned by a member of the
Credentials Committee as to whether he had any affidavit to
support his contention, however, he stated, "I must confess
that I have not. " The committee member retorted: "I must
say that you have presented some poor cases in this state. "
The Black and Tans were seated.

The Taft forces were so successful, not only in controlling the Southern delegates but in getting them seated,
that they attracted the ire and consternation of other Presidential hopefuls.   This dissatisfaction led to an announcement
by Representative James Burke of Pennsylvania, political
manager for Senator Knox, that there would be a fight on the
convention floor to reduce the representation of the Southern
States.   The sponsors of Mr. Burke's resolution argued that
the rights of the northern states which were necessary for
Republican electoral success had been handed over to delegations from southern states which never gave the party any
votes in the electoral college. [11] The Taft forces, in firm
control of the convention, defeated the resolution on the convention floor.

The 1912 convention was a repeat of the 1908 convention.   Taft once again used the Black and Tan delegates to
secure his nomination.   Although Taft was nearly assured of
renomination, competition came from ex-President Theodore
Roosevelt.   "Roosevelt came out of retirement to seek a third

term. . . .   Although winning most primaries, he was over-
whelmed by Taft's control of the state party organization and
the convention machinery. " Professor Burdette notes that
Taft "firmly decided to use all the powers of his office for
winning convention delegates. "[12]

At the convention "many of Taft's delegates, especially
in the South, had been chosen by party organizations in their
states and the Roosevelt forces raised the charge of theft. "
But Roosevelt's charges carried little weight because Elihu
Root, a Taft man, was elected temporary chairman of the
convention.   In reply to Roosevelt's charges of theft, "Root
ruled that each contested delegate could vote except in his
own case and the convention thereby supported its credentials
committee's favorable report on the Taft delegations. "[13] In
the final balloting Taft received 561 votes to 107 for Roosevelt.   After losing the nomination Roosevelt attended the Progressive Party convention, accepted the party's nomination
and attempted to build a Lily-white movement in the South.

All of the contests from the South--Alabama, Arkansas, Texas, Virginia, North Carolina, and Mississippi--were
decided in Taft's favor and all but two decisions of the Credentials Committee were unanimous. [14] It also came to the
light during the convention proceedings that a Roosevelt man
had approached many southern delegates with money if they
would bolt Taft and join the Roosevelt side. [15] Black delegates bolted excepted those who followed Roosevelt to the
Progressive Convention.   In 1912, "delegates from the Negro
dominated organization in the South accounted in large part
for Taft's renomination over former President Roosevelt. "
Commenting similarly, Professor Lewinson writes that "almost all the contests that were fought to a finish were decided in favor of the regular Black and Tan organization who
were for Taft. "

Elihu Root, Charles Evans Hughes and other Republican
aspirants did not firmly secure the southern delegations in
1916, as their predecessor, Taft, had done, and no clear
pattern emerged at the national convention.   Some Black and
Tan delegates, like the Lily-whites, sponsored Hughes; others
backed Root and some backed Roosevelt.   Hence, this time,
the seating contests were decided mainly on merit rather than
on attitude.   The major reason for this change was that the
Democrats were in power; Woodrow Wilson had been elected
in 1912 over Taft and had a good chance in 1916 of being re-
elected.   Republican delegates from the South therefore tried
to remain uncommitted as long as possible.

Consequently, the contests between Black and Tans and Lily-whites at the national convention were resolved in a mixed fashion. The fight in the Mississippi delegation ended up with both Taft factions being seated with one-half of the votes each. The Louisiana contest ended similarly: "Armand Romain, a white leader, controlled six of the twelve votes permitted to the state of Louisiana and Walter Cohen, a Black, controlled the other six. " Robert Church, the powerful Black boss from Memphis, and his group shared the votes with the seven white delegates from Tennessee. In the first district of Florida, a white man was seated over the Black contestant, C. H. Alston.[16]   The contest between the two factions in Georgia didn't involve racial matters but organizational structure. The group which supported Hughes was seated over the group which supported ex-Senator Elihu Root.[17] The clash in Arkansas was resolved in the same fashion.

With the seating contests resolved, the call for nomination voting got under way and Charles Evans Hughes received the nomination on the third ballot. The convention then moved to reform delegation representation from the South, passing a resolution which had been presented in 1912, but with one basic change, a reduction in the number of votes required by a delegation from 10, 000 to 7, 500.

The Republican convention of 1920 met in Chicago with three leading candidates: General Leonard Wood, Governor Frank O. Lowden of Illinois, and trailing far behind, Senator Hiram W. Johnson of California. Each man had done some pre-convention campaigning among some of the Black and Tan delegations but, says Professor Gerald Pomper, they "were unsuccessful. " Neither Wood nor Lowden won majority support for the Republican nomination.

When the convention convened a few of the contestants were pledged to General Wood and a few to Governor Lowden; and some were uninstructed. To heighten the already ambiguous situation there were numerous Black and Tan factional fights. South Carolina, Arkansas and Virginia had dual delegations. The other southern states--Florida, Georgia, Louisiana, Mississippi, North Carolina, Tennessee, Texas, and Alabama--had internal Black and Tan/Lily-white clashes over certain seats. For instance, fifteen of Georgia's seventeen seats were being contested by a group headed by a Black, Henry Lincoln Johnson of Atlanta. The Johnson-led Blacks were at first uncommitted but later came out for Lowden and were seated over the whites who favored General Wood. The

Black delegations from South Carolina, Arkansas and Virginia were rejected, and the Lily-whites were seated by the Credentials Committee. Blacks from Mississippi, North Carolina and Alabama who supported Lowden were seated. Wood supporters from Texas and Florida were seated. In Tennessee and Louisiana the seating contests were divided evenly between Lowden and Wood. [18]

The deadlock between Lowden and Woods continued to the tenth ballot, when a dark-horse candidate, Warren G. Harding, won. Before the convention adjourned, a new resolution was adopted to further decrease southern representation to only four at-large delegates. This, it was hoped would reduce the quadrennial scandal over southern Black delegates. The 1920 convention was an outright victory for the Lily-whites in the South.

Despite their losses, the Black and Tans made another attempt in 1924 to be recognized by the national convention. In some states, the Black and Tans held local, county and state conventions in accordance with party regulations. Some even attempted to sponsor political candidates, while others fused with the Lily-whites. The panoply of presidential hopefuls in 1924, which included Robert M. LaFollette, Senator Hiram Johnson, Herbert Hoover, Frank Lowden, Charles C. Davis and other lesser lights, had not made the usual pre-convention tour of the South to buy delegates. The major reason was that everyone expected Harding's vice president, Calvin Coolidge, who had become President in 1923 following Harding's death, to obtain the nomination without challenge. LaFollette and Johnson, however, made good showings in several primaries and raised the specter of uncertainty.

When the Credentials Committee opened its hearings at the Cleveland convention in June, the first contest heard involved the Black and Tan and Lily-white delegates from Georgia. The Black group, led by Henry Johnson of Atlanta, argued that their delegation was superior to the Lily-white faction recognized by President Harding because of its regularity in attending conventions and the delegations consistent support of the party. The Credentials Committee, however, hoping to clear up the long standing factional fight in Georgia, had already decided in favor of the Lily-whites. Just before the Committee read its decision publicly, Johnson, the Black and Tan leader, produced a letter written by President Harding to C. Bascom Slemp, the Secretary to President Coolidge, saying that recognition of the Lily-white faction in 1920 had been a blunder and suggesting that action be taken to alter the situation.   The letter was a trump card for Johnson and the committee voted 22 to 14 to seat the Black and Tan delegation. [19]

The Credentials Committee also voted to seat the Perry Howard Black and Tan delegation from Mississippi over the Lily-white faction.   All of the Joe Tolbert-led Black and Tan faction from South Carolina was also seated, although there were two challenges to his delegates from the fourth and sixth congressional districts in the state.   In the contest between Black and Tans and Lily-whites from the tenth Congressional district in Tennessee, the Black delegates were seated.   This district was in the Memphis area and was dominated by Black Republican Boss, Robert Church.   In the Louisiana contest, the Black and Tans, led by Walter Cohen, were also seated over the Lily-whites.   Thus, in 1924, the Black and Tans, at least those who brought challenges, won the day.   The Lily-whites, after this defeat in 1924, began to prepare for a comeback in 1928.   According to Professor Heard, "by 1928 in every southern state Lily-white organizations rivaled the 'regular' organizations or organizations traditionally controlled by Negroes. "

Hoover had twice been a candidate for the Presidency, in 1920 and 1924, and had lost both times.   When President Coolidge issued a statement in the summer of 1927, "I do not choose to run for President in 1928, " the Hoover forces set their plans in motion for a third try.   With two Republican factions existing in nearly every state Hoover had plenty of opportunities to bargain, and he began his pre-convention campaign in the same tradition as past Republican presidential hopefuls.   Writes Journalist Drew Pearson, "Rush Holland, former assistant Attorney General for Harry Daugherty, was the Hoover bagman who toured the South and paid off the Southern delegates. "[20]   Benjamin Davis, the Black G. O. P. National Committeeman from Georgia, revealed in sworn testimony before a Senate committee investigating Hoover's southern purchases after his inauguration, that he had "received $2, 000 of Hoover's money to pay the expenses of Georgia Republicans.   Prior to this payment Ben Davis was not for Hoover.   Afterwards he was.   Perry Howard, colored G. O. P. National Committeeman for Mississippi, also received $2, 000 of Hoover's money.   The Mississippi delegates voted for Hoover. "[21]   H. L. Mencken, commenting on the 1928 Republican convention, explains why United States Senator Charles Curtis didn't get more delegates

before the convention. It seems, wrote Mencken, that Ole
Charlie "lacked Lord Hoover's bar'l, could not find an angel
to finance him, and hence had to keep out of the Southern
states where only cash money counts."[22]   Although Hoover
had invaded the South with "cash money" he was not consistent in buying up delegations. He bought both Black and White
delegations, and at the convention, those who were pro-
Hoover, whites and Blacks alike, were seated.

When the Republican national convention convened on
June 12, 1928, in Kansas City, Missouri, several factional
contests emerged from sothern delegations.   From Texas
there were two delegations; the Black and Tans, led by a
white man, Harry Beck, were rejected in favor of the pro-
Hoover Lily-whites.   The Perry Howard Black and Taners
were seated over the Lily-whites from Mississippi because
they were pro-Hoover.   In the Louisiana contest, the Walter
Cohen Black and Tans who were Hoover men were seated, as
were the Lily-whites who were pro-Hoover.   Cohen was pro-
Hoover.

In other states, only certain seats were being chal-
lenged, including, for example, nine of the ten Florida seats,
three Georgia seats, four South Carolina seats, and three
Tennessee seats.   In the South Carolina case, all of the Joe
Tolbert Black and Tans were seated.   Robert Church, the
Black Boss of Memphis, was seated in Tennessee.   In Florida,
the pro-Hoover Lily-whites were seated over the Black and
Tans.

Summing up the 1928 convention, Professor Pomper
says that "Herbert Hoover, after a long pre-convention campaign and with the tacit endorsement of the Administration,
held a substantial lead and was easily nominated after Lowden,
his major opponent, withdrew. " Professor Burdette adds that
Hoover's "search for advance commitment by delegates had
been well organized and his opposition was scattered among
five candidates without decisive backing.   The convention
nominated Hoover on the first ballot.... "

Soon after his inauguration Hoover declared that "successive Presidents had long wished to build up a Republican
party in the South, such as would commend itself to the citizens of the southern states. " Hoover then commended the
"existing Lily-white state committees in Virginia, North Carolina, Alabama, Arkansas, Louisiana, Texas and Florida. "
In South Carolina, Georgia, and Mississippi, "recent expo-

sures of abuse in the sale of patronage" necessitated the reorganization of the party in those states, and Hoover indicated that "the duty of reorganization rests with the people
of those states, and all efforts to that end will receive the
hearty cooperation of the Administration."[23] "If these three
states are unable to initiate such reorganization," Hoover insisted, "the different Federal departments will be compelled
to adopt other measures to secure advice as to the selection
of Federal employees."

Prior to his inauguration, Hoover created a separate
campaign committee to drum up the white southern vote independently of the Black and Tan state organizations.   In
Texas, where the two committees clashed, the Black Republican leader quit and openly declared himself for Al Smith,
the Democratic candidate.

In short, Hoover used the Black and Tan delegates to
secure his nomination and afterwards dropped them and promoted the Lily-whites.   Once in office, Hoover removed the
Negro Committeeman from Georgia, Ben Davis, helped launch
a senatorial investigation of Perry Howard's dealings in Mississippi, forced Walter L. Cohen out of a federal post in
Louisiana, and pushed Robert Church in Tennessee into the
background.[24]   Hoover delivered a mortal blow to Black and
Tanism on the national level.   In every state he openly endorsed the Lily-white movement and worked closely with it,
at the same time suppressing the Black and Tan Republicans.
Like Hayes, Garfield, Arthur, and Harrison, Hoover was
seeking to develop a new strategy to rejuvenate the Republican
party in the South.   His sponsorship of lily-white organizations in the southern states, he hoped, would attract southern
democrats to the Republican fold--but the long-range strategy
failed.

During Hoover's term Black and Tanism went into its
final phase, declining rapidly after his inauguration.   Although
Howard was acquitted of the charges brought against him,
Cohen in Louisiana recovered and Robert Church in Tennessee
continued, Black and Tanism as a force in Republican National Convention politics was never the same again.   When
the 1932 Republican convention convened, Black and Tanism,
for the first time since the 1880's, was no longer a major
issue.   Several Black and Tan groups, however, like the Joe
Tolbert group in South Carolina and the Perry Howard-led
faction in Mississippi, remained in existence.

In 1932 Ole Tireless Joe Tolbert's faction ran into some difficulty, losing some of its seats for the first time to a new lily-white group led by J. C. Hambright. Joe's group recaptured the seats in 1936, but lost them permanently in 1940. However, Black and Tan groups continued to challenge the Lily-white forces until 1956.

Commenting on the rise of the new Lily-white movement in South Carolina, an elderly Negro Republican stated that:

> The Nigger is a gone baby in South Carolina politics. In 1876 Wade Hampton put red shirts on Niggers and said just help us get rid of Carpetbaggers this once--after that he and they didn't need the Nigger no mo![25]

These were prophetic words: when the new lily-white Republican movement got firmly seated, the Black members were chopped, for disciplinary reasons. Before getting entrenched, however, the Lily-white Republicans in South Carolina bragged about the caliber of their Black membership. A leader of the new movement remarked:

> Right now, we have four Niggers in Philadelphia. In 1932 we had such a good bunch of Niggers up there, they took up with the ones from Pennsylvania and Ohio, who helped us get recognized... Herbert Hoover and Taft sponsored our delegation mostly on account of them... I tell you what we did. We went out to the College [Black South Carolina State] and got the best educated ones we could find... We got the best known Nigger preacher in the state....[26]

By 1942, the Blacks who had helped the lily-whites get seated were dropped.

In Mississippi, the Howard Black and Tans were challenged each year by the Lily-whites who put a slate of independent Republican electors on the state ballot each four years from 1920 through 1956. But each year the Howard faction was seated. There is some indication in the literature that Eisenhower used the Black and Tans from Mississippi to secure his first ballot nomination. After 1956, and the death of Perry Howard in 1961, the Black and Tans from Mississippi collapsed. In 1960 they were given honorary seats at the convention.

In retrospect, it is somewhat ironical that the two longest lasting Black and Tan groups were the ones most criticized as corrupt and scandalous. These most deplored and best known of all the Black and Tan Republicans, however, were seated by the national convention until almost the last man among them had faded from the scene.

Decline and Fall

The two basic reasons for the collapse of the Black and Tans as a force in national convention politics were the Lily-whiteism and the New Deal.

Lily-whiteism as sponsored by Hoover in 1928 led to a major withdrawal of Blacks from the Republican party in the South. "The success of the Hoover invasion of the South in 1928," writes Professor Bunche, "spelled the doom of the Black influence in Southern Republican organization. Lily-whiteism was given a great fillip and today the Negro is largely only on the fringes of Republican activity in the South." For the most part this is still true in the mid-seventies, in both north and south, although Bunche's remarks were made over thirty years ago.

Benjamin Davis, who resigned in 1928 from his Republican post of National Committeeman--a position he had held for 15 years--indicated in a 1939 interview that "the Republican party in Georgia now is just a few poor whites who meet every four years for the purpose of controlling patronage." Mrs. George Williams, former Black Republican Committeewoman from Georgia, put it thusly;

> I was the first Republican Committeewoman from the State of Georgia and the first Negro Committeewoman in the Country... I am a Republican from principle... I have always voted the Republican ticket. In 1932 Walter Brown and Herbert Hoover Lily-whited the party in Georgia... I have stumped this entire state for the Republicans--but I wouldn't do it now. [27]

In Georgia, the Lily-whites took over the party after the 1928 convention. In the pre-Hoover days, there had been four to six Black district chairmen, but in 1939 there were no Black district chairmen and only about thirty-five Black county chairmen among the one hundred and fifty-nine counties. Be-

fore 1928, Black Republicans controlled the state's Republican
central committee; by 1939 they had only three members on
it.   Today the situation is even worse; hardly any party positions in the state are held by Blacks.

In Louisiana, a Black dentist, the leader of the young
Black Republican organization in Baton Rouge, indicated in
1940 that "the turning over of the leadership of the Republican
party to the Lily-whites by Hoover hurt the strength of the
party very much.   It discouraged and alienated Negroes and
did not attract the anticipated number of whites. " He further
indicated that in New Orleans the number of Black Republicans dropped from 750 in 1932 to 500 in 1936.   In Baton
Rouge the number had fallen from 130 to 95 by January, 1940.

In sum, Lily-whiteism not only depleted what few followers the Republicans had in the Black community; it also
made it difficult for younger Blacks to join.   The result is
that in nearly every southern state today, there are very few
Blacks in the Republican party.

The other force which led to the final collapse of Black
and Tanism was the social, economic and political recognition
and relief that the New Deal brought Black Americans.   In
1936, when the New Deal had successfully reached down to
the Black masses, Blacks made their move on the national
level to the Democratic party.   Although they had been supporting the party on the local and state levels, allegiance had
generally been given to the Republican party on the national
level.   But in 1936 nearly eighty-five percent of the Black
vote went to the Democrats.   Jobs, money and social recognition destroyed the old political allegiance to the party of
Lincoln. [28]

In assessing the impact of Black and Tan Republicanism, one is forced to conclude, with Professor V. O. Key,
that it had been of little utility or concern to Blacks, except
those who wanted to be "convention delegates, party function-
aries, or patronage farmers. "

Goldwater, Nixon, and Black Republicans

In 1964 Barry Goldwater became the Republican Presidential nominee and ran on a strong states' rights and anti-
civil rights platform.   In Congress he had voted against the
controversial 1964 Civil Rights Act.   He carried five southern

states.   This was only the third time in history that the
South had bolted the Democratic ticket.

Goldwater's position was basically conservative and
against extension of equal rights to Black Americans.   At
this time, 1964, Blacks were in the midst of their greatest
social revolution and the Goldwater conservatism clearly
could not possibly attract Southern Blacks back to the Republican fold.

In 1968 Richard Nixon continued the conservative trend
started by Goldwater, securing his nomination with the aid of
Senator Strom Thurmond of South Carolina.   In return for
Thurmond's political influence, Nixon tried to repay his political debt to the South by attempting to name to the Supreme
Court two conservative Southerners: Clement Haynsworth
from South Carolina and Harrold Carswell from Florida.   In
other instances, he pursued a policy of slowing down integration in the South and spoke out against busing of students to
achieve balanced integration in the schools.

No Republican President in recent history, in fact,
has made any really meaningful attempt to attract Blacks
back into the party of Lincoln.   Although during Eisenhower's presidency the Supreme Court rendered the historic
Brown decision in 1954 and Ike nationalized and sent in federal troops to Little Rock in 1956 to help school desegrega-
tion, he has not really been regarded as a President who
fostered civil rights.   In contrast, Democratic Presidents
like Roosevelt, Truman, Kennedy and Johnson have done much
in this century to aid Blacks and their actions have done
much to foster Black loyalty to the Democratic party.

However, not all Blacks today are Democrats.   Even
in the South there are some Blacks who are Republicans.
Their efforts to re-attract other Blacks to the Republican
fold, however, have been stymied by Southern Republican conservatism and the heavy emphasis on law and order and on
states' rights.   If the Republican Party is to attract more
Blacks, in either the North or the South, it will have to move
away from its contemporary conservatism and demonstrate
more concern for Black needs and priorities.

An opportunity for the Republicans exists, however,
because a tremendous number of Black independent parties,
movements and candidates have been emerging in the South
since the late sixties.   These independent movements indicate

that Blacks are dissatisfied with the Democratic party but are
blocked from meaningful participation in the Republican organization, either in the region or nationally.

Thus, Republicanism still faces a dilemma in the
seventies. In the South it is still a political program in
search of a following. In the beginning it had Black support
in the South, then deliberately subordinated those supporters
and finally eliminated them. Meanwhile, in over 90 years,
from 1878 to the present, it still has not been able to attract
to its fold the whites whom it has wooed so long.

A southern Republican policy may yet be found, but
the correct one, devoid of racism, has not yet surfaced.

Notes

1. Heard, op. cit., p. 96.

2. Key, op. cit., p. 292.

3. Heard, op. cit., p. 118.

4. In 1916 the National Republican Convention voted to allow
   one delegate for each district and one additional delegate for each Congressional District in which votes
   for Republican Presidential electors were not less than
   7,500. See W. F. Nowlin, The Negro in American
   National Politics (Boston: Stratford Co., 1931), p. 73.

5. For a partial list of Hanna-McKinley Southern tours see
   Clarence Bacote, "Negro Office-holders in Georgia
   under President McKinley," Journal of Negro History
   (1939), pp. 217-219.

6. Gerald Pomper, Nominating the President: The Politics
   of Convention Choice (New York: W. W. Norton, 1966),
   p. 287.

7. See "Many Republicans Contest," New York Times (May
   28, 1900), p. 2.: "Republican Committee Settles Contest," Ibid. (June 15, 1900), p. 1.; and "Sentiment
   of the State Delegation," Ibid. (June 16, 1900), p. 1.

8. W. E. B. Dubois, "The Republican and the Black Voter,"
   The Nation (1920), pp. 757-758.

9. "Few Delegation Contests, " New York Times (April
    30, 1904), p. 3. "Alabama Contest, " Ibid. (June
    21, 1904), p. 2. ; "Lily-whites Keep Up Fight. "
    New York Times (April 21, 1904), p. 2. "National
    Committee" Ibid. (June 22, 1904). "Negro Dele-
    gate Mistaken For Hotel Bellboy. " Ibid. (June 20,
    1904), p. 2.

10. "24 Seats Won by the Taft Men, National Committee
    Seats Administration Delegates in Alabama and Arkan-
    sas... " New York Times (June 16, 1908), p. 1. ;
    "Lousiana for Taft" New York Times (May 8, 1908).
    p. 2. "Tennessee Contests" Ibid. (June 12, 1908),
    p. 4. ; "Negro Question in Virginia, " Ibid. (June
    13, 1908), p. 2.

11. "Want to Reduce Delegation--Allies to Offer a Resolu-
    tion Cutting Down Southern Representation, " New
    York Times (June 14, 1908), p. 3.

12. Burdette, op. cit. , p. 73.

13. Ibid.

14. "Taft Advisees Open Contest Hearing" New York Times
    (June 4, 1912), p. 1. ; "Taft Wins in All Cases, "
    Ibid. (June 8, 1912), p. 10; "Taft Wins in First
    Contest, " Ibid. (June 6, 1912), p. 2; and "Contest
    Bitterly Fought to the End," Ibid. (June 16, 1912),
    p. 5.

15. "Row in Georgia Caucus," New York Times (June 18,
    1912), p. 2.

16. "62 Contests Are Decided, " Ibid. (June 6, 1916), p. 2.

17. "Party Split in Georgia, " New York Times (April 13,
    1916), p. 7; "Decision Deprives Hughes of Votes, "
    Ibid. (June 2, 1916), p. 2; "Georgia Fight Causes
    Delay, " Ibid. (June 3, 1916), p. 4.

18. See "122 Contests before National Committee, " New
    York Times (May 29, 1920), p. 17; "Lowden Men
    Gain in First Contest, " Ibid. (June 1, 1920), p. 1;
    "Woods Gain two Contested Seats, " Ibid. (June 2,
    1920), p. 2.

19. "Win With Harding Letter--Johnson Delegates From

Georgia are seated, " New York Times (June 5, 1924), p. 2.

20.   Quoted in Heard, op. cit. , p. 123.

21.   Ibid.

22.   H. L. Mencken, Making a President (New York: Alfred Knopf, 1932), p. 27.

23.   The forgoing relies heavily on Lewinson, op. cit. , p. 173.

24.   Ibid. , p. 172-178.

25.   Quoted in Bunche, op. cit. , p. 1191.

26.   Quoted in Ibid. , p. 1187.

27.   Quoted in Ibid. , p. 1183.

28.   Walton, Black Politics, Chapter 7.

APPENDIX

TABLE I

Southern Black Delegates to Republican National Conventions, 1868-1944
(Partial listing)

Year	Names of Delegates	States
1868	P. B. S. Pinchback	Louisiana
	James H. Harris	North Carolina
	H. E. Hayne	South Carolina
	G. T. Ruby	Texas
1872	William V. Turner	Alabama
	William H. Grey	Arkansas
	Josiah T. Walls	Florida
	J. H. Armstrong	Florida
	William H. Gleason	Florida
	Edwin Belcher	Georgia
	Jefferson F. Long	Georgia
	A. W. Stone	Georgia
	B. K. Bruce	Mississippi
	James Hill	Mississippi
	J. R. Lynch	Mississippi
	George W. Price, Jr.	Mississippi
	James H. Harris	Mississippi
	J. W. Williamson	Mississippi
	A. J. Ransier	South Carolina
	H. J. Maxwell	South Carolina
	S. A. Swails	South Carolina
	W. B. Nash	South Carolina
	F. H. Frost	South Carolina
	Robert Smalls	South Carolina
	R. B. Elliott	South Carolina
	G. T. Ruby	Texas
	Robert Norton	Virginia
	P. J. Carter	Virginia
	R. G. L. Paige	Virginia
	John Robinson	Virginia
	Ross Hamilton	Virginia
1876	Jeremiah Haralson	Alabama
	Green S. W. Lewis	Alabama

	M. W. Gibbs	Arkansas
	John R. Scott	Florida
	Henry M. Turner	Georgia
	P. B. S. Pinchback	Louisiana
	J. T. Settle	Mississippi
	J. J. Spellman	Mississippi
	J. D. Cessar	Mississippi
	James H. Harris	North Carolina
	W. P. Mabson	North Carolina
	Robert B. Elliott	South Carolina
	Stephen A. Swails	South Carolina
	Joseph H. Rainey	South Carolina
	William J. McKinley	South Carolina
	William B. Nash	South Carolina
	Robert Smalls	South Carolina
	Lawrence Cain	South Carolina
	R. Allen	Texas
	N. W. Cuney	Texas
	B. K. Bruce	Mississippi
	P. J. Carter	Virginia
	Ross Hamilton	Virginia
	W. N. Stevens	Virginia
1880	Ben. S. Turner	Alabama
	James T. Rapier	Alabama
	M. W. Gibbs	Arkansas
	Joseph E. Lee	Florida
	James Hill	Mississippi
	H. C. Carter	Mississippi
	J. H. Harris	North Carolina
	George W. Price, Jr.	North Carolina
	Stewart Ellison	North Carolina
	R. B. Elliott	South Carolina
	Samuel Lee	South Carolina
	C. M. Wilder	South Carolina
	Wilson Cook	South Carolina
	W. J. Whipper	South Carolina
	W. F. Meyers	South Carolina
	W. H. Holland	Texas
	N. W. Cuney	Texas
	Peter J. Carter	Virginia
	J. W. Poindexter	Virginia
	H. Clay Harris	Virginia
	B. K. Bruce	Mississippi

Table I (cont'd.)

1884	Frank H. Threat	Alabama
	M. W. Gibbs	Arkansas
	Joseph E. Lee	Florida
	William G. Stewart	Florida
	A. N. Wilson	Georgia
	P. B. S. Pinchback	Louisiana
	James Hill	Mississippi
	John R. Lynch	Mississippi
	B. K. Bruce	Mississippi
	James H. Harris	North Carolina
	J. E. O'Hara	North Carolina
	John H. Williamson	North Carolina
	J. M. Freeman	South Carolina
	Paris Simpkins	South Carolina
	C. M. Wilder	South Carolina
	Wilson Cook	South Carolina
	E. H. Deas	South Carolina
	J. C. Napier	Tennessee
	S. A. McElwee	Tennessee
	N. W. Cuney	Texas
1888	John W. Jones	Alabama
	Frank H. Threat	Alabama
	Samuel Petty	Florida
	P. B. S. Pinchback	Louisiana
	John R. Lynch	Mississippi
	James Hill	Mississippi
	T. W. Stringer	Mississippi
	J. J. Spelman	Mississippi
	James H. Harris	North Carolina
	J. H. Williamson	North Carolina
	Robert Smalls	South Carolina
	Paris Simpkins	South Carolina
	E. H. Deas	South Carolina
	Samuel A. McElwee	Tennessee
	Isham F. Norris	Tennessee
	N. W. Cuney	Texas
	C. M. Ferguson	Texas
1892	Joseph E. Lee	Florida
	John G. Long	Florida
	John R. Lynch	Mississippi
	George W. Gayles	Mississippi

	James Hill	Mississippi
	Henry P. Cheatham	North Carolina
	John C. Daney	North Carolina
	George C. Scurlock	North Carolina
	James H. Young	North Carolina
	E. H. Deas	South Carolina
	Paris Simpkins	South Carolina
	N. Wright Cuney	Texas
	C. M. Ferguson	Texas

1896	H. V. Cashin	Alabama
	Joseph E. Lee	Florida
	John G. Long	Florida
	Walter L. Cohen	Louisiana
	S. W. Green	Louisiana
	James Hill	Mississippi
	Robert Smalls	South Carolina
	C. M. Wilder	South Carolina
	C. M. Ferguson	Texas

1900	H. V. Cashin	Alabama
	Joseph E. Lee	Florida
	John G. Long	Florida
	Henry W. Chandler	Florida
	J. W. Lyons	Georgia
	Walter L. Cohen	Louisiana
	John R. Lynch	Mississippi
	James Hill	Mississippi
	Robert Smalls	South Carolina
	E. H. Deas	South Carolina
	Charles M. Ferguson	Texas
	Fred Harris	Arkansas

1904	Joseph O. Thompson	Alabama
	John W. Jones	Alabama
	H. V. Cashin	Alabama
	Fred Harris	Arkansas
	Joseph E. Lee	Florida
	Henry W. Chandler	Florida
	J. W. Lyons	Georgia
	Walter L. Cohen	Louisiana
	E. H. Deas	South Carolina
	William F. Myers	South Carolina
	C. M. Ferguson	Texas
	William M. McDonald	Texas

Table I (cont'd.)

1908	Joseph O. Thompson	Alabama
	William R. Fairley	Alabama
	Frank H. Lathrop	Alabama
	Joseph E. Lee	Florida
	Henry W. Chandler	Florida
	Isaac Jenkins	Florida
	Judson W. Lyons	Georgia
	J. Madison Vance	Louisiana
	Flournoy Rivers	Tennessee
	Walter L. Cohen	Louisiana
1912	J. A. Jones	Arkansas
	Joseph E. Lee	Florida
	W. A. Watts	Florida
	W. A. Lucas	Florida
	M. Paige	Florida
	William James	Georgia
	S. S. Broadnax	Georgia
	J. C. Styles	Georgia
	R. B. Butts	Georgia
	W. E. Penn	Georgia
	R. A. Holland	Georgia
	Louis H. Crawford	Georgia
	M. B. Morton	Georgia
	Charles T. Walker	Georgia
	A. N. Fluker	Georgia
	S. S. Mincey	Georgia
	Walter L. Cohen	Louisiana
	F. H. Cook	Louisiana
	J. Madison Vance	Louisiana
	E. W. Sorrell	Louisiana
	B. V. Baranco	Louisiana
	W. W. Phillips	Mississippi
	P. W. Howard	Mississippi
	R. R. Church, Jr.	Tennessee
	W. H. Love	Texas
	W. M. McDonald	Texas
	Fred Harris	Arkansas
1916	F. V. Lathrop	Alabama
	Joseph E. Lee	Florida
	Walter L. Cohen	Louisiana
	D. W. Sherrod	Mississippi

1920	Joseph E. Lee	Florida
	S. S. Mincey	Georgia
	Benjamin J. Davis	Georgia
	Walter L. Cohen	Louisiana
	B. V. Baranco	Louisiana
	D. W. Sherrod	Mississippi
	H. M. Daily	Mississippi
1924	Benjamin J. Davis	Georgia
	Walter L. Cohen	Louisiana
	B. V. Baranco	Louisiana
	Perry W. Howard	Mississippi
	S. D. Redmond	Mississippi
	Robert R. Church	Tennessee
1928	S. A. Jones	Arkansas
	Benjamin J. Davis	Georgia
	Walter L. Cohen	Louisiana
	P. W. Howard	Mississippi
	S. D. Redmond	Mississippi
	C. J. Butler	Mississippi
	R. R. Church	Tennessee
1932	S. A. Jones	Arkansas
	John L. Webb	Arkansas
	Benjamin J. Davis	Georgia
	W. H. Harris	Georgia
	James Lewis, Jr.	Louisiana
	Perry W. Howard	Mississippi
	Fred H. Miller	Mississippi
	S. D. Redmond	Mississippi
	J. B. Woods	Mississippi
	Eugene P. Booze	Mississippi
	Charles H. Isaacs	Mississippi
	N. J. Frederick	South Carolina
	Webster Porter	Tennessee
	R. R. Church	Tennessee
1936	S. A. Jones	Arkansas
	S. L. Greene	Arkansas
	B. J. Davis	Georgia
	A. T. Walden	Georgia
	Dr. Sol C. Clemons	Georgia
	James Lewis	Louisiana
	Dr. J. A. Hardin	Louisiana

Table I (cont'd.)

1936 (cont'd.) Perry W. Howard   Mississippi
               W. J. Box   Mississippi
               F. H. Miller   Mississippi
               S. D. Redmond   Mississippi
               C. J. Butler   Mississippi
               J. B. Woods   Mississippi
               J. H. Oldham   Mississippi
               E. P. Booze   Mississippi
               W. I. Peek   South Carolina
               E. W. Bowler   South Carolina
               A. J. Collins   South Carolina
               B. T. Smith   South Carolina
               T. H. Pinckney   South Carolina
               W. L. McFarlan, Sr.   South Carolina
               C. G. Williams   South Carolina
               W. M. Howard   South Carolina
               R. R. Church   Tennessee

1940   S. A. Jones   Arkansas
               J. Leonard Lewis   Florida
               Benjamin J. Davis   Georgia
               Sam B. Solomon   Georgia
               James Lewis, Jr.   Louisiana
               Perry W. Howard   Mississippi
               S. D. Redmond   Mississippi
               W. J. Box   Mississippi
               Fred H. Miller   Mississippi
               E. L. Patton   Mississippi
               H. M. Daily   Mississippi
               C. T. Butler   Mississippi
               J. B. Woods   Mississippi
               Robert R. Church   Tennessee
               I. M. A. Myers   South Carolina
               James Brier   South Carolina

1944   Benjamin J. Davis   Georgia
               James Lewis, Jr.   Louisiana
               Perry W. Howard   Mississippi
               S. D. Redmond   Mississippi
               M. H. Daily   Mississippi

TABLE II

Votes for the Black and Tan Republicans
in South Carolina--1936, 1944, and 1952

Year	Black and Tan Vote	Votes Received
1936	Tolbert Faction (Black and Tans)	953
	Hambright Faction (Lily-whites)	693
1944	Regular Republicans (Whites)	4, 547
	Tolbert Faction (Black and Tans)	63
1952	Regular Republicans (Whites)	158, 289
	Tolbert Faction (Black and Tans)	9, 793

Source: Luman H. Long, ed., 1968 World Almanac (New York: Doubleday Company, Inc., 1967), p. 227, 235.

TABLE III

Votes for the Black and Tan Republicans in Mississippi--
1928, 1936, 1940, 1944, 1948, 1952 and 1956.

Year	Black and Tan Vote	Votes Received
1928	Independent Slate (Whites)	26, 202
	Howard-Redmond (Black and Tans)	524
1936	Howard-Redmond (Black and Tans)	2, 760
	Rowland (Whites)	1, 675
1940	Independent Republicans (Whites)	4, 550
	Regular Republicans (Black and Tans)	2, 814
1944	Independent Republicans (Whites)	7, 859
	Regular Republicans (Black and Tans)	3, 728
1948	Regular Republicans (Black and Tans)	5, 043
1952	Regular Republicans (Black and Tans)	112, 966
1956	Regular Republicans	56, 372
	Black and Tans - Grand Old Party	4, 313

Source: Luman H. Long, ed., 1968 World Almanac (New
          York: Doubleday Company, Inc., 1967), p. 227,
          235.

TABLE IV

Number of Black Delegates to
Republican National Conventions,
1868-1972

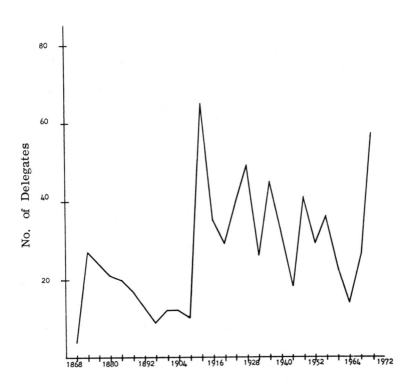

ELECTION YEAR

NOTE: Each Interval Represents a Four Year Period

BIBLIOGRAPHY

BOOKS

Agar, Herbert. The Pride of the Union. Boston: Houghton Mifflin, 1950.

American Political Science Association. Toward a More Responsible Two-Party System. New York: Holt, Rinehart & Winston, 1959.

Aptheker, Herbert, ed. A Documentary History of the Negro People in the United States. New York: Citadel Press, 1969.

Arnett, H. M. The Populist Movement in Georgia. New York: Columbia University Press, 1922.

Bennett, Lerone, Jr. Before the Mayflower. Baltimore: Penguin Books, 1968.

_____. Black Power U. S. A. Chicago: Johnson Publishing Company, 1967.

_____. What Manner of Man. Chicago: Johnson Publishing Company, 1964.

Botkin, B. A., ed. Lay My Burden Down: A Folk History of Slavery. Chicago: Phoenix Books, 1961.

Brewer, J. Mason. Negro Legislators in Texas. Dallas: Mathis Publishing Company, 1935.

Brisbane, Robert. The Negro Vanguard. Valley Forge: Judson Press, 1970.

Buni, Andrew. The Negro in Virginia Politics, 1902-1965. Charlottesville: University Press of Virginia, 1961.

Burdette, Franklin L. The Republican Party: A Short His-
        tory. New York: D. Van Nostrand Company, 1968.

Casdorph, Paul. A History of the Republican Party in Texas,
        1865-1965. Austin: The Pemberton Press, 1965.

Clark, John B. Populism in Alabama, 1874-1896. Auburn:
        1927.

Coulter, E. Merton. William G. Brownlow--Fighting Parson
        of the Southern Highlands. Chapel Hill: University of
        North Carolina Press, 1937.

Cox, LaWanda & John H. Politics, Principles and Preju-
        dices, 1865-1866. Glencoe: Free Press, 1963.

Curry, R. O. Radicalism, Racism and Party Realignment:
        The Border States During Reconstruction. Baltimore:
        Johns Hopkins Press, 1969.

Democratic State Executive Committee. Democracy v. Rad-
        icalism. Raleigh, N. C. , 1884.

DeSantis, Vincent. Republicans Face the Southern Question--
        The New Departure, 1877-1897. New York: Green-
        wood Press, 1969.

Donald, David. The Politics of Reconstruction, 1863-1867.
        Baton Rouge: Louisiana State University Press, 1965.

Douglas, W. O. Mr. Lincoln and the Negro. New York:
        Atheneum, 1963.

DuBois, W. E. B. Black Reconstruction in America. New
        York: Russell & Russell, 1962.

Elversveld, Samuel. Political Parties: A Behavioral Anal-
        ysis. Chicago: Rand McNally, 1964.

Foner, Eric. Free Soil, Free Labor, Free Men. New
        York: Oxford University Press, 1970.

Foner, Philip S. , ed. The Life and Writings of Frederick
        Douglass, Vol. II. New York: International Publish-
        ers, 1950.

Franklin, John Hope. Reconstruction: After the Civil War.

Chicago: University of Chicago Press, 1961.

Gillette, William. The Right to Vote. Baltimore: The
Johns Hopkins Press, 1969.

Goldwin, Robert, ed. Political Parties U. S. A. Chicago:
Rand McNally, 1968.

Gordon, A. H. Sketches of Negro Life and History in South
Carolina. Columbia: University of South Carolina
Press, 1971.

Green, F. M., ed. Essays in Southern History. Chapel
Hill: University of North Carolina Press, 1949.

Greenstein, Fred. The American Party System and the
American People. Englewood Cliffs, N. J.: Prentice-
Hall, 1963.

Hackney, Sheldon. Populism to Progressivism in Alabama.
Princeton: Princeton University Press, 1969.

Hare, Maud Cuney. Norris Wright Cuney. New York: The
Crisis Publishing Co., 1913.

Heard, Alexander. A Two-Party South. Chapel Hill: University of North Carolina Press, 1952.

Herring, P. The Politics of Democracy. New York: Norton,
1940.

Hines, Margie. Negro Suffrage and the Florida Election
Laws, 1860-1950. Durham: North Carolina College,
1953.

Hirshson, Stanley P. Farewell to the Bloody Shirts: Northern
Republicans and the Southern Negro, 1877-1893. Chicago: Quadrangle, 1968.

Holloway, H. H. The Politics of the Southern Negro. New
York: Random House, 1969.

Howard, Perry H. Political Tendencies in Louisiana, 1812-
1952. Baton Rouge: Louisiana State University Press,
1957.

Jackson, L. P. Negro Officeholders in Virginia, 1865-1895.

Norfolk: Quids Quality Press, 1945.

James, Judson L. American Political Parties. New York:
Pegasus, 1969.

Key, V. O. Politics, Parties and Pressure Groups. New
York: Thomas Y. Crowell, 1958.

_____. Southern Politics in State and Nation. New York:
Vintage Books, 1949.

Lawson, Kay. Political Parties. New York: Charles
Scribner's Sons, 1968.

Lewinson, Paul. Race, Class and Party: A History of Negro
Suffrage and White Politics in the South. New York:
Russell & Russell, 1963.

Logan, Rayford. The Betrayal of the Negro. New York:
Collier Books, 1965.

_____. The Negro in the United States. Princeton, N. J.:
D. Van Nostrand, 1957.

Lynch, John R. The Facts of Reconstruction. New York:
Bobbs-Merrill, 1970.

Mabry, William A. The Negro in North Carolina Since Reconstruction. Durham: Duke University Press, 1940.

McPherson, James M. The Negro's Civil War. New York:
Vintage Books, 1965.

_____. The Struggle for Equality. Princeton: Princeton
University Press, 1964.

Mencken, H. L. Making a President. New York: Alfred A.
Knopf, 1932.

Miller, William D. Mr. Crump of Memphis. Baton Rouge:
Louisiana State University Press, 1964.

Milner, John T. White Men of Alabama Stand Together,
1860-1890. Birmingham, 1890.

Moos, Malcolm. The Republicans: A History of Their Party.
New York: Random House, 1956.

Morton, Richard L. The Negro in Virginia Politics. Char-
        lottesville: The University of Virginia Press, 1919.

Myrdal, Gunnar. An American Dilemma. New York: Harper
        & Row, 1962.

Nathans, Elizabeth S. Losing the Peace: Georgia Republi-
        cans and Reconstruction, 1865-1871. Baton Rouge:
        Louisiana State University Press, 1968.

Nowlin, W. F. The Negro in American National Politics:
        A Study of the Negro in America National Politics
        Since 1868. Boston: The Stratford Company, 1931.

Official Proceedings of the Constitutional Conventions of the
        State of Alabama, 1901.

Olbrich, E. The Development of Sentiment on Negro Suf-
        frage to 1860. Wisconsin: The University of Wis-
        consin Press, 1965.

Pomper, Gerald. Nominating the President: The Politics
        of Convention Choice. New York: W. W. Norton,
        1966.

_____ and D. Herzberg, eds. American Party Politics.
        New York: Holt, Rinehart & Winston, 1966.

Porter, Kirk H. A History of Suffrage in the United States.
        Chicago: University of Chicago Press, 1918.

_____ and D. B. Johnson, eds. National Party Platforms,
        1849-1964. Urbana: University of Illinois Press, 1966.

Price, H. D. The Negro and Southern Politics: A Chapter
        of Florida History. New York: New York University
        Press, 1957.

Proceedings of the Republican National Convention, 1856-1896.
        Minneapolis, 1893.

Quarles, Benjamin. Black Abolitionists. New York: Oxford
        University Press, 1969.

_____. Lincoln and the Negro. New York: Oxford Uni-
        versity Press, 1962.

Richardson, Joe M. The Negro in the Reconstruction of Florida, 1865-1877. Tallahassee: Florida State University Press, 1965.

Riker, William. The Theory of Political Coalitions. New Haven: Yale University Press, 1968.

Rossiter, Clinton. Parties and Politics in America. Ithaca: Cornell University Press, 1963.

Schattschneider, E. E. Party Government. New York: Rinehart, 1942.

Shaftner, John T. A Colored Man's Exposition of the Acts and Doings of the Radical South from 1865 to 1876 and its Probable Overthrow by President Hayes' Southern Policy. Jacksonville: Gibson and Dennis, Steam Book and Job Printers, 1877.

Simpkins, Francis Butler. Pitchfork Ben Tillman. Baton Rouge: Louisiana State University Press, 1967.

Sindler, Allan P. Political Parties in the United States. New York: St. Martin's Press, 1966.

Sorauf, Frank J. Party Politics in America. Boston: Little, Brown & Co., 1968.

Stampp, Kenneth M. The Era of Reconstruction, 1867-1877. New York: Vintage Books, 1965.

Stanley, J. Randall. History of Gadsden County. Quring, Florida, 1948.

Taylor, A. A. The Negro in Tennessee, 1865-1880. Washington, D. C.: Associated Publishers, 1941.

Wallace, John. Carpetbag Rule in Florida. Jacksonville: Da-Costa Printing and Publishing House, 1888.

Walton, Hanes, Jr. Black Political Parties. New York: Free Press, 1972.

_____. Black Politics: A Theoretical and Structural Analysis. Philadelphia: J. B. Lippincott, 1972.

_____. The Negro in Third Party Politics. Philadelphia:
    Dorrance, 1969.

Washington, B. T.   Up From Slavery.   New York: Double-
    day, 1922.

Wesley, Charles.   Neglected History.   Ohio: Central State
    College Press, 1965.

Wharton, Vernon.   The Negro in Mississippi.   New York:
    Harper Torch Books, 1965.

Wiley, B. I.   Southern Negroes, 1861-1865.   New Haven:
    Yale University Press, 1965.

Williamson, Joel.   After Slavery: The North in South Caro-
    lina During Reconstruction, 1861-1877.   Chapel Hill:
    University of North Carolina Press, 1965.

Winston, Robert.   It's a Far Cry.   New York, 1937.

Woods, F.   Black Scare.   California: University of Cali-
    fornia Press, 1968.

Woodward, C. Vann.   The Origin of the South, 1877-1879.
    Baton Rouge: Louisiana State University Press, 1951.

Work, Monroe V., ed.   The Negro Yearbook.   Tuskegee,
    Alabama, 1912.

ARTICLES AND PERIODICALS

Alexander, Thomas B.   "Ku Kluxism in Tennessee, 1865-
    1869, " Tennessee Historical Quarterly (September,
    1949), 195-219.

Bacote, Clarence A.   "Negro Officeholders in Georgia Under
    President McKinley, " Journal of Negro History (July,
    1959), 219.

_____. "Some Aspects of Negro Life in Georgia, 1880-
    1908, " Journal of Negro History (July, 1958), 186-
    213.

Bage, Elvena S.   "President Garfield's Pronouncement, "
    Negro History Bulletin (June, 1951), 195-197.

Barnes, Johnny W.   "The Political Activities of the Union
    League of America in North Carolina, " Quarterly Re-
    view of Higher Education Among Negroes (October,
    1952), 141-150.

Bell, Howard.   "National Negro Conventions of the Middle
    1840's: Moral Suasion v. Political Action, " Journal
    of Negro History (October, 1957), 247-260.

Bentley, George R.   "Freedmen's Bureau in Florida, "
    Florida Historical Quarterly, XXVIII (July, 1949), 29.

Brown, Charles.   "Reconstruction Legislators in Alabama, "
    Negro History Bulletin (March, 1963), 198-201.

Cox, LaWanda & John H.   "Negro Suffrage and Republican
    Politics: The Problem of Motivation in Reconstruction
    Historiography, " in Gatell and A. Weinstein, eds.,
    American Themes.   New York: Oxford University
    Press, 1968.

Cuson, R. F.   "The Loyal League in Georgia, "   Georgia
    Historical Quarterly (June, 1936).

DeSantis, Vincent.   "Negro Dissatisfaction with Republican
    Policy in the South, 1882-1884, " Journal of Negro
    History (January, 1951), 152.

_____.   "The Republican Party and the Southern Negro,
    1877-1897, " Journal of Negro History (April, 1960),
    85.

Douglass, Frederick.   "The Republican Party--Our Position,"
    Frederick Douglass Paper (December 7, 1855).

DuBois, W. E. B.   "The Republican and the Black Voter, "
    The Nation (1920), 757-758.

Dyer, Brainerd.   "One Hundred Years of Negro Suffrage, "
    Pacific Historical Review (February, 1968), 3.

Dykstra, R. & Hahn, H.   "Northern Voters and Negro Suf-
    frage: The Case of Iowa, 1968, " Public Opinion
    Quarterly (Summer, 1968), 207.

Farris, Charles D.   "The Re-Enfranchisement of Negroes in
    Florida, " The Journal of Negro History (October,
    1954), 264.

Fishel, Leslie Jr.   "Northern Prejudice and Negro Suffrage,
       1865-1870, " Journal of Negro History (January, 1954)
       8-26.

_____. "The Negro in Northern Politics, 1870-1900, "
       Mississippi Valley Historical Review (December, 1955),
       466-489.

Fox, Dixon.   "The Negro Vote in Old New York, " Political
       Science Quarterly (June, 1917), 252-275.

Halsell, Willie D.   "Republican Factionalism in Mississippi,
       1882-1884, " Journal of Southern History (February,
       1941), 84-101.

_____. "James R. Chalmers and Mahoneism in Missis-
       sippi, " Journal of Southern History (February, 1944),
       37-58.

Hoffman, E. D.   "The Genesis of the Modern Movement for
       Equal Rights in South Carolina, 1920-1939, " Journal
       of Negro History (October, 1959), 363-369.

House, Albert V. , Jr.   "President Hayes' Selection of David
       M. Key for Postmaster General, " Journal of South-
       ern History (1938), 91.

Jackson, L. P.   "The Educational Efforts of the Freedmen's
       Bureau and Freedman's Civil Societies in South Caro-
       lina, 1862-1872, " Journal of Negro History (January,
       1923), 1-40.

Osborn, George C. , ed.   "Letters of a Carpetbagger in
       Florida, " Florida Historical Quarterly, XXXVI (Jan-
       uary, 1958), 259.

Post, Louis F.   "A Carpetbagger in South Carolina, " Journal
       of Negro History (January, 1925), 20.

Riddleberger, Patrick W.   "The Break in the Radical Ranks:
       Liberal vs. Stalwarts in the Election of 1872, " Journal
       of Negro History (April, 1959), 136-157.

Russ, William Jr.   "Registration and Disfranchisement under
       Radical Reconstruction, " Mississippi Valley Historical
       Review, XXX (1934), 163-180.

_____. "Radical Disfranchisement in Georgia, 1867-
1871, " Georgia Historical Quarterly (September, 1935)
178-207.

Shugg, Roger W. "Negro Voting in the Ante-Bellum South, "
Journal of Negro History (October, 1936), 357-364.

Simpkins, Frances B. "The Ku Klux Klan in South Carolina,
1868-1871, " Journal of Negro History (October, 1927),
621-647.

Sindler, Allan P. "Bifactional Rivalry As an Alternative to
Two-Party Competition in Louisiana, " American Political Science Review (September, 1965), 641-662.

Smith, Harvard W. "The Progressive Party and the Election
of 1912 in Alabama, " The Alabama Review, IX (1956),
5-22.

Stanley, John L. "Majority Tyranny in Tocqueville's 'America: The Failure of Negro Suffrage in 1846', " Political Science Quarterly (September, 1969), 428.

Talmadge, John E. "The Death Blow to Independentism in
Georgia, " Southern Historical Quarterly (December,
1955), 37-47.

Taylor, A. A. "The Negro in South Carolina During Reconstruction, " Journal of Negro History (October, 1924),
384.

Thorpe, Earle E. "William Hooper Council, " The Negro
History Bulletin, XIX (1956), 85-86.

Walton, Hanes, Jr. "Another Force for Disfranchisement:
Blacks and the Prohibitionists in Tennessee, " Journal
of Human Relations (First Quarter, 1970), 728-738.

_____. "Blacks and Conservative Political Movements, "
Quarterly Review of Higher Education Among Negroes
(October, 1969), 177-183.

_____. "The Negro in the Progressive Party Movement, "
Quarterly Review of Higher Education Among Negroes
(January, 1968), 17-26.

_____ and James Taylor. "Blacks, the Prohibitionists

190   Black Republicans

and Disfranchisement, " Quarterly Review of Higher Education Among Negroes (April, 1969), 66-69.

Weeks, S. B. "The History of Negro Suffrage in the South," Political Science Quarterly, IX (December, 1894), 673-703.

Wesley, Charles H. "Lincoln's Plan for Colonizing the Emancipated Negroes, " Journal of Negro History (January, 1919), 11-12.

_____. "Negro Suffrage in the Period of Constitution-Making, 1785-1865, " Journal of Negro History, 32 (April, 1947), 143-168.

_____. "The Participation of Negroes in the Anti-Slavery Political Parties, " Journal of Negro History (January, 1941), 39-76.

Work, Monroe V. "Some Negro Members of Reconstruction Conventions and Legislatures and of Congress, " Journal of Negro History, V, 63-125.

UNPUBLISHED MATERIAL

Brittain, Joseph M. "Negro Suffrage and Politics in Alabama Since 1870. " Unpublished Ph. D. thesis: Indiana University, 1957.

Bunche, Ralph. "Political Status of the Negro. " Unpublished manuscript prepared for the Gunnar Myrdal Study.

Clepper, L. D. "Republican Politics in Louisiana from 1900-1952. " Unpublished Master's thesis: Louisiana State University, 1950.

Corlew, R. E. "The Negro in Tennessee, 1870-1900. " Unpublished Ph. D. dissertation: University of Alabama, 1954.

Dumas, Joseph. "The Black and Tan Faction of the Republican Party in Louisiana, 1908-1936. " Unpublished Master's thesis: Xavier University, 1943.

Fishel, Leslie. "The North and the Negro, 1865-1900: A Study in Race Discrimination. " Unpublished Ph. D.

dissertation: Harvard University, 1953.

Gelb, Joyce. "The Role of Negro Politicians in the Demo-
    cratic, Republican and Liberal Party of New York
    City. " Unpublished Ph. D. dissertation: New York
    University, 1969.

Ownes. Susie Lee. "The Union League of America. " Un-
    published Ph. D. dissertation: New York University,
    1943.

Queener, V. M. "The Republican Party in East Tennessee,
    1865-1900. " Unpublished Ph. D. dissertation: Indiana
    University, 1940.

Quillian, B. O. "The Populist Challenge in Georgia in the
    Year 1896. " Unpublished thesis: University of
    Georgia, 1948.

Shadgett, Olive H. "A History of the Republican Party in
    Georgia from Reconstruction Through 1900. " Unpub-
    lished Ph. D. thesis: University of Georgia, 1962.

Shafner, Terrell H. "The Presidential Elections of 1876 in
    Florida. " Unpublished Master's thesis: Florida State
    University, 1961.

Smith, Allen Chandler. "The Republican Party in Georgia. "
    Unpublished Master's thesis: Duke University, 1957.

Snowden, I. G. "The Political Status of the Negroes in the
    United States with Particular Reference to the Border
    States. " Unpublished Ph. D. dissertation: Indiana
    University, 1943.

Tucker, Mary Louise. "The Negro in the Populist Movement
    in Alabama, 1890-1896. " Unpublished Master's thesis:
    Atlanta University, 1957.

Uzee, P. D. "Republican Party in Louisiana from 1877-
    1900. " Unpublished Ph. D. dissertation: Louisiana
    State University, 1950.

INDEX

Abolitionists 1, 30
Africa 12
Afro-American Democratic
  League 79
Alabama 69-85
Alabama Democratic Asso-
  ciation 85
Alcorn, James 34
Allen, John W. 75
Allen, Richard 64
Allison, W. B. 58, 66,
  153
Alton, C. H. 157
AME Zion Quarterly 91
American Party (Know
  Nothings) 1
Ames, A. 130
Amnesty Act 35
Anderson, R. B. 114
Anglo African 18, 28
Anti-Slavery Party 21
Aptheker, Herbert 27, 28
Ard, E. C. 128
Arkansas 123-128
Arthur, Chester 38, 39,
  65, 87, 88
Athens Blade 51
Atlanta Constitution 50
Atlanta Republican 52
Avery, Moses B. 70

Bacote, Clarence 44, 60
Bassett, Ebenezer 21
Belcher, Edwin 50
Bennett, Lerone 17, 28,
  36, 43, 125

Berman, Amos 5
Bifactionalism 2
Billings, Liberty 99
Black & Tans 39, 40, 43,
  45, 46, 47, 49, 50, 51,
  52, 55, 56, 57, 58, 59,
  60, 61, 63, 64, 65, 66,
  67, 68, 69, 70, 73, 76,
  77, 78, 79, 80, 81, 82,
  83, 84, 85, 87, 88, 89,
  90, 96, 97, 98, 102, 103,
  104, 109, 115, 116, 120,
  121, 126, 127, 128, 131,
  135, 136, 137, 141, 151,
  152, 153, 159, 163, 164
Black Codes 128
Black Delegates 14, 20, 41,
  59, 62, 68, 70, 86, 93
Black Democrats 73, 75,
  93, 101, 103, 107, 110,
  111
Black Farmer Alliance 78
Black Freedmen 31
Black Knights of Labor 78
Black Militia 125
Black Nationalism 109
Black Populist 79, 89, 90
Black Reconstruction 23,
  24, 30
Black Republicanism 1, 6,
  16, 17, 23, 25, 47, 62,
  67, 69, 86, 89, 92, 98,
  103, 105, 106, 108, 110,
  112, 116, 122, 123, 126,
  128, 129, 131, 165
Black Suffrage 10, 11, 116,
  118, 119

Blacks 12, 63, 94, 102,
  111, 120
Blain, James 65
Blair, Frances 9
Blass, Carter 97
Bleven, Jere 79
Blount, J. H. 127
Bolte, Edwin H. 68
Booze, Mary 134
Bowen, Christopher 111
Bradley, A. A. 51, 52
Bradwell, William 100
Brayton, Elery M. 111
Brown, Joseph 34
Brown, T. H. 54
Brownlow, William C. 117,
  118, 119
Bryant, J. E. 50
Bruce, B. K. 131
Buchanan, James 8
Buck, A. E. 52, 56
Bull Moose Progressive
  Party 85
Bulter, W. C. 113
Bunche, Ralph 163
Burdette, Franklin 6, 12,
  26, 28, 160
Burford, H. C. 84
Buttain, J. 71
Byrd, Jonas 107

Callaway, A. H. 86
Campbell, Tunis 51, 52,
  53
Carpetbaggers 31, 32, 34
Carswell, Harrold 165
Carlyle, Richard 103
Casdorph, Paul 62
Cashin, H. U. 81
Chamberlain, D. A. 109
Chase, Salmon 20
Church, R. R. 121, 157,
  159, 160, 161
Civil Rights Acts 23, 164
Civil War 24
Clanton, James H. 70

Clarkson, K. C. 83
Clemenceau 24
Cleveland, Grover 57, 88
Cohen, Walter L. 68, 69,
  134, 154, 157, 159, 160,
  161
Colonization 9, 10, 12, 13
Colored People Convention
  of South Carolina 105
Colored Republican Club 15
Congressional Radicals 117
Constitutional Amendments
  13th: 21, 24
  14th: 21, 24, 117
  15th: 21, 24, 30
  16th: 31
Coolidge, Calvin 158, 159
Council, William H. 77
Creager, R. B. 66
Crump, E. H. 121, 122
Cullum, S. M. 58
Cuney, Norris W. 45, 65,
  66
Curtis, Alexander 76
Curtis, Charles 159

Davis, Benjamin 61, 159,
  161, 163
Davis, Charles 158
Davis, E. J. 62, 63, 64
Davis, Julius 84
Dayton, William L. 7
Delany, Martin D. 109, 110
Democrats 3, 4, 18, 23,
  24, 35, 107, 110
Dent, T. M. 51
Deveaux, J. H. 51, 54, 56
Disfranchisement 84, 104,
  114, 157
District of Columbia 22
Dobbs, John 61
Douglas, Stephen 12
Douglas, W. O. 27
Douglass, Frederick 3, 4,
  5, 7, 8, 15, 16, 18, 21,
  26, 27

Dred Scott decision, 15
DuBois, W. E. B.   68
Dyer, Brainerd 28
Dystra, R. 27

East Tennessee News   122
Edmonds, Helen 91
Eight Ballot Box Law 112
Eisenhower, David 162
Elections of 1856 8
Emancipation Proclamation
   13, 17
Emmett, Robert 6
Equal Rights League 31,
   48, 58, 62

Farmer, James 141
Ferguson, H. 66
Ferguson, Jesse 81
Few, James 54
Finley, Jesse T. 102
Fishel, Leslie 140
Fisk, Clinton B. 116
Fleming, James G. 140
Flowers, Jack 19
Foner, Eric 9, 12, 26,
   27, 28
Foner, Philip 26
"Force Bill" 23
Ford, Levi 75
Fort Sumter 17
Free Blacks 3, 4, 9, 14
Free Soiler Party 4
Freedmen Bureau 21, 22,
   71, 92, 98, 105, 116
Fremont, John C. 6, 7,
   9, 18
Fugitive Slave Bill 5
Fusionists 79, 89, 91

Garfield, James 39, 64,
   94
Gee, Banky 88
Gelb, Joyce 140, 141

Gerald, J. Bates 115
Gibbs, Jonathan 100, 101,
   102
Gibbs, Mifflin 125
Gillette, William 20, 29,
   30, 43, 119
Gleaves, R. H. 108
Goldwater, Barry 165
Gomillion v. Lightfoot 85
Grant, Ulysses 20, 21
Greeley, Horace 120
Green, John T. 109
Greenbackers 77, 112
Grey, William 123, 125
Griggs, N. M. 95
Guthrie, William 89

Hackney, Sheldon 82
Hahn, Michael 13, 27
Hambright, J. C. 113,
   115, 162
Hamilton, A. J. 63
Hampton, Wade 162
Hampton Red Shirts 110
Hanna, Mark 41, 57, 58,
   151, 153
Haralson, Jere 76
Harding, Warren G. 66,
   133, 158
Harris, James 86
Harrison, Benjamin 38, 39,
   40, 58, 77, 132
Hart, Ossian B. 100, 102
Harvey, Q. William 77
Hashell, A. C. 113
Hati 21
Hawkins, Monroe 123
Hay, John 100
Hayes, R. 38, 39, 94, 110
Haynes, James W. 108
Haynsworth, Clement 165
Heard, Alexander 151
Heflin, Senator 121
Hendley, Charles 78
Hendrix, B. L. 115
Henry, Sam 36, 37

Herring, Pendleton 1, 25
Hill, James 131, 132, 136
Holtzolaw, William H. T.
   82
Hood, J. W.   86
Hoover, Herbert 41, 61,
   66, 135, 158, 163
Howard, Perry 133, 135,
   136, 159, 160, 161, 162
Howard, Redmond 134
Hughes, Charles E.   154,
   156, 157
Humphreys, B. G.   128
Huntsville Gazette 77
Huntsville Journal 82
Huntsville Republican 81

Jaybird - Woodpecker War
   65
Jenkins, W. K.   88
Jim Crowism 25
Johnson, A. N.   80
Johnson, Andrew 31, 93,
   117
Johnson, D. B.   26
Johnson, Henry Lincoln
   157, 158, 159
Johnson, Thomas 123
Jones, Marshal 112

Key, V. O.   1, 2, 121,
   152, 164
Kolb, Reuben 78, 79, 80
Kolbite 79
Knox, John B.   82
Ku Klux Klan 36, 37, 72,
   90, 119, 124

La Follette, Robert M.   158
Lamar, L. Q. C.   136
Langston, John 95
Lee, Thomas 70
Leevy, I. S.   115
Lewis, Tom 88

Liberal Republicans 35, 88,
   125
Liberty Party 4, 14
Lily Whites 2, 39, 45, 46,
   47, 103, 115, 120, 127,
   135, 137, 140, 160, 163
Lincoln, Abraham 6, 10,
   13, 14, 15, 17, 18, 19,
   22, 116
Lincoln Brotherhood 99
Lincoln Emancipation Clubs
   115
Lincoln Independent Party
   140
Lincoln Liberty Tree 15
Linden, Glenn 28
Lindsay, John 141
Little, Indiana 85
Little Rock, Arkansas,
   Gazette 126
Logan, R.   28, 43
Loguen, J. W.   5
Long, Jefferson 51, 52
Longstreet, James 52
Louisiana 14
Love, E. K.   58, 59
Lowden, Frank 133, 157
Loyal League 36, 62, 99
Lucas, James K. P.   76
Lusk, James 36, 37
Lynch, John 36, 44, 130,
   131, 132, 136

McClellan, George B.   18
McDonald, W. M.   66, 134
Mackey, A. C.   111
Mackey, E. W.   112
McKinley, William 40, 41,
   57, 58, 59, 60, 67, 151
Macon County Democratic
   Club 161
McPherson, James 28
Mallory, A. C.   65
Mann, Horace A.   134
Marbry, William 86, 87
Martin, William 101

Mason, J. W. 123
Matthew, E. H. 81
Meas, George 112
Memminger, R. W. 111
Mencken, H. L. 159, 160
Military Reconstruction Acts
  31, 48
Miscegenation 24
Mississippi Plan 36
Mississippi State Constitu-
  tional Convention 129
Mitchell, J. 98
Modocs 131
Montgomery, Isaiah 40
Montgomery Advance 16
Monticello Constitution 103
Morgan, Edwin 6
Mosely, Robert 78
Moses, F. J. 108
Moses-Gleaves Ticket 108
Mosley, L. T. 132
Mound, Bayou 134
Muldihill, M. J. 133, 134
Muller, J. E. 140
Multiple Ballot Box Law
  103, 104
Murphy, William 123
Murray, George W. 113

NAACP 68
Nash, William Beverly 105
National Convention of
  Colored Men 18
National Equal Rights League
  18
National Freedmen Conven-
  tion 105
National Political Abolition-
  ists Convention 16
National Union Republican
  Party 130
Negro Suffrage Convention
  14
New Deal 163, 164
New Orleans 13
New York 14

New York Tribune 101
Nilblack, Silas 102
Nixon, Richard 164, 166
Norcross, Jonathan 52, 53
Norfolk Journal and Guide
  98
North Carolina 13
Norton, R. 95

Ohio 15
Ohio Colored Men Convention
  15
Olbrich, Emil 27
Osborn, Thomas 98

Party Cleavage 1
Patillo, Walter 88
Payton, John 117
Pearce, Charles 101
Pearson, Drew 159
Philadelphia National Union
  Convention 117
Pickens County Sentinel 113
Pike, Albert 117
Pledger, William 51, 52,
  54, 55, 56, 57, 59
Political Parties 1
Pollard, Joseph 97
Pomper, Gerald 153, 157
Porter, Kirk 26
Proceedings of Republican
  National Conventions 1856-
  1896 26

Quarles, Benjamin 14, 16,
  19, 27, 28
Quay, Matthew 58, 59

Radical Abolitionists Party
  1, 14
Radical Republicans 30, 105
Ransier, A. J. 107
Rapier, J. T. 70

Readjusters 94, 95, 96
Reconstruction 17
Reconstruction Act of 1867
  31, 109
Rector, Henry 123
Redmond, S. D. 133
Reed, Harrison 102
Regulators 72
Republican National Conven-
  tions 1860, 15; 1868, 20;
  1904, 154; 1908, 154;
  1912, 155; 1916, 156;
  1916, 156; 1920, 133, 158;
  1924, 159; 1928, 159, 160,
  161; 1956, 162; 1960, 162
Republican Party 1, 9, 10,
  33, 42, 100, 106, 108,
  112, 166
Richmond Planet 97, 98
Riddleberger, Patrick 85
Riker, William 34, 43
Robinson, Jackie 141
Robinson, Solon 101
Rockefeller, Nelson 141
Roosevelt, Theodore 84
Root, Elihu 157
Ruby, C. T. 63
Rucker, Henry 51
Russ, William Jr. 44
Russell, Daniel 85

Samuel, Richard 123, 127
Saunders, William 99, 101
Savannah State College 58,
  60
Scalawags 31, 32, 34
Scott, James 75
Scruggs, E. 84
Second Reconstruction Act
  70
Shadgett, Olive 48
Sherman, John 64
Shorter, Caesar 75
Sinclair, Tom 130
Sindler, A. 25
Slavery 6, 19

Slemp, C. 158
Smalls, Robert 111
Smith, Al 135
Smith v. Allwright 85
Smith, Gerrit 7, 16
Smith, J. McCone 5
Southern Delegates 152
Spencer, E. O. 136
Stampp, K. 43
State Convention of Colored
  Men (New York) 8
Stern, Willie 82
Steven, Bill 80
Stevens, T. 22, 124
Sumner, C. 22
Supreme Court 5, 85
Sweat, Isham 86
Syracuse, New York 5

Taft, William H. 84, 111,
  154
Taylor, F. T. 121
Texas 62
Threat, Frank H. 72
Tillman, Benjamin 90, 113
Tolbert, Joseph 41, 114,
  161, 162
Trigg, Joseph M. 122
Turner, H. M. 51, 52
Tuskegee Civic Association
  33

Union League 22, 32, 48,
  71, 86, 92, 98, 105, 118
Unionists 31

Volstead Act 69

Walden, A. T. 61
Walls, Josiah T. 102
Walterson, Harvey 117
Walton, Hanes 25, 26, 27
Warner, A. J. 80

Washington, B. T.   40, 81,
    82, 84, 154
Watkins, William T.   14, 15
Webster, E. A.   111
Wedowee Randolph Toiler   78
Weekly Defiance   52, 53, 54
Wesley, Charles   26, 27, 28
Whip   5
White, George   89
White, James T.   123, 125
White Cape   72
Wilkerson, George   84
Wilkerson, W.   121
Wilmont, David   6
Wilson, Woodrow   156
Wimbly, A. T.   68
Wimbs, Ad.   81, 83
Wimbush, C. C.   51, 57
Wood, Leonard   66
Woods, Forrest   24, 28, 29
Woodward, C. Vann   44
Wright, R. R.   51, 59

Young, P. B.   98